Practicing Writing

Pittsburgh Series in Composition, Literacy, and Culture

David Bartholomae and Jean Ferguson Carr, Editors

practicing writing

THE POSTWAR DISCOURSE OF FRESHMAN ENGLISH

Thomas M. Masters

With a Foreword by Janice M. Lauer

UNIVERSITY OF PITTSBURGH PRESS

Published by the University of Pittsburgh Press, Pittsburgh, Pa., 15260
Copyright © 2004, University of Pittsburgh Press
Manufactured in the United States of America
Printed on acid-free paper
10 9 8 7 6 5 4 3 2 1

Library of Congress Cataloging-in-Publication Data
Masters, Thomas M.
   Practicing writing : the postwar discourse of freshman English / Thomas M. Masters ;
with a foreword by Janice M. Lauer.
      p. cm. — (Pittsburgh series in composition, literacy, and culture)
   Includes bibliographical references (p.   ) and index.
   ISBN 0-8229-4236-4 (acid-free paper)
   1. English language—Rhetoric—Study and teaching—United States—History—20th
century. 2. Report writing—Study and teaching (Higher)—United States—History—
20th century. 3. World War, 1939–1945—United States—Influence. I. Title. II. Series.
   PE1405.U6M375 2004
   808'.042'0711073—dc22

                                                                2004013589

*This book is dedicated to all those whose voices are rarely heard—
the students and teachers whose experience constitutes
the discursive practice of freshman English.*

Contents

Foreword

IN THE LAST DECADE, the field of Rhetoric and Composition has been developing a significant body of literature on composition instruction in the nineteenth and the first half of the twentieth centuries. Thomas Masters's *Practicing Writing* offers us an important addition to that scholarship. When I read his text about freshman English in the postwar period from 1947 to the late-1950s, I encountered a narrative I had lived through when beginning to teach in the 1950s. His account is so astute that I vividly recalled the circumstances that prompted a number of us to work so hard in the 1960s for a disciplinary field that would equip us to challenge the "current-traditional paradigm."

One of Masters's important contributions to this scenario is an interpretive frame of six presumptions of freshman English, which he uses as lenses through which to analyze his archival data. These six beliefs, however, do not characterize just the postwar period, but still haunt many of our classrooms today. His first presumption, *instrumentality* or service, identifies freshman English's ambitious goals: providing a capsule liberal education, advancing the dominant political ideology, fostering democracy, teaching reading to enable students to discern important ideas in their other subjects, producing good citizens though academic literacy, and teaching writing to help students express the content they have learned. *Priority* or marginality names an emphasis on craftsmanship, requiring a background in ideas and tools (grammar, style, organization, and development). *Efficiency* describes a constant fine-tuning of the curriculum, modifying teaching strategies but never substantially effecting change. *Individuality* points to an emphasis on self-expression, a presumption in conflict with a goal of conformity to certain social and political roles. *Transmission* characterizes the belief that powers and qualities are transmitted to students "by unseen yet effective means"; that values and skills are *absorbed* through students' encounters with selected texts. The last presumption, *correspondence*, identifies the belief that reading and writing should model the text as an "organic construct of interdependent meaning." Thus, *Practicing Writing* not only educates but holds up a mirror for us.

Masters's text also provides an impressive example of multimodality, as it draws on the historical work of other scholars like Crowley, Berlin, Connors, and Brereton and on theories such as Michel Foucault's notions of power and discursive practices, and interlaces them with empirical research. In response to critics' calls for more extensive archival work in this area, Masters gives a rich account of three composition programs: Northwestern University, Wheaton College, and the University of Illinois (Chicago and Urbana). He bases his narrative on multiple sources: reports and records of departments and committees, faculty bulletins and catalogs, student publications, personal papers of faculty members (tests, teaching notes, student papers, articles, and book reviews), interviews with forty people, textbooks, and journal articles. In these three different kinds of institutions, Masters finds a number of similar features in their freshman English programs. For example, their first priority was to instill in students a code of correctness and style, and all of these programs emphasized reading and discussion of canonical literature. They felt obliged to develop students' ability to compose acceptable prose, and the purpose of assignments was to enable students to prove they had mastered a type of discourse like description or exposition, with content making little difference. Each program engaged in regular modifications to the curriculum but was resistant to change.

These features also mark many programs today. What Masters didn't find in these programs was attention to such matters as invention, readers and discourse communities, multiple drafts, revision, or peer collaboration—interests of scholars later in the emerging field of Rhetoric and Composition. Reading this account provides us with a perspective on our continuing struggles to extricate ourselves from these presumptions and practices.

Masters uses details from the archives of three institutions to create a powerful mosaic that illustrates these presumptions. His in-depth account is lucid, intelligent, and also cautionary. As he says in the conclusion, freshman English of this period is a phenomenon with a "durable ideological apparatus," both tenacious and elastic—stretching to the present or appearing in new guises.

JANICE M. LAUER
Reece McGee Distinguished Professor of English
Purdue University

Preface

ANYONE WHO HAS TAKEN, taught, or administered a 100-level college course should find value in *Practicing Writing*. I suspect that anyone interested in the intellectual, cultural, and social development of the United States after World War II would also find it interesting. I have written this study, however, with two particular audiences in mind: academics from any field who are interested in literacy issues; and English scholars and practitioners, especially in the discipline of Composition.

Many presume that the perennial problem of students' "illiteracy" has a simple, straightforward solution. Mike Rose calls this "the myth of transiency"—"the belief . . . in the American university that if we can just do *x* or *y*, the problem will be solved—in five years, ten years, or a generation—and higher education will be able to return to its real work" ("Language of Exclusion" 355). David Russell connects Rose's myth with the seductive, misguided expectation that the complex problems of academic literacy can be solved via simple reforms: "New forms of remediation continually hold out the promise that, with enough organization and cooperation, drill and reinforcement, students can be trained to write once and for all; that Americans will again possess this elementary skill, this component of general education, and teachers can get on with their 'real' work: teaching specific information" (*Writing in the Academic Disciplines* 165). *Practicing Writing* shows how for a decade the faculties at Northwestern University, Wheaton College, and the University of Illinois (Urbana and Chicago) tried to do *x, y, z,* and beyond, but the "problem" of freshman English resisted a solution. I hope that the anecdotes, examples, facts, and discussion of this study will maintain the interest of those both inside and outside English departments, and will show how the history of freshman English is important not only to those who teach it, but to everyone who has a stake in students' literacy.

David Russell explains why it is important that academics outside of Composition understand its history: "In the end, a narrow focus on the history of composition courses may actually reinforce the myth of transience, since it may credit freshman English with a larger or more cohesive effect than it has ever had. . . . Simply reforming freshman English (again) will not adequately address the deeper issues of writing acquisition: the nature of academic writing, its relation to disciplinary formation and perpetuation, and its relation to students' access to professional communities" (32). *Practicing Writing* should help anyone who cares about postsecondary education appreciate the complexity and the challenge of something seemingly as simple as offering or, harder yet, reforming a course that is supposed to teach undergraduates how to write.

A Note on the Sources of This Study

The principal sources for this study have come from the archives at Northwestern University, Wheaton College, the University of Illinois (Urbana), and the Special Collections of the University of Illinois at Chicago. At Northwestern I examined records from the office of the dean of liberal arts; the English department; catalogs; the personal papers of faculty members who had taught or administered freshman English, including Fred Faverty, Wallace Douglas, Jean Hagstrum, Ernest Samuels, and Harrison Hayford; as well as copies of an intramural newsletter concerning the course, "The English 'A' Analyst." The archives at Wheaton contain a file of minutes from the Department of English from 1949 to 1964, both committee meetings and departmental meetings. I also examined the personal papers of Clyde Kilby and Peter Veltman, as well as copies of student publications, student-written history research papers, catalogs, a faculty-prepared style book, the minutes of faculty meetings, and copies of the faculty bulletin. The Urbana archives include catalogs, student publications, the personal files of Charles Roberts, and the records of the University Senate Committee on Student English. At the University of Illinois at Chicago I examined catalogs, records of the Humanities department, the chancellor's files, copies of student publications, and the personal papers of Falk S. Johnson, who directed the Division of Rhetoric from 1949 to 1966. I also found departmental and personal records in the English department offices in Urbana and in Chicago.

My research included telephone and personal interviews and correspondence with approximately forty persons who had taught or administered freshman English in these four programs. The teachers included Ernest Samuels, Jean Hagstrum, Wallace Douglas, and Harrison Hayford at Northwestern; Robert Warburton, Peter Veltman, and Paul Bechtel at Wheaton; Lynn Altenbernd and George Hendricks at Urbana; and Marion Kerwick, Chadwick Hansen, Mary Sidney, Arthur Greenwald, Bernard Kogan, and Falk Johnson at Chicago.

I wish to acknowledge the help of the archivists, without whom this study would have been impossible. These include Patrick Quinn at Northwestern; Thad Voss, David Malone, and David Osielski at Wheaton; William J. Maher and Ellen Swain at Urbana; Carolyn Adams at the Champaign County Historical Archives; and Alan Kovac, Douglas Bicknese, and Mary Diaz at Chicago. Others who have been helpful in critiquing this study during the many stages of its long, slow birth have been Patrick McGann, Rance Conley, Carol Severino, David Jolliffe, Peter Hales, William Covino, David Russell, Don Mitchell, Dennis Baron, Janice Lauer, Jean Ferguson Carr, David Bartholomae, and the anonymous reviewers from the University of Pittsburgh Press. I would like to thank Christina Acosta for her editorial help, Anne Masters for her research assistance, and my wife, Kathleen Lynch Masters, for her honest feedback and encouragement. Finally, I owe a special debt to David Spurr, who helped me conceive the plan of this study and guided me through its earliest drafts.

Practicing Writing

Introduction

People know what they do; they frequently know
why they do what they do; but what they don't know
is what what they do does.

MICHEL FOUCAULT

N THE LAST TWENTY-FIVE
YEARS, NO ACADEMIC SUBJECT HAS received as much scrutiny as rhetoric and composition. John Brereton claims that "historians of composition have created the single most impressive body of knowledge
about any discipline in higher education" (*Origins* xiv). Anyone with a
serious interest in composition as a discipline has come to understand
the principal features of its history and theory: origins of present practices in the late nineteenth century; the gulf between the sweeping
scope of classical rhetoric and the marginal space that writing instruction has occupied in the academy; the subjugation of a "low" composition to a "high" literature within English departments, where writing
instruction usually resides; the ways in which the pedagogies and actions and products of teachers and students alike can be interrogated
via all of the contemporary schools of criticism. Without doubt, those
who study the discipline as well as those who practice it know far more
about what they do, and why they do what they do, than I did, for example, when I began teaching English in 1968.

I

Still, as I read those studies, from Albert R. Kitzhaber's *Rhetoric in American Colleges, 1850–1900* to the most recent articles in *Pre/Text, Rhetoric Review, College English,* or *College Composition and Communication,* I sense a difference between many scholarly conclusions about writing instruction and my experience as a teacher. Brereton also notes a limitation in the familiar histories. "Most historians have regarded rhetoric as the ideal, composition as a fall from grace, and the last two decades as the beginnings of a great recovery" (*Origins* xiii). He points out that because of their "genuine interest in the philosophical underpinnings of nineteenth-century rhetoric," and because theory, as represented in books and articles, is more accessible for study, some historians have emphasized philosophy, theory, and ideology at the expense of actual classroom practices (xii).[1] In their attempt to document the history of writing instruction in American higher education, scholars have tended to study the most accessible kinds of evidence—textbooks, monographs by acknowledged leaders and experts in the field, journal articles, descriptions of writing programs, syllabi, biographies of notable teachers, administrators, and theoreticians.[2]

A specific example from one of the standard histories of rhetoric and composition illustrates how a historian has described the theoretical framework for classroom practices without examining adequately the practices themselves. In *Rhetoric and Reality,* James Berlin proposes to examine both the theoretical as well as the practical. "In examining the variety of rhetorics that have appeared in the English departments of American colleges in the twentieth century, I will . . . be concerned with the rhetorical theories that have appeared, as well as with the epistemological and ideological elements to which they are related. But I want also to examine the concrete classroom practices to which these theories have led" (5). Berlin aims to proceed from theory, philosophy, and ideology to the experience of teachers and students. Once he had established a theoretical basis, however, what evidence of "concrete classroom practices" did Berlin actually investigate?

In "The Communications Emphasis: 1940–1960," the fifth chapter of his study, Berlin analyzes rhetoric courses during the postwar era. In discussing how communications courses included concepts taken from general semantics, Berlin cites programs at the University of Iowa and the University of Denver as examples of a conservative and a liberal approach. He found evidence of events at Iowa in a collection of essays edited by Earl James McGrath, *Communication in General Education,* dated 1946. Berlin selected evidence of classroom practices in the Denver course from a *College English* article, also from 1946, by faculty members Levette Davidson and Frederick Sorenson. Having presented the content and pedagogy of the courses as explained in these two sources, Berlin summarizes the limited penetration of communications courses into university curricula in a parenthetical comment: "At most schools, current-traditional rhetoric continued to be the central approach of composition instruction" (*Rhetoric and Reality* 104). Although Berlin aims to examine "concrete classroom practices," he relies solely on one book and one article for information regarding what was happening in the classrooms at Iowa and Denver and then lumps all of the particular experiences that happened elsewhere under one general title: "current-traditional."[3] Brereton points out the hazard of reducing the daily experience of thousands of teachers and students to a convenient label. "Interpreting the history of composition as a loss and then a revival of rhetoric has given a partial view, a view that explicitly devalues almost a century of teaching and learning. And an unwieldy name like current-traditional, one that almost scorns precision, is about on a par with 'Dark Ages' as a satisfactory investigative or taxonomic tool" (*Origins* xiii).[4]

Several other commentators have observed the lack of attention to everyday classroom experience in the histories of our discipline. As early as 1982, in "Is There a Text in This Class?" Susan Miller notes that most histories of the discipline might best be categorized as histories of what had been published, rather than of what had happened in the classroom. In 1987 Stephen North writes, "There is little evidence as yet to suggest that Composition's Historians have tried other avenues: private collections, small town or school libraries, attics and garages; or the people themselves, teachers and students, either for written or oral material" (74). Brereton notes in his 1995 study, "In searching for the ideologies, historians sometimes ignored the actuality of the experience of students and teachers, curriculum planners and administrators. Indeed, we rarely looked at the writing itself" (xiv). In his 1994 article, "Composing English Studies," Richard E. Miller critiques the approaches of Gerald Graff (*Professing Literature*) and Evan Watkins (*Work Time*), both of whom he claims neglect the importance of the material conditions of teaching. Miller calls for an approach to institutional history focused more directly on "the solicitation and treatment of student writing" (174). He cites Edward Said's injunction in *The World, the Text, and the Critic* that critical work begin "with concrete instances drawn from everyday reality that lie outside or just beyond the interpretive area necessarily designated in advance and thereafter inscribed by every theory" (242). Miller suggests:

> Investigating . . . the actual work of reading and writing students are required to do within a given educational system, the textbooks produced by educators alongside their reforms, personal accounts of the educators' teaching practices, and moments when educators quote student writing in their texts—this kind of institutional history would help to rescue the student from theoretical oblivion, make possible a critique of departmental and curricular reform proposals on pedagogical grounds, and provide a record of the range of local solutions to the problems all English departments face in teaching students how to read and write in the academy ("Composing English Studies" 177).

The kind of history North, Brereton, and Richard Miller call for would look quite different from the kind of work historians have offered previously. The established histories usually begin with an exposition of the generally accepted statements of theory at a given time, then proceed with illustration via specific examples from program descriptions, textbooks, and articles. A practice-based history would begin with a detailed examination of the particulars of writing and its instruction at a given moment in history and proceed to a description of the presumptions that constitute the discursive practice in which those particulars are bound up.

PRACTICING WRITING provides an example of how to undertake such a project. In *As If Learning Mattered*, Richard Miller comments on the methodology that a practice-based historian needs to follow: "One always studies what one can, shaping a project in response to what can be found, what can be reasonably argued" (45). Even if I can study only "what one can," I have chosen a particular academic discourse, a particular time in history during which it was operating, and the archives of four particular schools. The first step in explaining this study is to clarify those crucial choices.

I have chosen a historical period with clearly defined boundaries and far enough in the past that I could look at the material with some perspective, yet recent enough that I might still find the kinds of evidence that seem to have been neglected in previous histories. Like Kitzhaber, Douglas, Crowley, Connors, Berlin, and many others, I have chosen to look at the most common site of writing instruction in American colleges and universities—freshman English.

While reading *Rhetoric and Reality,* I understood that the post–World War II era in the United States might provide suitable boundaries and content. It has a clear beginning and end, commencing with the returning wave of veterans in 1947 and concluding with the educational reforms in the late 1950s, after the launch of Sputnik. It is a placid period of the "return to normalcy" between the economic and political turmoil of a great world war and the worldwide social revolution of the 1960s. As Berlin points out, however, "Economic, political, and social developments between 1940 and 1960 had placed in motion a current of ideas that would profoundly affect the teaching of writing" (119). Some of these developments include the rise and fall of the general education approach, including general semantics and structural linguistics; the calling into question of traditional practices including the teaching of prescriptive grammar; the revival of classical rhetoric; the establishment of a professional organization for teachers of composition; the sudden increase in the sizes and numbers of college campuses that began with the returning veterans and continued with children of the baby boom; the introduction of what Richard Lloyd-Jones, in his biography of Richard Braddock, has called "mass education" based on the American industrial model of economies of scale (Brereton, *Traditions* 157).[5]

Selecting a particular course and a particular era is a relatively straightforward act compared with choosing the materials to examine. John Brereton notes in *The Origins of Composition Studies in the American College, 1875–1925* that archival evidence abounds. "University archives have large quantities of student essays, course syllabi, lecture notes, and teaching materials" (xv). The question, however, remains "How to choose?" In a letter, David Russell told me, "I have tried to look at colleges which might be 'typical,' but the more schools I look at the harder that becomes."

Wallace Douglas wrote to me, "When I first contemplated the history of the teaching of composition and realized the dimensions of the task, I simply retreated. . . . Is there any principle of selection to organize the search? I couldn't think of any, nor can I now." With due respect to such cautions, I offer this explanation of how I selected archives for this study.

James Berlin has identified a time and place in which the "supremacy of eighteenth-century rhetoric" gave way to "a commitment to serving all the citizens of society—not just an aristocratic elite" (*Rhetoric and Reality* 58). The time was just after the Civil War, and the place was the American West. The Morrill Act of 1862, according to Robert Connors, "brought a large new population of students to American colleges and helped to found the major state universities, which would become important sites for composition teaching over the next five decades" (*Composition-Rhetoric* 9). David Russell concurs, noting that "in the decade following the Civil War, as the economy expanded rapidly in the North and West, colleges responded to the utilitarian chorus and began the dramatic changes that would create the modern university and define its role in the new rationalized, urban-industrial society of modern America" (*Writing in Academic Disciplines* 46).

My own background suggested looking in the Midwest for "particulars of writing and its instruction." The self-effacing, dutiful, hard-working, and productive nature of middle America reflects the qualities I associate with freshman English. In 1965 just after the period *Practicing Writing* explores, I took English 100 G, Rhetoric and Composition, at Lewis College (now Lewis University) in Lockport, an old industrial town on the Illinois and Michigan canal thirty-five miles southwest of Chicago. My twenty-four classmates and I were the sons of tradespeople, clerks, bookkeepers, salesworkers, mechanics, teamsters, and small business owners. The professor, Jeff Stiker, was gruff, taciturn, acerbic, and insightful. He was a scholar of eighteenth-century British literature, but never intimated that he considered freshman English less significant than other courses in the department. He never articulated any particular critical vision of the subject, nor did he claim that success in his class would bring us any greater benefit than avoiding academic probation. He taught from the *Harbrace College Handbook,* and from Maurice B. McNamee's *Reading for Understanding,* which provided the springboard for discussions and essays on the purpose of a college education, the order of nature, heroism, and the nature of logic and propaganda. I have no graded papers from that course, as Stiker recollected them before he would give us our final exam. When we asked him why he wanted them back, he commented with a wry smirk, "All the composition teachers gather them up. We make a big bonfire and dance around it to celebrate the end of the semester."[6] I suspected that reading the records and papers of people like Jeff Stiker would reveal an unembellished, unselfconscious view of this most practical of academic experiences.

After contacting English departments and college and university libraries throughout the region, a process much like panning for gold, I hit pay dirt in four places—the University of Illinois, both its original campus in Urbana as well as the one in Chicago; Wheaton College, in Wheaton, Illinois; and Northwestern University, in Evanston, Illinois. Each school had had meticulous people in its English department; their archivists had taken the initiative to gather and organize as much material as they could persuade their colleagues to deposit; and each possessed a distinct institutional identity. Although I had no way to predict the connections I would find among the four, the more I dug through the rich veins of "ore"—departmental minutes, committee records, annual reports, intramural publications, published and unpublished articles, and personal papers—the more I found common threads in the histories of these very different schools and in the experiences of the students and teachers of freshman English.

THE UNIVERSITY OF ILLINOIS is a prototypical midwestern public university. From the west facade of Davenport Hall, the original agriculture building, the words of founder Jonathan Baldwin Turner still remind students of his original vision for the school: "Industrial education prepares the way for a millennium of labor." Turner, much like his counterpart at Wheaton, Jonathan Blanchard, had come from the East with strong views about social inequality. He studied the classics at Yale until 1827, when he set out for the frontier with the notion of bringing intellectual and social enlightenment to the wilderness. In 1833 Turner established Illinois College at Jacksonville. Turner remained there for fifteen years, until the town's proslavery forces demanded his resignation due to his fiery abolitionism ("Tradition at the University of Illinois" 3–4).

For Turner, "industrial" did not signify the merely mechanical, but suggested "a new sort of technological education which would assert the dignity and importance of the practical sciences—engineering and agriculture—that elite universities had traditionally looked down upon" ("Tradition at the University of Illinois" 4). His "Illinois Industrial Association" argued for publicly funded universities, open to the "industrial classes," not just the children of the privileged. The Association persuaded Senator Justin Morrill of Vermont to introduce the Morrill Land Grant College Act, which Lincoln signed in 1863. Turner's vision was realized in 1867 when Illinois Industrial University was established in Urbana.

The experience of Charles H. Shamel, who began his studies there in 1886, illustrates the nature of education at Illinois Industrial:

> [On] . . . Monday Shamel was successfully examined in algebra, philosophy, physiology, botany, and rhetoric. On Thursday, having paid the required fee of $22.50 and made an $8 deposit for laboratory expense, he began work in German, chemistry, geometry, and trigonometry. . . . Friday evening brought his first meeting of the Philomathean Literary Society. Together with required chapel and military drill, these experiences introduced Charles Shamel to the heart of American higher learning as it was practiced in a land grant university toward the end of the nineteenth century. (Johnson and Johanningmeier 3)

In 1885 the university changed its name from Illinois Industrial University, "which many interpreted to mean either a reformatory or a charitable institution in which compulsory manual labor figured prominently" (Solberg 3), to the University of Illinois.

In 1894 the university separated its rhetoric offerings into two departments: rhetoric, and oratory and oral rhetoric. The first head of the rhetoric department, Thomas Arkle Clark, followed a career trajectory that presages those of many other men profiled in *Practicing Writing*. He studied at the University of Chicago and at Harvard, but never completed a degree beyond the bachelor's in literature he had earned at the University of Illinois. Although he headed the Department of Rhetoric, he "cherished literature because it transmitted the cultural tradition" (Solberg 66). He published many textbooks that were used in elementary and secondary schools. He "cared about students and was skillful at advancing both his own and his department's interests" (Solberg 66). Within six years, his diligence earned him a promotion to acting dean of the college.

The qualities of Thomas Clark's department have continued throughout the history of the University of Illinois. As the "Outline of Rhetoric 1" from 1907 shows, the courses at Illinois were based on "the kind of mass production model" commonly found at midwestern universities after the turn of the twentieth century (Brereton, *Origins* 470). Through the work of men such as Bernard Jefferson, Charles Roberts, Harris Wilson, and Arnold Tibbetts, Illinois exemplified the common sense, tightly managed, critically unselfconscious approach to the teaching of writing that many schools have emulated. In their "Memorial to Charles Walter Roberts," delivered after Roberts's death in 1968, his colleagues John Hamilton, Frank Moake, and Harris Wilson noted that "if one had been asked to name the most distinguished and influential director of the basic college writing course in the United States, one would have to name Charles Roberts. . . . Large numbers of Illinois Ph.D.s who taught English composition under his direction . . . [have] become directors of composition and heads of departments in other colleges and universities throughout the United States."

In the late 1940s Illinois faced an unprecedented challenge, as did almost all colleges and universities in the United States. The returning wave of veterans used their GI Bill benefits to seek a degree. Chadwick Hansen, who attended Yale under the V12 program, taught at the University of Illinois at Chicago from 1975 to 1995. In a letter, he described the circumstances that led to establishing the undergraduate division at Chicago. "In July of 1943 . . . the Navy, through its V12 program, began sending large numbers of young men to college simply because they had done well on intelligence tests. . . . These bright but poorly prepared students presented a genuine problem to the colleges and universities, and that problem was compounded many times over by the flood of veterans who went to college after the war on the G.I. Bill." To accommodate these veterans, Illinois set up "undergraduate divisions"

around the state to take pressure off the campus in Urbana by delivering general education courses at satellite locations. Only one eventually
evolved into a degree-granting institution. For its first nineteen years,
it was known by the name of the municipal lakefront structure that was
pressed into service as a temporary campus—Navy Pier. Arnold Hartoch,
who taught German there, eulogized the campus after it had moved to
a new, permanent location in 1965:

> Navy Pier! The University of Illinois, Chicago Undergraduate Di-
> vision, born August 1946, died February 1965. Gone, but not for-
> gotten.
>
> A half-mile long dark, dank corridor, a steep flight of stairs to
> the east end "head house," classrooms made of plywood (where else
> could Shakespeare compete with movies on Hygiene?), paint pur-
> chased from railroad salvage, icy cold winters, boiling hot summers,
> cursing truckers down the middle road, freighters, trade shows—.
>
> But oh, what students! First, the veterans, older, wiser, driven by
> the desire to learn, to make up for lost time; the gradual influx of
> teenagers from high school, not as "driven" as the veterans, but all
> good students and fine people. . . .
>
> If there was one characteristic which distinguished Navy Pier, it
> was the feeling of togetherness, everyone working as a team against
> the physical facility, against the experiences of a great war, against
> the gaps in the formal learning of the students, to achieve the ul-
> timate objective—an educated person. (unpublished document)

Part of the legacy of Illinois is the way in which Turner's notion of education for the "industrial classes" was adapted to meet the needs of urban
adults who had survived the boredom and horror of World War II, and
saw the university as a means of achieving social, emotional, and financial
order. The rhetoric program at Navy Pier was directed by Falk Johnson,
who had served with a radio intelligence company in Europe during
World War II. He and his colleagues—a very different group from the
cadre of graduate students who taught the course in Urbana—followed
Roberts's program for the most part, but modified it to serve their particular needs.

The oldest institutions of higher education in the Midwest are not
state sponsored. As settlers spread west of the Allegheny Mountains,

the new communities often felt the need to declare their identity by founding a college. The federal government empowered individual states to grant college charters as they saw fit, resulting in a uniquely American system of many small colleges, rather than a few centralized national institutions as might be found in Europe. According to Harold Williamson and Payson S. Wild, by 1860 the difficulties of transportation on the frontier as well as democratic notions of universal education—at least for males—led to the founding of over 800 small colleges in the American West, although only 180 managed to achieve any sort of permanence (1–2). Paul Bechtel, in his history of Wheaton College, notes another motivation. "In . . . the midwestern states east of the Mississippi—Ohio, Indiana, Illinois . . . nearly all of the colleges were Christian. . . . Hoping to transform a spiritual wilderness into a Christian society, these men [eastern revivalists who had been educated at Yale, Princeton, or Dartmouth] made a frontal attack on the ignorance and secularism of the rapidly expanding upper Mississippi Valley" (*Wheaton College* 7). One such school, Illinois Institute, was founded in 1853 by a small antislavery Wesleyan congregation from Batavia, Illinois. The financial crash of 1857 imperiled the fledgling college, so the trustees recruited Jonathan Blanchard, a nationally known abolitionist who had been president of Knox College in Galesburg, to head the Institute. Blanchard, a skillful fund-raiser, persuaded local landowner Warren L. Wheaton to donate fifty acres of prime real estate. In exchange, the school would change its name to Wheaton College. Blanchard assured him, "This will at least save your heirs the expense of a good monument" (Bechtel 20).

Inspired by Oberlin, which became the first coeducational college in the country when it admitted four female students in 1837, Blanchard considered educational opportunity for women a social cause as important as prison reform and the abolition of slavery (Bechtel 24). The "Gentlemen" and "Ladies" adhered to a strict code of conduct. They had to attend all college exercises, including church services, recitations, and examinations. They could not "leave town, be out at night, [or] leave their rooms during study time" and were enjoined from "offensive or indecent conduct, the propagation of infidel principles, profaning the Sabbath, the use of liquors or tobacco, careless use of fire, or entering the marriage relation while a member of the college." The students' lives were tightly scheduled, with classes from 8:00 until 11:30 every morning and from 1:00 to 4:00 in the afternoon, with evening study from 7:30 to 9:30 (27).

Under Blanchard's leadership, students pursued a classical curriculum. Freshmen and sophomores studied Cicero, Livy, Horace, and Tacitus in Latin; and Xenophon, Thucydides, and the Pauline Epistles in Greek. In addition, they took algebra, geometry, trigonometry, analytics, and calculus. Juniors took mechanics and hydrostatics, chemistry, mineralogy, pneumatics, optics, electricity, astronomy, geology, physiology, and either French or German. Senior year included psychology, political economy, the United States Constitution, history, and "philosophy of the plan of creation, evidences of Christianity . . . elements of biblical criticism, and intellectual and moral history." Art and music were offered as noncredit courses that could be taken for an extra fee (Bechtel 23). Students engaged in debate, declamation, original essays, and poetry through literary societies that met, as did the one Charles Shamel attended at Illinois, on Friday afternoons. Originally there was a single society, the Beltionian; Blanchard separated the women into their own, the Aeolian Society (27). By the mid-1930s, twenty years after the college had moved away from a strict classical curriculum and had instituted elective courses including English, these societies had gained even more popularity. In addition to the Beltionian and Aeolian Societies, the college had added Excelsior, Aristonian, Philalethean, Boethallian, Naitermian, and Ladosian to accommodate the growing student body (136). These societies declined in popularity after World War II, but did not disappear from campus life completely until the late 1950s.

Bechtel notes that before the turn of the century rhetoric consisted in oral recitation, taught by Blanchard himself. A catalog from the late 1880s states: "For 'rhetorical work, the President of the College meets the Freshmen, Sophomores, and Juniors once each week. The plan is a complete and practical course in Oratory'" (56). Around the turn of the century, the classical curriculum at Wheaton began to unravel under pressure from an increasingly scientific approach in the rest of academia. In 1917 the college established departments. In Wheaton's arrangement at that time, logic and rhetoric were taught by Professor Darien Straw, who headed the Department of Social Sciences (79). By the 1930s the college had grouped its various departments into six divisions, a structure that remained for many years: Language and Literature; Bible; Philosophy, Psychology, and Education; Music and Expression; Science and Mathematics; History and Social Science; and Physical Education. The classical system that relied upon the talents and personalities of a few strong professors gave way to a system of liberal education that would "prepare the student to enter a life that will have breadth, depth, and elevation—a life that, though increasingly dependent on technology, transcends technology's demands." Required general education courses included those in the Bible, psychology, literature, science or mathematics, theology, and history, as well as six hours in rhetoric, taught by members of the English department (123).

During World War II, Wheaton faced many of the same issues as did Illinois. In 1943 a contingent of 250 young men came to the campus under the auspices of the Army Specialized Training Program. Shortly after the war, the returning GIs swelled the population of the campus and changed its tone. "Matured by travel and peril, by tough discipline, and by their awareness of the value of an education, they were eager to compensate for the lost years" (Bechtel 183). As did colleges and universities across the country, Wheaton struggled to deal with the new ethical and ideological framework of post–World War II America. Where the likes of Robert Hutchins, Mortimer Adler, Norman Foerster, and Mark Van Doren proposed to revitalize society through a new humanism, the faculty at Wheaton sought to articulate the particularly Christian contribution their school could make to postwar reconstruction. During a retreat at Winona Lake, Indiana, in September of 1946, they came to a consensus about how Wheaton would face the challenges of the postwar milieu. They acknowledged the value of the Renaissance concept of innate human value and dignity, as did the new humanists; but, in the words of Cornelius Jaarsma, a professor of philosophy: "The frame of reference for all evaluation in the Christian college comes from the Scripture as God's special revelation. . . . Our entire liberal arts curriculum belongs in this framework. All classroom teaching should be oriented toward this end" (184). At the conclusion of his description of Wheaton's centennial celebration, Paul Bechtel, chair of Wheaton's English department from 1966 to 1977, sums up the values that first motivated a small group of Wesleyan antislavery activists to establish Illinois Institute, values that endured through more than a century:

> The Centennial. . . . was a time to remember the pioneers from
> New England—strongly influenced by Puritanism and the evangel-
> ical movements of Charles G. Finney [a famous lawyer-turned-
> evangelist of the 1830s who became the first professor of theology
> at Oberlin, and an acquaintance of Jonathan Blanchard]—who
> brought to the Illinois prairies the idea of a liberal arts education
> undergirded by a theistic vision of life which confessed the sover-
> eignty of God and founded its intellectual development on Hebrew-
> Christian sources. (229)

The social issue of abolition may have galvanized the founders of
Wheaton, but the college and those who taught there never confused
mere social activism with the dissemination of Christian values. In the
1950s faculty still had to subscribe to its "Standards of Faith and Doctrinal Platform."

Later in this study, I will analyze how Wheaton's Christian concept
of a liberal arts curriculum played out in Writing 111 and 112, their postwar freshman English classes. The career of Peter Veltman, who was
hired in 1948 to teach those classes, exemplifies the writing program at
Wheaton. Like Charles Roberts, he had begun his career as a high school
English teacher and after making a move to the college level became involved in freshman English issues, both at his institution and in a larger
context. In 1953, for example, both Veltman and Roberts performed
small roles in the annual meeting of the Midwestern English Conference, held at the Northern Illinois State Teachers College (now Northern Illinois University). Like Thomas Arkle Clark, Veltman managed
to escape the confines of freshman English by moving into a deanship.
Although Veltman and his colleagues inhabited a vastly different educational milieu than did those at Illinois, the scene of teaching in which
freshman English operated during the postwar era was remarkably similar at both schools.

Like Wheaton, Northwestern University came to life in the 1850s,
inspired by a Christian vision. When Illinois achieved statehood in 1818,
Chicago was a muddy trading outpost defended by a small military gar-
rison. By midcentury, however, the city had grown to 30,000 people and
had developed a lively economy based on transportation, manufacturing,
grain trading, and meatpacking. Wisconsin had colleges at Madison,

Beloit, and Appleton (Lawrence); Indiana had one at Greencastle (Indiana Asbury, later renamed DePauw); Michigan had been founded at Ann Arbor in 1837; and other colleges operated in Illinois at Jacksonville (Illinois College); Galesburg (Knox); and Lebanon, near St. Louis (McKendree). Williamson and Wild note that the majority of the American colleges established during the first half of the nineteenth century came about through the impetus of religious denominations, in particular the Presbyterians and Congregationalists before the 1830s, and soon after the Methodists.

In midcentury Chicago, Methodists outnumbered all other Protestant denominations; a group of nine "members of this congregation . . . took the initiative in founding a university to make higher education available to . . . Methodist youth" (2). They aimed to serve young people from the original Northwest Territory, which had since been divided into the states of Ohio, Indiana, Illinois, Michigan, Wisconsin, and a portion of Minnesota. Hence, they chose the name "Northwestern University." Of the nine men, only one—John Evans, after whom Evanston, the town that grew up next to the university, was named—had a college education (at the Lynn Medical College in Cincinnati). All, however, were successful members of the middle class: three ministers, three attorneys, and two businessmen. On 31 May 1850, after the men knelt in prayer in Grant Goodrich's law office at Lake and Dearborn in Chicago, they resolved that "the interests of *sanctified* [emphasis in original] learning required the immediate establishment of a University in the northwest, under the patronage of the Methodist Episcopal Church" (Williamson and Wild 3).

The founders invoked "the interests of *sanctified* learning," intending that the university be conducted with a religious atmosphere so that "the regenerate heart . . . be accompanied and directed by an enlightened intellect to give man the full image of his Maker" (Williamson and Wild 5). Nevertheless, their purpose was more practical than doctrinaire. They conceived of Northwestern as a regional university that would prepare students for "the practical duties of life" (5). In their request for support sent to the six Methodist conferences in the region, they noted that "our church ought to have plenty of laborers," meaning that the university would train students to perform useful roles in society.

Northwestern and Wheaton appear to have been founded to advance explicitly religious principles; a deeper examination, however, reveals why they have turned out to be such different institutions. Although Wheaton was not affiliated with any specific denomination, it aimed to bring Christianity to the "spiritual wilderness" of the Midwest. The college hired faculty and admitted students only if they subscribed to a statement of faith that eventually was codified into a nine-point "Doctrinal Platform." Northwestern, in contrast, was founded by men from a distinct denomination, but their goals were far more general. They aimed to develop skilled workers for the society in which the church members happened to live. Northwestern's charter specified that trustees be appointed by the Methodist Episcopal conferences in the original Northwest Territories, but students and faculty were not required to subscribe to a specific religious faith (5). A statement by John Evans reveals what underlay the intentions of these Methodists in establishing a university for the Chicago area, and also the caliber of institution they anticipated: "It would cost at least a thousand dollars less for each son we may educate in the proposed university than to send him to Yale or Cambridge" (Williamson and Wild 3).

By 1854, when the property for a campus north of Chicago had been acquired and an endowment had been raised, the trustees announced their design for Northwestern: "As the institution is designated to be a university—at least in the full American sense of the term—with its different departments, it might appear an oversight to confine our organization to the faculty of a single department, viz.: the College of Literature, Science and the Arts; but we judge this arrangement best adapted to the wants of the country" (Williamson and Wild 9). Although they began with one college, the trustees also discussed developing professional schools. They rejected founding their own medical school, as Chicago already had the well-established Rush Medical College (at which Charles Evans, one of the founders, held a professorship); but they endorsed a future law school, to be established "at no distant day in connection with our present faculty" (9). Other schools soon followed: Music (1895), Engineering (1909), Education (1920), Speech (1921), and Journalism (1921). By way of contrast, Wheaton did not organize its faculty into departments until 1917. Unlike Wheaton and Illinois, Northwestern was founded as an all-male institution. It did not acquire the Women's College until 1873.

At the beginning, a Northwestern student's life resembled what he would have experienced at Illinois or Wheaton. The "Regulations" published in December 1866 forbade "smoking . . . drinking or keeping spirituous liquors; playing at cards; profane, rude, or indecent language; noise, or any irregular conduct tending to disturb the peace of the community; and all practices opposed to morality and good order or unbecoming a gentleman." These same regulations specified a system of "marks" to be levied against students for "unexcused delinquencies" including absences or tardiness to "recitation, reading compositions, declamation, or church . . . absence from prayers . . . violation of study hours, or impropriety of conduct in chapel, at recitation, or elsewhere." If a student reached forty-eight marks in a given term, he would be removed from the university (Williamson and Wild 14). Students were expected to attend classes or study three hours every morning, three every afternoon, and every evening after seven o'clock. The faculty informed parents of students' academic performance as well as their attendance at recitations, at daily prayers, and at the two Sunday religious services (31). In letters home, Elmer Sims described his first experience at Northwestern in 1874: "They have the most examining here, and they are terrible hard. Folks need not say that this is not a good school." After a bit more experience, Sims's assessment became harsher: "A student is a slave, a slave to his studies. He leaves home and has to work hard and anxiously or if he doesn't he will have to drop out" (31). Although women were eligible to take courses throughout the university's offerings, they seemed to have confined themselves to the study of literature and the fine arts (30). As at Illinois and Wheaton, students' social life revolved around the weekly meetings of undergraduate debating societies. The Hinman Society, named after Northwestern's first president, was established in 1855, the Adelphic Society in 1860, and the Ossoli Literary Society for women in 1874 (Williamson and Wild 33). The few opportunities that did exist for coeducational activity—class parties, winter sleigh rides and summer boating excursions on Lake Michigan—were carefully supervised. As Mrs. Andrew Brown, wife of one of the trustees noted, "Our ingenuity was sometimes taxed to the utmost to provide amusement for young people who might not indulge in card playing or dancing" (34).

As at Illinois and Wheaton, rhetoric at Northwestern began as a branch of oratory. In 1868 Robert McLean Cumnock came to Evanston as a professor of divinity at the Garrett Theological Seminary. He soon became a popular figure, eventually heading a School of Oratory that was named after him (in 1920 it became part of the School of Speech, now the Department of Performance Studies). Like Blanchard at Wheaton, he embodied the ideals of literacy typical of the old college. One former student described him: "He was not interested in . . . our present day political and social institutions. He knew little of the literature of his day. He was a heroic figure from an earlier age, an age which expressed itself in scrupulous devotion to duty (to one's work)" (Graff, *Professing* 49–50). Toward the end of the century, however, his notion of rhetoric gave way to the kind of freshman composition course that Harvard had instituted in 1872. According to their "Report of the Committee on Composition and Rhetoric" of 1892, Charles Francis Adams, Edwin Lawrence Godkin, and Josiah Quincy describe the content of English A at Harvard as: "(1) elementary instruction in the theory and practice of English Composition, and (2) an introduction to the study of English Literature. The theory is taught throughout the year by lectures; the practice is obtained in short weekly themes, written in the classroom and criticized by the instructors" (Brereton, *Origins* 75).

"English A" first appears in Northwestern's course catalog in 1891. The listing includes only a mention of the required text, Richard Chenevix Trench's *English Past and Present.* Presumably, this course would have resembled its eponymous counterpart at Harvard. In 1892 J. Scott Clark began to teach the class. Clark was an early proponent of "giving to the rhetorical training in our schools a more practical character" (quoted in Kitzhaber, *Rhetoric* 209). In the preface to his *Practical Rhetoric,* published in 1886, he railed against other textbooks in which "the pupil is led through a labyrinth of abstractions bearing such names as 'Invention,' 'Taste,' 'Deduction,' 'Simplicity,' 'Partial Exposition,' 'Feeling,' 'Perfection,' 'The Sublime,' 'The Picturesque,' 'The Graceful,' 'The Novel,' 'The Wonderful,' and so on, until he becomes lost in a theoretical maze, while he goes on writing and speaking in the same obscure, clumsy forms that he used before he ever saw a Rhetoric" (quoted in Kitzhaber, *Rhetoric* 208). Clark continued to teach English A until his untimely death from appendicitis in 1911, but his influence continued, as Clark had changed the focus of the introductory rhetoric course from elocution to written composition. English A remained in Northwestern's catalog of courses until it was dropped in 1968, but its basic content did not change. In his contribution to "Freshman English Courses in Twelve Illinois Colleges" for the *Illinois English Bulletin* in 1951, Ernest Samuels comments: "We do not give special instruction in 'oral' English" (15). Evidently the spirit of Cumnock still haunted English A. Samuels went on to describe a course that had two basic objectives: developing writing skills, including mechanics, style, correctness, and sense of audience; and developing "a full and appropriate response to what deserves to be called 'literature'" (16–17).

Given Northwestern's straitlaced origins, it is interesting to note that by the 1950s "pundits from other colleges, notably the University of Chicago, nicknamed Northwestern 'Country Club U' for its alleged emphasis on social life" (Pridmore 190). The reaction of the editors of the *Daily Northwestern* just after V-J Day suggests what campus life had become: "Ah, Peace—Ah, Men. Those strange 2-legged creatures wearing trousers which you may have seen around campus are MEN. . . . And for the feminine element, too, the lean years are over. Peace, its [*sic*] wonderful!" (Williamson and Wild 243). The end of the war brought more to campus than the renewal of Homecoming, the Waa-Mu show, and fraternity and sorority activities; in 1948 veterans swelled to an enrollment of 10,704. According to Williamson and Wild, "For several years the tone of student life was much influenced by the maturity and serious mindedness of the large number of veterans . . ." who "maintained a high level of academic achievement . . . [and] remained deeply concerned about national and international developments" (243).

In the postwar era, English A continued to be required of incoming freshmen, except for those who scored in the top 10 percent on an entrance examination. The English department during this era had many luminaries: Ernest Samuels, the Pulitzer Prize-winning biographer of Henry Adams; Harrison Hayford, the expert on Melville; Richard Ellmann, the biographer of William Butler Yeats and James Joyce; Bergen Evans, whose wildly popular "Introduction to Literature" class led him to fame as a television personality (and to notoriety for his involvement with the ill-fated "$64,000 Question"). Many of these senior professors taught English A at one time or another, but none devoted himself to it as did Wallace Douglas. As an undergraduate at

Cornell, Douglas had studied with Porter Perrin, who in the 1930s was objecting to poor composition pedagogy. In "The Remedial Racket," Perrin wrote: "These [handbook] exercises obviously violate the lone principle that present teachers of composition have salvaged from the 2,500 years of the discipline of rhetoric, that one learns to speak and write by speaking and writing" (384). Douglas brought the wit and passion of his mentor Perrin and his forebear J. Scott Clark to his efforts to reform the teaching of writing in college, as well as in elementary and secondary schools. In a memo to his department chair, Jean Hagstrum, Douglas wrote: "On the whole, it seems fair to say that nearly everything that is wrong with the way school teachers now approach their children and writing is a result of the fact that the teachers base their teaching of 'writing' on whatever conceptions they were able to derive from the 'rigorous writing courses' that they had in college" (15 May 1973). As Roberts and Johnson epitomized what freshman English was at Illinois and Veltman did so at Wheaton, we can understand what it meant to work in freshman English at Northwestern during the postwar era through Douglas's education, personality, and professional career.

I can sum up the ways in which Illinois, Wheaton, and Northwestern represent the apparent diversity in American higher education by describing the official seals they use to represent themselves. The original seal of the University of Illinois (now supplanted by a stylized "logo") includes an outer band that contains the phrases "University of Illinois" and "Chartered 1867." This band encircles a design with the words "Learning & Labor" hovering above a glowing open book. On one page of the book is written "Agriculture" and on the other "Science and Arts." Placed below the book are a plow, an anvil, and a small steam engine. True to Jonathan Baldwin Turner's populist vision for the new university, all the words of the emblem are in English, not Latin or Greek, and the images eschew the classical motifs that many schools use. The objects represent Illinois's break from the classicism typical of the old college, and from education directed toward the needs of the children of the powerful.

Wheaton College has no seal, but its stationery and other materials that represent the school contain a stylized drawing of the bell tower of the original "Main Building" (now called Blanchard Hall) completed in 1872, below which are written the words "For Christ and His Kingdom." The bell, used since that time to mark the time and important events at the Wheaton campus, is engraved with the date of installation, the name of the school, and the school's motto in Latin: *Christo Et Regno Ejus* (For Christ and His Kingdom). John L. Stratton, who headed the fund-raising effort for that original bell, commented: "The trade winds passing the Tower have kissed the bell and circled the globe with its message. Missionaries across the seas have heard it in their dreams" (Bechtel 34). Just as Jonathan Blanchard came to the Midwest in the 1830s "hoping to transform a spiritual wilderness into a Christian society," so Wheaton still seeks to use the liberal arts in a missionary spirit to transform not only middle America, but the world.

Northwestern University's official seal features three concentric circles. The outermost displays the words "Northwestern University," the name of the territory that the school was founded to serve, and the date of its founding, 1851. The second circle contains the Latin words, *Quaecumque Sunt Vera* (Whatsoever things are true), a phrase from the Epistle to the Philippians 4:3. In this particular part of the letter, Paul is encouraging the community to note: "Whatsoever things are true . . . honest . . . just . . . pure . . . lovely . . . of good report; if there be any virtue, and if there be any praise, think on these things." Below this phrase is a branch of laurel, the classical symbol of Apollo, and therefore of accomplishment in the arts and sciences. The innermost circle contains an open book surrounded by rays of light. On the book is written a Greek phrase from the Gospel of John 1:14, which translated says: "The Word . . . full of grace and truth." The scriptural phrases recall that the Methodist founders aimed to promote "*sanctified* learning," and the classical designs and language of the seal suggest their desire to create a university that would rival the best schools of the Northeast. The classic typeface used in the seal was designed by Frederic W. Goudy of Chicago. "Emerging from the same historical and cultural milieu as the University, the Goudy typeface might be said to reflect midwestern values: Its straightforward, self-assured, and unpretentious character makes it an appropriate choice for Northwestern" ("Northwestern University Identity System" 3).[7]

Those same qualities, "straightforward, self-assured, and unpretentious," also suggest my choice of these three midwestern schools as the basis for this study. Although they differ from one another in terms of their historical origins, their educational ideology, and their development, together they provide what I consider honest, true evidence of the practice of freshman English in the postwar era.

IN THE PREFACE TO *The Methodical Memory,* Sharon Crowley characterizes her work as "a deconstruction, rather than a history" (xiv). Crowley explains from a theoretical point of view why current-traditional rhetoric has remained "the most pervasive discursive practice ever used in writing instruction" (xiii).[8] I grapple with that same pervasive discursive practice from another point of view. In *The Methodical Memory,* Crowley asks, "What happens to classical invention when it is assimilated into the new rhetoric of the nineteenth century?" I ask, "What dichotomies pervade and support the structure of freshman English in the postwar era?" I take the representations of the practices of freshman English that I found in the archives and in my interviews as a text to be "solicited" in a Derridean sense, to reveal its structure, the source of its power, and the mechanism of its durability.

Perhaps I can better identify my "terministic screen" by comparing and contrasting this study with *Composition-Rhetoric.* Connors begins with a much larger—yet more general—archive, and he attempts to tell a much more sweeping narrative. Yet, he resists the "historiographic" label, claiming "the ideologies and theories have plenty of servants already" (21). He locates his study within his own experience: "My training had been New Rhetorical. . . . Criticizing the older methods of teaching writing . . . was an almost automatic task for one beginning historical study" (19). I have been trained as a pedagogue, and during my first twenty years of teaching, I kept afloat by reading James Moffett, Janet Emig, John Mellon, and Mina Shaughnessy, trying to find someone who could help me make sense of what I perceived as nearly random patterns of success and failure in my classroom. Beginning in 1980, my first attempt to interrogate my own experience as a teacher fell under what Stephen North has dubbed the "experimentalist" approach. Eight years later, while approaching my comprehensive exams, I sought some sort of a rhetorical Euclid to impose order on the chaos of my knowledge. At first I grasped at what I could find—Derrida, Lyotard, Foucault, Heidegger, Bourdieu, Jameson—but then began to read Berlin, North,

Lunsford, Crowley, Connors, and Kitzhaber, authors who could help me put my own experience into historical perspective. Out of the lumber room of my research and experience, some of it theoretical, much of it practical, emerges this book. Like Connors, I am convinced that "the more deeply I looked, the more I could see myself and my colleagues and friends in the words and works of people . . . for whom, just as for us, times were always clangingly modern and pressures were always great, paper grades were always due, and tomorrow was always mysterious" (20). My goal is not to show the benightedness of our forebears, but to look long and hard at all the evidence I could find of the actual experiences of real teachers and students, and to try to perceive what gave shape to their lives in the classroom.

Apart from the conviction that other descriptions and analyses of freshman English did not capture my self-recognition of being a student and a teacher, I did not enter into this research with a preconceived notion of what I might find or what I might prove. Certainly, my exposure to postmodernist analysis has influenced the way I have read the text of freshman English, and my exposure to the historiographers of composition has created a context for the raw data I found. The presumptions I have identified and named, however, originated not from me or other scholars, but from the material itself. Doing this research was not like searching through the haystack of evidence for a needle of truth; or finding some sort of Rosetta Stone that, if decoded, would allow me to make sense of an unintelligible language; or laying my hands on the smoking gun that would allow me to assign guilt where it belonged. In selecting a metaphor for my experience, I would say it was much more like cleaning out my mother's attic after she had passed away. I knew those boxes of notes, photos, clippings, letters, postcards, and souvenirs meant *something*, and I had a general sense of how they represented her life. But in arranging them I had no design to follow. Ultimately, I had to decide which items had real significance or none, which I could connect so as to reveal patterns in her life, and finally how to organize those patterns so as to create a story. I threw many things away, but in the end assembled a memory book that has some rough coherence.

Practicing Writing is also such a memory book. In it, I identify a system of presumptions that reveals the shape of the discursive practice of freshman English at a given time, or at least its local representation at Illinois,

Wheaton, and Northwestern. In the first part of this study, "The Discourse of Freshman English," I describe the system of rules and categories for thinking, speaking, and writing within which participants of freshman English operated. This system consists of six paradoxical presumptions. These names have not been selected from an established list of "keywords" such as Raymond Williams's; rather, I have tried to find common terms that captured the sense of the events I perceived. In some cases, these terms have been used by other writers as well, but not always with the denotation or connotation that I intend. I discuss in each chapter the etymology of the name I give to a particular facet of this discursive practice and distinguish between my and other usages with which it may be confused.

Before all else, freshman English was taken to be a "service" course, a concept discussed in chapter 1, "Instrumentality." As a service course, freshman English was considered universal; but by virtue of this universality, it could not claim any particular content as its own, and so it was confined to the margins of academic discourse. The marginality of the course is treated in chapter 2, "Priority." Because freshman English was a marginalized activity, intellectual interest in the actual content of the course was displaced, making what was taught under the heading "freshman English" almost arbitrary and leaving the field open to constant pedagogical innovation, features discussed in chapter 3, "Efficiency."

In chapter 4, "Individuality," I argue that teachers and students alike believed that the students' development as writers depended on their ability to render honest and accurate accounts of themselves as individuals; yet this individuality was the expression of a "self" carefully constructed according to an academic model of order and rationality. In their development as individuals, students were expected to accomplish two goals through reading: their enlightenment by means of the cultural values transmitted to them via their contact with serious literature, and their coming to realize the complex, organic unity of texts via close reading. These beliefs are discussed in the next two chapters, entitled "Transmission" and "Correspondence." I argue that these beliefs are problematic because the presence of cultural value and organic unity derive not from the texts themselves, as was supposed, but from the readers' self-construction according to Arnoldian ideals and New Critical theory, both of which tacitly informed reading in freshman English.

The second part of the study, "The Practice of Freshman English," takes up how this system of paradoxical beliefs and values operated as the rules for the practices of freshman English during the postwar era. "The Course," chapter 7, presents the activities and materials used in freshman English classrooms, the benefits claimed for having taken or having taught the course, and its essential unalterability, despite frequent attempts at pedagogical innovations. In "The Student," chapter 8, I analyze samples of writing that students produced in their freshman English classes so as to bring to the foreground the particular "intransitive" subjectivity to which they were expected to accommodate themselves. In the next chapter, "The Teacher," I examine the problematic position of the teacher of freshman English—both as a member of the faculty at a particular school and as a member of a profession. Here I present the biographies of four exemplary men—Wallace Douglas of Northwestern, Peter Veltman of Wheaton, Falk Johnson of Navy Pier, and Charles Roberts of Illinois.

SOME HISTORIANS ASSUME that as a consequence of knowing the history of their discipline, teachers will develop more enlightened pedagogies.[9] In my concluding chapter, I will explain how practitioner-based history can enable teachers to bring about far more important and subtle changes than adopting a more self-reflexive theory or choosing and deploying more effective means of delivering education. Practice-based history reveals what Richard Miller has called the "bureaucratic constraints that both enable the academic enterprise and limit its scope" (*Learning* 210). *Practicing Writing* suggests how to develop the "far more sober and supple intellectual persona" that Miller calls for in order to cope with such constraints (*Learning* 41). Becoming critically conscious of one's scene of teaching can be dangerous. One risk is to see teaching as simply too overwhelming to contemplate, and so to retreat into routine. Another is to see the problems as hopelessly complicated, and so abandon teaching entirely. A third is to think that critical consciousness makes one too sophisticated for the dirty work of the classroom; those who remain must be intellectually inferior. Such responses to recognizing the problematic nature of teaching lead to bitterness, judgment of others, or abandonment of the field. A more authentic response to understanding the complicated nature of teaching practices is to appreciate what Miller calls "the grammar of the culture" (24) of schools. He notes the tremendous stability of this type of culture: "Educational systems . . . have assumed a historically produced character that manifests itself in our time as an immensely complex bureaucracy with an inherent resistance to structural change" (23). Critically enlightened teachers tend to suspect bureaucracy and seek ways to circumvent or eliminate it. A more useful way to approach the challenge of educational reform, however, is to accept that schools cannot be freed of bureaucracy; they exist to serve bureaucratic ends: "This is what all teachers do, regardless of discipline or position in the academic hierarchy: they solicit, assess, and respond to student work; they perform the bureaucratic function of sifting and sorting individuals" (36). As it is impossible to be a teacher and not be, to some extent, a bureaucrat, Miller calls for effective "intellectual bureaucrats" who would have remarkable but not impossible abilities. These would include "tolerance for ambiguity, an appreciation for structured contradictions, a perspicacity that draws into its purview the multiple forces determining individual events and actions, an understanding of the essentially performative character of public life, and a recognition of the inherently political character of all matters emerging from the power/knowledge nexus" (213). Like Richard Miller, I hope that practitioners in composition as well as in many other fields might realize that "*constraining* conditions are not *paralyzing* conditions" (213).

The Discourse of

Freshman English

Instrumentality

$\mathcal{O}$N THE 1950S FRESHMAN ENG-
LISH WAS CONSIDERED A "SERVICE" course, that is, one designated as
the instrument by which students were prepared (or indoctrinated) for
other disciplines in the university. From its beginnings, "English"—first
literature and later composition—entered the college curriculum to serve
ancillary purposes. In *Professing Literature,* Gerald Graff describes the "pre-
professional era" of the early nineteenth century, during which literature served ends other than the understanding of literature itself. "There
was nothing wrong with treating literature in an instrumental way—as
an illustration of grammar, rhetoric, elocution, and civic and religious
ideals" (19). Susan Miller cites George Gordon, a nineteenth-century
literature professor at Oxford, who describes the "triple function" of
literature: "to delight and instruct us, but also, and above all, to save our
souls and heal the State" (*Textual Carnivals* 20). In less doctrinaire language,
Arthur Applebee offers five reasons for the acceptance of English literature as a subject in the nineteenth century. "The teaching of literature
for the first time met all requirements that could be put upon a subject
for study: usefulness, discipline, moral value, interest, even patriotism"

(29). From its inception, English as a discipline (including composition) had to justify its presence in the curriculum by instrumentalizing itself.

In his dissertation, "Captive Audiences: Composition Pedagogy, the Liberal Arts Curriculum and the Rise of Mass Higher Education," John Heyda documents the debate in early-nineteenth-century British universities over the relative merits of the classics or science as "centrally educative subjects." William Riley Parker, Wallace Douglas, Gerald Graff, Susan Miller, and many others have noted that the history of English in American colleges—including the introduction of freshman English at Harvard in the 1870s—is in a way the story of English replacing Classics as the "centrally educative subject." Within the English departments at American universities, one subject has carried the centrally educative (i.e., instrumental) function more than any other—the first-year course.

I use the term "instrumentality" to name the set of practices, common in American colleges and universities in the postwar era, by which academic literacy was inescapably reduced to a set of skills that students were expected to acquire by taking a particular course.[1] Once students had "had" this course, they were expected to be able to satisfy whatever demands for reading, writing, speaking, listening, and thinking they might encounter within or without the academy. A further consequence of instrumentality has to do with its impact on the notion of "literacy" within the academy. Because literacy became equated with broad notions of "reading," "writing," "speaking," "listening," or "thinking," the entire topic, a potentially powerful location for intellectual investigation, was dissipated into the realm of mere technique. Almost anything could be invoked as an agent of such "skills"—as I explain in the next chapter, "Priority," which explains how attempts to find stable content for the course led to constant yet fruitless innovation.

This chapter will present the general goals—both those of the academy, and those of society at large—that students and teachers of freshman English assumed (or were assigned) during the postwar era. Given those goals, the course was invested with certain specific practices, both in the classroom and within the institution as a whole. Given the nature of the course in which they found themselves caught up, both students and teachers assumed instrumental functions within the academy.

In 1965 National Council of Teachers of English commissioned Robert Gorrell to write a chapter on introductory composition courses for its survey, *The College Teaching of English*. Gorrell identified the general assumptions concerning the freshman course:

> In a sense, freshman English is popularly regarded as a kind of capsule liberal education, a way of filling the gaps that appear as specialization increases. The course is accepted and required with the hopes that it will work not one but a series of major miracles: that it will change the language habits of many students so that they will become adept in the dialect of standard English, that it will produce students who have ideas, can find facts to develop them, and can organize and present material clearly and persuasively, that it will train students to read expository prose rapidly and accurately and also to appreciate and interpret literature, that it will make students think clearly and logically, and so on. (92)

The outcomes Gorrell mentioned—proficiency in standard English; thinking, fact-finding, organizing; reading speed, accuracy, and interpretation; logic—are not content-specific. Unlike courses in other disciplines, freshman English existed to satisfy the demands of the student's real reasons for attending the university. Freshman English was a means to what students themselves and the faculty acknowledged as more important ends.

Gorrell's statement also illustrates the tension that the instrumental function of the first-year course causes. On the one hand, freshman English assumed the duties of providing a "capsule liberal education," the locus of academic literacy. Gorrell's phrase "produce students" suggests that it was not intended to convey a particular body of information or even to deal with a body of information; rather, it served to remake persons in an academic image and likeness. On the other hand, Gorrell states the impossibility of a single course producing such effects. For freshman English to "produce students" as expected would constitute "a series of major miracles." As would-be miracle-worker, freshman English became a scapegoat for the rest of the academy. It was necessary as an instrument of academic literacy, thereby relieving all other disciplines from responsibility for the quality of students' spoken and written language. It was also necessary as a place to direct the blame when mass-produced graduates failed to live up to expectations that hearkened back to a golden age when all students supposedly achieved the kinds of competencies Gorrell describes.

By providing all students at the academy with a "capsule liberal education," freshman English also undertook the task of advancing the dominant political ideology. After World War II and the ensuing East-West tension, American higher education assumed its share of responsibility for fostering democracy in a world that tended toward less valid, more dangerous ideologies. Society in general and colleges in particular expected that graduates would provide the enlightened leadership that participatory government demands. As the instrument of academic literacy, freshman English bore the brunt of these expectations. In "Rhetoric and the Quest for Certainty" (1962), Hans Guth summed up the role of the course as an instrument of local-level democracy: "No college department . . . recognizes as its specialty the responsible use of language in nontechnical communication. On the other hand, our graduates, as school board members, newspaper editors, PTA chairmen, and chamber of commerce presidents will participate in such communication—though they may never have been led to examine its rhetorical structure for moral implications" (135). Guth connected the responsibility of freshman English to produce academically literate students with the university's responsibility to produce good citizens. No other discipline was willing to "deal with such matters as the byways of innuendo," but Guth saw that if teachers mustered their "self-confidence and self-respect," "Freshman English, which at its least inspiring dwindles into a service course, can be a crucial part of a student's liberal education" (136). Only the course that touches *all* students—freshman English—could prepare the citizenry for the rhetorical demands of modern citizenship.

In "The One-Legged, Wingless Bird of Freshman English" (1950), Kenneth Oliver connected freshman English with citizenship in broader terms, but in doing so invested the course with even greater responsibility as an instrument of democracy. Arguing against Harold Allen's proposals to base the course on communication theory, Oliver wrote: "Either Americans will continue to discover and express their own personal, individual experiences, convictions, points of view, regardless of what sways the crowd, or collectivism will strengthen its hold upon both ideas and action. . . . Vigorous, effective, sincere personal expression may lead to that maturity of thought which can prevent from developing Hitlers and Politburos at too tragic a rate among us" (5). It was not enough to produce graduates who could run newspapers, school boards, and chambers of commerce. For Oliver, the fate of democracy—and therefore of the entire world, given his culture's understanding of the American experience during and after World War II—depended upon the personal expression that no course taught or promoted, save freshman English. Only if individuals learned to express their "inner selves," Oliver claimed, could society stem the tendency toward the horrors of "collectivism." Oliver's words suggest the seriousness attached to the course. He saw it as the sole instrument within the academy by which democratic ideology could be promoted.[2]

Notably, Oliver does not claim that "discover[ing] and express[ing] . . . personal, individual experiences, convictions, points of view, regardless of what sways the crowd" would help Americans address other social issues that provoked public debate in the 1950s. In their papers, students often addressed topics such as McCarthyism, the perils of the atomic age, racism, anti-Semitism, and sexism, but teachers and administrators did not use freshman English as a forum for these issues.

In subsequent chapters, I will use examples of student writing on controversial topics to explain how the course did not employ such subjects (or the controversial books and articles often used as models) as topoi at which genuine public dialogue might commence. Instead, the discourse of freshman English included them as it did the notion of a "liberal education" so as to contain and neutralize them within the prevailing social and political ideology.

Commentators such as Guth and Oliver called attention to the significance of freshman English in American democratic life, but the language of catalogues and textbooks obliquely devalued the course. Those who taught freshman English characterized it as a temporary means to the permanent, truly valuable ends of an academic education.

Discussing the place of literature in English A, the freshman course at Northwestern, Harrison Hayford (1956) acknowledged that the course must serve the needs of students whose interests lie in disciplines other than the liberal arts, such as commerce, journalism, education, engineering, music, or speech. He commented: "It would be impossible to do in one basic freshman course all the things that validly might be done. . . . We emphasize composition because we think it is what the students most obviously need and what focuses the educative processes germane to the area most usefully for them and for us as their teachers" (45). Students in English A needed composition, in other words, to further their careers as managers, journalists, teachers, engineers, musicians, or performers, both in the academy and afterwards.

The University of Illinois *Stylebook of English* (1951) introduced students to their work in Rhetoric 101 and 102 with these words: "Good English, spoken and written, will be expected of you as a college graduate. Almost every survey of the requirements for success in any career emphasizes the necessity of capable expression of facts and ideas. . . . To assure your preparation for the future, the University requires you to express yourself in clear, concise English" (University Senate Committee on Student English 1). The *Stylebook* deems literacy important because it serves practical purposes in the students' futures. No matter which careers students may pursue, they must "express [themselves] . . . in clear, concise English" in order to succeed. Without doubt the *Stylebook*'s assertion is valid to the system within which it was constituted. Management, law, science, engineering, medicine, all professions require (or at least are facilitated by) a command of "good English, spoken and written." However, except for departments within liberal arts such as English itself and a few token experiments elsewhere,[3] colleges or professional curricula within the university did not assume responsibility for developing the literacy of their graduates. Responsibility for academic literacy remained within the boundaries of freshman English.

Freshman English, then, assumed general goals as a capsule liberal education and as an introduction to political and professional discourse. Given these goals, the content of the course—reading and writing—becomes instrumentalized. Reading becomes the means to getting at what is important in substantial subjects; writing becomes the expression of the content one has learned. Prefaces to the anthologies used in the freshman course describe reading as a method, or tool. Myron Matlaw and James Stronks, the editors of *Pro and Con* (1960), state: "Reading with greater comprehension will not only improve your grades and help you in all your college courses; it will, beyond these short-term benefits, stimulate your mind and broaden your understanding and experience" (xiv). Like an investment, literacy produces both short-

and long-term profits. To use another metaphor, literacy is an obstacle to be overcome in order to obtain both external and internal benefits. In *Readings for College English,* a text used at Northwestern in the early 1950s, John C. Bushman and Ernst G. Mathews describe the value of their book in improving students' reading skills: "The discussion questions in this book present 'laboratory' work in the techniques of good reading; the patterns established are for the most part transferable to all types of reading" (ix). Here, reading is presented as a scientific endeavor. Students arrive at general principles via laboratory experiments and then apply them in the "real" world.[4] Both sets of editors encourage the students to consider the material their texts contain as having only temporary value. Having completed the course, students retain a general sort of skill, or power; in and of themselves, the actual selections they had read have no intended value. Learning to read as a college student, then, is a means. Once a student has succeeded in freshman English, she or he is capable of achieving much more important ends, such as social or professional position, specialized (and therefore valuable) knowledge, or economic or political power.

Like reading, writing also became an instrument. Oscar J. Campbell's "The Failure of Freshman English" outlines the two major objectives for freshman courses in English: development of mechanical skill (the less important) and training in thinking. Regarding thinking, Campbell claims that the freshman course is meant to allow the student new to the university "opportunity to articulate [his new intellectual acquisitions]." As an instrument of articulation, writing becomes a secondary or supportive skill by which primary or significant "intellectual acquisitions" can be transmitted (177–85).[5] Herman Bowersox, head of the freshman English program at Roosevelt University, wrote in 1955 that the purpose of the freshman Composition course is practical—"to provide the student with skill in the production of the kind of discourse, chiefly exposition and argument, that he needs in his other classes and in later life" (39). As part of the content of a course that is itself an instrument for the rest of the academy, writing becomes a tool. This tool will undoubtedly prove useful to those who acquire it, but it has no particular interest for anyone but those who must teach the students to use it.

The mechanistic undertones of freshman English reveal an instrumentality that extended the responsibility of those who taught the course far beyond the limits of their classrooms. Even though they had no control over students who had completed the course, teachers found themselves responsible for writing performed across the entire range of the university's offerings, and for the progress of students as they advanced toward graduation. Sometimes teachers of freshman English were implicated by forces outside their control, such as complaints of students' illiteracy from other faculty members or employers of the university's graduates. Sometimes they implicated themselves.

In March of 1960, the Senate Committee on Student English in the undergraduate division at the University of Illinois, Chicago (Navy Pier),[6] distributed a copy of a memo that Donald W. Riddle, head of the Division of Social Sciences, had distributed to his department. Riddle had given an exam on which five of twenty-one students exhibited "deficiencies"; two were so poorly written that he lowered their grades. He took it upon himself to inform his colleagues, the committee (and indirectly, the rest of the faculty), of the problem. In his memo, Riddle explained his approach to poor student English, which included marking all errors in spelling and grammar, lowering grades due to substandard writing, and using the "yellow slips," stickers that staff from any discipline could use in order to refer a student to the English department for remedial help. The committee's use of Riddle's memo illustrates the practical effects of instrumentality on students, teachers, and on the institution.

Riddle felt a certain responsibility to further academic literacy; otherwise, he never would have written the memo. Nevertheless, he did not perceive that his responsibility lay in dealing with the source of the problem. He wrote, "I do not assume the duty of teaching rhetoric. But I consider it my duty to cooperate with the Committee on Student English." He could spot problems in his students' writing, but either could not or would not deal with their causes. For that, individual students were referred back to the Department of English, and the problem of illiteracy itself was turned over to the Committee on Student English. The committee used Riddle's experience as an example of what other faculty should do, in particular that they should use the yellow slips so that students who needed another dose of freshman English could get it. Everyone involved—Professor Riddle, the members of the committee, the faculty at large who read the memo when the committee distributed it, even the students who had written poorly in the first place—turned to the designated instrument of academic literacy for the solution to their problem.

Seven years earlier (18 December 1953), Fred Faverty, chair of the English department at Northwestern and head of the Committee on Students' Use of English, received a memo very similar to Riddle's from Economics professor Frank W. Fetter. He had been moved to write because "two recent student reports . . . spurred me to organize some ideas that I have expressed in silence to myself a number of times." He was bothered by the carelessness he found in the papers, which were poorly organized and contained many errors in spelling and syntax. The students offered excuses—they had not been asked to write a paper since freshman English and were out of practice; no other professors had criticized their work; if the content of the paper was accurate, they presumed that formal errors made no difference. Fetter noted that many faculty had seen such deficiencies and heard such excuses, but they had taken no action because the College of Liberal Arts lacked a clear mechanism for reporting substandard writing, and because the problem was so widespread that they did not know where to begin. He proposed that Faverty's committee develop some sort of "short printed form" that faculty could use to report students who produced "deficient work," and proposed that Faverty approach the dean of the college to make a statement clarifying "that the improvement in the student use of English is not just a policy of the English department, but is part of the educational program of the College of Liberal Arts."

In effect, Fetter was asking for the same sort of response to the problem of poor student English that Riddle had sought. Like Riddle, he tried to deal with the problem that arose in his own classroom and also tried to encourage his colleagues to do their share to help students improve the quality of their writing. Neither he nor Riddle, however, sought noninstrumental approaches to the problem of student writing. Neither acknowledged that he may have given assignments too ambitious for the length of time students had to write them, that his students may have been unfamiliar with the conventions of writing in his discipline, or that he had assumed improperly that a single introductory course could furnish students with such "training in English" that they could produce skillful prose wherever it might be called for. Instead, the incidents were used to intensify pressure upon the freshman English course and its teachers to deal with the problems of academic literacy, and so absolve others of responsibility.

Another incident from the files of the Senate Committee on Student English at Navy Pier illustrates instrumentality in a different way. In their annual report to the faculty at the end of the 1953–1954 academic year, the committee proposed a plan for "attempting to establish next year the tradition that students here use good English in all their University work." This plan consisted of a promotional program featuring stories in the student newspaper and a series of posters placed around the campus each week encouraging a heightened awareness of the advantages of correct and forceful expression. Their memo states, "During one week, for example, the program may stress the fact that vocational and social advancement may be helped by good English and hurt by poor English." In this case, freshman English instructors were spared responsibility for coordinating the program, but the promotion itself becomes a surrogate for the course. Those who would attempt to "establish . . . [a] tradition" of literacy by means of advertising believe that good English will come about via the operation of an instrument. Academic literacy, itself an instrument, is to be achieved instrumentally. The archives do not contain any further mention of this program, but Riddle's memo six years later suggests that students had not yet been led to establish the desired tradition.

At Wheaton College, the Department of English itself raised the issue of seemingly incompetent writing among juniors and seniors. Instructors had noticed that other departments were accepting writing that would never be tolerated in Writing 111 and 112 (Wheaton's name for freshman English). The English faculty felt frustrated because the work they had put into developing the writing skills of freshmen had been wasted when their colleagues allowed upperclassmen to backslide. The minutes of the department meeting on 20 May 1955 report the thoughts of one professor: "Why [can't] we . . . maintain the same high standards in other departments' courses? Is it honest to give a young man a diploma (which indicates that he has satisfied the English Department requirements), and then let him go into a pastorate and mangle the church bulletin?" The moral urgency expressed at that meeting led them to bring their case to the entire faculty. The agenda for the faculty meeting states that the Department of English wished to present "the need for every faculty member to cooperate in keeping the level of written English at Wheaton as high as possible."

Confronted with the limits of their power as instruments of literacy, those responsible for freshman English did not absolve themselves of responsibility for students no longer under their control. Instead, the Wheaton Department of English accepted the responsibility imposed upon them with a zeal that reflected the evangelical temper of the college. They perceived their duty not only to offer a course, but to ensure competence in academic literacy for all students. Their colleagues at Illinois shared a similar self-perception. *Standards in Freshman English,* published at Urbana in 1956, stated that once students had completed Rhetoric 101 they "can, and will henceforth, write correctly and effectively even under pressure" (3). Their colleagues in other departments gladly let the English faculty attempt to enforce such dictums.

Clyde Kilby and other members of the Department of English at Wheaton requested the opportunity to present their plea at a general faculty meeting. During three separate sessions in early 1956, Kilby called for a number of changes in the policies of the college, including requiring all faculty to scrutinize student work for correctness and style; setting up auxiliary services such as a referral system, remedial courses, and a writing clinic; and various hortatory efforts on the part of the administration to encourage better writing. Kilby's requests produced predictable results. The faculty asked the English department to develop and distribute a checklist that professors could attach to student papers. Any students reported as deficient by two or more of their instructors would be remanded to the English department.

The checklist itself (nearly identical to forms used for the same purpose at Urbana and Navy Pier) contained a statement in boldface capital letters followed by three evaluative comments:

THE ENGLISH IN THIS PAPER IS UNACCEPTABLE

__ It appears to be the result of carelessness. In the future I shall expect you to write with more care.

__ The English in this paper is so poor that your grade has been lowered.

Write with more care.

— You should take this paper to the English Department, where corrective measures will be suggested. Do this within the next week; then return this paper to me.

The checklist itself suggests how the faculty in disciplines other than English read student writing. Detached from the texts themselves, "English" is an added feature to their "real" substance. Other disciplines disavow problematic discourse and remand it the English department. In the marginal space occupied by freshman English, teachers assumed the roles of police or physicians. They had to work with language that the rest of the academy refused to recognize because it violated laws or displayed such a lack of "health" that it needed therapy. Students who exhibited carelessness knew the law, but disregarded it, like motorists who run stop signs or ignore the speed limit. Students who displayed "poor" English revealed a deeper problem, a deficiency due to substandard nurturing or lack of development.

Three years later, in the annual report of the English department for 1959–1960, C. J. Simpson, the acting chair, suggested how attempting to highlight the problem of student writing at Wheaton only drove it further into the shadows. In that year, only ten students had been reported to the English department as deficient in their writing. Simpson commented, "Ten is not a large number. It seems to mean that in general our students write quite acceptably, or that some instructors are quite lenient in the standard of writing they will accept. I fear the latter is more likely to be true than the former."

Instruction in writing at Northwestern University also bore the imprint of instrumentality. In 1935 the faculty established a Committee on Students' Use of English. This committee exercised the "power to make and enforce regulations necessary to secure a reasonable command of English by students whose work is reported to it." Unlike its counterpart at Illinois, the committee at Northwestern wielded only symbolic power.[7] It seems to have produced only one regulation, a warning in the university's catalog of undergraduate offerings: "No student seriously defective in the use of English, either spoken or written, will be recommended by the faculty of the College of Liberal Arts. Written papers seriously defective will not be acceptable in any department of the College and work unacceptable on this score will be reported with the evidence to the committee" (from "Minutes of the Faculty of the College of Liberal Arts," Northwestern University, 10 December 1935). Although no evidence reveals that a student was ever reported to the committee, let alone not "recommended" (presumably, for graduation), documents from the university's archives suggest that the "students' use of English" did not meet the faculty's standards.

In his annual report to Dean Simeon E. Leland in 1961, department chair Jean Hagstrum discussed the continuing dissatisfaction with English A10 (English A had been renumbered in 1956):

> The problems that continually arise in English A10 are among the most complex that we as an English department must face. . . . I am convinced that the American freshman, even in a university with a selected enrollment, is badly in need of a year of instruction in written exposition. It will not do to say, as some have, that our students are getting better in English. Admittedly they are. . . . We recognize now that the use of language is like the wearing of appropriate clothes in only superficial ways. The highest use of language, on the contrary, represents the activity of the mind on its newest frontiers and is inextricably related to the entire educational process. A good university ought not to abandon compulsory exposition as its students get better but ought instead to lift the course to their level and beyond—and give everyone an opportunity of taking it. Such a course would be of inestimable value during the rest of the student's academic career and, if he is in a position of responsibility, during the rest of his life.

As Guth and Oliver had suggested, Hagstrum saw the course as a tool not only for academic success, but also for all of the other activities a college graduate might encounter in life, especially those of greater social value and responsibility. Moreover, Hagstrum's statement reveals the boundless expectations invested in the course. No student lay beyond the need for freshman English. As students grew in their skill, the responsibility of the course grew all the greater. The more proficient the students became, the more important freshman English became.

In 1968 Northwestern rethought its educational philosophy. Hagstrum headed the faculty committee that set forth "new approaches to undergraduate education at Northwestern." One of the new approaches the committee enacted was the demise of English A10.

> The English Department has now abandoned the monolithic, multi-sectioned freshman course in composition for a series of courses that illustrate the range and method of modern scholarship in English. . . . Although it will offer advanced work in composition to interested students, the English Department can no longer be expected to serve as the stylistic and compositional chaplain to the entire University. It must . . . not consume all its energies in a service course of dubious benefits. (*A Community of Scholars* 14)

In abolishing English A10, the faculty avoided the problem of instrumentality, but did not resolve it. They admit the bankruptcy of an instrumental approach to academic literacy ("a service course of dubious benefits"), but frame the issue not in terms of the function or value of language within the academy but in terms of power and obligation. The English department excused itself from duties as "chaplain"—the military or hospital officer who does not fight and die, or dispense cures and perform surgery, but only "counsels the suffering." Instead, the members of the department become implicated more thoroughly in the "real work" of the academy, where they could expend their energies in ways more suited to their talents and dispositions. Perhaps they were wise to escape the dilemma of freshman English, but their action does not solve the problem Hans Guth raises of "teachers [who] are understandably reluctant to leave the solid ground of a rigorously defined specialty and venture into the area where students learn to distinguish the responsible from the irresponsible" ("Rhetoric" 135). The Northwestern decision to limit the English faculty to what they considered their proper discipline reveals one way of avoiding the problem of instrumentality. No one articulated the perception that the freshman course resided in an inextricably instrumental position, and that the only way to escape that trap was to abolish the course. Nevertheless, from a critical perspective forty years later, we can see that the department at Northwestern intuited the inherently instrumental paradox of offering such a course.

The very existence of the University Senate Committee on Student English at the University of Illinois (Urbana) exemplifies how freshman English served as an instrumental agent of academic literacy. Executive Secretary Jessie Howard documented the history of the committee in "The Qualifying Examination in English: Background" (1962).

She located its origin in the "criticism of poor English among many of [the university's] graduates" in the late 1930s. In 1940 the Board of Trustees pressured the university president, Arthur C. Willard, "to see that serious consideration be given to the matter" (University Senate Committee 1). A number of committees conducted studies of the problem and surveyed faculty opinion. As a result, in 1941 the Senate implemented a system by which freshmen were required to take two semester-length courses, Rhetoric 1 and 2. Those who scored low on the placement exam took a noncredit remedial course, Rhetoric 0, as well. Students who received a grade lower than a "B" in Rhetoric 2 took the English qualifying examination. Those who failed were assigned another semester of writing instruction, Rhetoric 5. Later, these courses were renumbered as 100, 101, 102, and 200. During its twenty-seven years of operation, the University Senate Committee on Student English implemented a number of projects in order to ascertain the level of students' writing performance and to raise it. The committee published the *Stylebook of English,* a required text for all students at the university. It established a writing clinic where those not enrolled in rhetoric courses could remedy their writing deficiencies. It frequently scrutinized students and faculty alike through surveys and studies. It revamped the rhetoric offerings, eliminating the remedial course for freshmen and establishing an intensive publicity program in order to stimulate better teaching in the high schools. It tinkered with the relationship between the English qualifying examination and Rhetoric 200, eventually making the course optional.

Despite considerable efforts by the committee, the hundreds of instructors in the Rhetoric program, and the thousands of students who took the courses and exams, the committee's own evidence suggests that during the postwar era students at the University of Illinois did not show improvement relative to standards of correctness and expectations that they write in a particular academic style. After a decade under its revised standards for student English, the committee issued "The University of Illinois Faculty Looks at Student English." The report, based on a questionnaire distributed to the entire faculty in 1954, states: "The available evidence indicates that the problem of unsatisfactory student English still exists. Members of the faculty still express critical opinions of students' English. Grades given in Freshman Rhetoric and English qualifying examinations show that substantial portions of the student body lack the ability to write good English" (1).

In a document accompanying this particular report, the committee also analyzed responses to the question, "What is your reaction to the proposition that, as a University faculty member, you should accept some responsibility for improving the written English of your undergraduate students?" Although 58 percent responded "agree strongly," the committee concluded: "The fact that a faculty member proposes some measure for the improvement of student English or that he endorses such a proposal is no sign that he will help to put the proposal into practice" (16). The committee's own evidence revealed that every proposal for enlisting faculty cooperation in improving or maintaining students' English —publishing the *Stylebook,* distributing "Pink Slips" (checklists similar to the "yellow slips" used at Navy Pier), distributing background studies and suggestions for incorporating writing assignments into courses outside the Division of Rhetoric, conducting faculty symposiums, engaging in various types of publicity—proved ineffective. As did their colleagues at Wheaton, Navy Pier, and Northwestern, those responsible for freshman English at Urbana found that the rest of the faculty claimed to value "good English," but even in the face of obvious deficiencies were not willing to displace the responsibility for teaching good English away from a single, instrumentally conceived course.

Evidence of the problematic nature of freshman English as an instrument of academic literacy also includes data concerning the students' performance and attitudes. Between 1947 and 1960, the percentage of students who failed the English qualifying examination rose from 13.3 (1946–1947) to 55.2 (1960–1961). In 1965 Wilmer A. Lamar and Ruth E. McGugan, of the Division of Rhetoric at Urbana, surveyed first-year students in Rhetoric 101 and 102, students who had taken the courses two or three years before, as well as the instructors. Of the older students who responded, 94 percent disagreed with the statement "Rhetoric should be required only of English majors," and 91 percent disagreed with "Rhetoric is a useless preparation for my career." These figures suggest that students from a wide variety of specializations perceived their experience in the rhetoric classes to be valuable. Nevertheless, 54 percent agreed with the statement "My writing is pretty much the same after the course as before." Fewer yet (41 percent) agreed that "I have continuously tried to improve my writing on the basis of this course."

Only one-third (between 30 and 35 percent) could agree with statements such as: "The writing techniques that I learned have improved my work, and consequently my grades, in other courses"; "the course improved my day-to-day use of correct grammar"; "the course caused me to change my style of writing"; or "I noticed that my spelling improved as a result of the course" (68–69). Like the faculty, these students claimed to have found value in what Robert Connors calls "composition-rhetoric," but when pressed found little in their actual writing practices that revealed any real change. The students' felt sense that the course had provided them with something useful belies Connors's assertion that "during the Modern Period, it becomes a truism that student dislike for Freshman Composition is exceeded only by the dislike of its teachers" (*Composition-Rhetoric* 13). He acknowledges that "composition-rhetoric" fulfilled "potent social and pedagogical needs" (7), suggesting that even during the "modern period," when Connors alleges that the course "remained a scholarly backwater and a professional avocation, a drudgery, and a painful initiation ritual" (14–15), a complex phenomenon was unfolding under the title "Freshman English." Broad-brush labels such as "current-traditional rhetoric" and other generalizations about the post–World War II era mask the subtle interplay of experience among teachers and students of freshman English.

Ironically, a course that assumed the general goal of providing a "capsule liberal education" contradicts itself in two ways. The claims of service to the liberal arts and to democracy are belied by the specific issues with which freshman English teachers and students typically concerned themselves, like the correction of surface-level errors. Moreover, instead of fostering the beliefs and practices commonly held to be "liberal," for example freedom and originality, as the instrument of academic literacy, freshman English became the agent of an ideology that reinforced strict rules and conformity.

NOT ONLY DID instrumentality motivate many of the practices of the course itself; it also affected the lives of the students and faculty involved in freshman English. When language itself is instrumentalized, those involved with such language also inescapably become instruments themselves.

No matter how humane or visionary administrators and teachers might have been, the instrumental nature of freshman English reduced students to the status of raw material. They were valuable not because of their individual potential or innate worth as human beings, but because they were grist for the machine of freshman English. John Heyda refers to this aspect of the course when he describes the vacuousness of early-twentieth-century textbooks for freshman English: "In spite of the fine talk, by Channing [Boylston Professor of Rhetoric at Harvard from 1819 to 1851] and others, of social equality, justice, and the wonders of an 'improved society,' composition instruction had clearly failed to define the student as anything but an object, a mere tool of liberal educational policy" ("Captive Audiences" 149). The firm but friendly talk in text-books and course materials about future academic, social, and financial benefits of having taken freshman English masks what students became within it.

Now and then, a submerged hostile reality broke the polite surface. Karl Dykema, who served as chair of the Conference on College Composition and Communication in 1953, wrote "The Problem of Freshman English in the Liberal Arts College" (1951). Dykema discussed the tension between the liberal rhetoric with which freshman English was presented, and the rigid expectations that students had to meet. He named as one undercurrent of this tension the survival of English departments themselves. "It is the special problem of freshman English in the liberal arts college to see that the course is so conducted that it will meet its proper objectives and yet not discourage students from electing courses in literature" (4). The "special problem" for the instructors, then, is to balance what they must do for the academy (indoctrinate the students rigorously in academic literacy) against what they would choose to do (attract large enough numbers to maintain courses in the fields in which they have been trained and which they wish to teach—in short, courses desirable to them). Students became tokens in this struggle between the beliefs and desires of the institution as a whole, and those of a smaller constituency of common interest, the Department of English.

During a meeting at Wheaton College in 1956, the members of the English department were discussing the possibility of exempting some students from general education requirements, including Writing 111 and 112. One instructor, Helen Siml deVette, had been so successful in teaching expository writing that her students had been able to win prizes in national competitions. She observed that it would be unfortunate to allow the fifty best writing students to escape the English department completely when they were the very ones who should be trained in writing. For this instructor, students were resources for the advancement of the program itself. She did not object because the talented students to be exempted would not be able to meet the requirements of the college, but because they would siphon off what little recognition freshman English had been able to achieve.

William Riley Parker has pointed out that students in freshman English became the capital upon which teachers and departments tried to base their power and status. In "Where Do English Departments Come From?" he describes the mechanism whereby the raw material of freshman English enrollees provided the basis upon which English departments became so prominent in the university. "It was the teaching of freshman composition that quickly entrenched English departments in the college and university structure" (11). It had an even more profound effect upon those who taught. Once students had fulfilled their requirements they were free of the engine of freshman English, but many instructors never escaped. Freshman English was staffed for the most part by the powerless of academia: graduate students, new faculty struggling for tenure, or those who had despaired of ever achieving a tenure-track position and were content with teaching only the required course. According to Robert Connors, what Oscar J. Campbell wrote in 1939 held true for the postwar era: "At the bottom of almost every large English department lies a kind of morass of unhappy, disillusioned men and women which poisons all its fairer regions" (*Composition-Rhetoric* 203).[8] In his survey, Gorrell found this pattern of staffing to be one of the common denominators of freshman English across the nation in the 1950s. Ironically, the one course considered important enough to be made a universal requirement could only be staffed, for the most part, with conscripts. It is doubly ironic that the more conscientious these conscripts proved to be, the less likely they were to advance within academia.[9] In "Freshman English in America" (1965), Martin Steinmann commented: "Often the able, conscientious teacher of freshman English never gets his Ph.D. At the end of seven years, or whatever the limit is, he is turned out of post-graduate school and his job and, while looking for work as a textbook salesman, copy-editor, or junior-college teacher, has ample leisure to contemplate his folly" (393–94). Anyone who tried to work what Gorrell called the "several major miracles" expected of freshman English found that the demands of teaching the course left one unable to devote sufficient time to the work that would bring advancement, especially completing one's dissertation. Those who began in freshman English and survived usually did so by subverting the overt purpose of the course. They either taught just well enough to escape judgment as incompetent, or made the course into one they could teach comfortably, usually some sort of literary survey.[10]

A poll of the rhetoric staff at Urbana by Charles Roberts in 1942 revealed that their primary interests in high school had been books and literature. Virtually all had majored as undergraduates in English literature and were doing graduate work in order to teach advanced courses in literature. Few thought it worthwhile for the department to offer a graduate course in the teaching of composition. In "Provisions for Rhetoric and the Rhetoric Staff," a 1951 update of Roberts's survey, the University Senate Committee on Student English found that these characteristics had not changed in the intervening nine years and commented: "The teaching of rhetoric is likely to be regarded as only a chore, a temporary means of livelihood, a 'blind-alley job,' a dreary routine from which escape is to be found at the earliest possible moment" (4). In a paper delivered at the Conference on College Composition and Communication in 1958, Dudley Bailey clearly connected the instrumentality of freshman English as a course, and the instrumentalization of those who taught it. "Like the janitors, we provide a 'valuable service' for our various colleges. But we are not really a part of any of them. Our own colleagues in English look upon us with friendly toleration—if they are not overly candid—or outright contempt—if they are starchy and honest. Only at our conventions do we assume any importance in the scheme of things; and I have often thought of this convention as the largest wound-licking convocation in the teaching profession" (232).

The essential instrumentality of freshman English and its ramifications suggest why certain approaches to reform did not work. Plans to raise the self-expectations and performance of teachers or students of freshman English without seeking to realign the expectations and responsibilities for academic literacy within the university only made things worse. Plans for improvement in "literacy" that did not also deal with the context within which freshman English had to operate raised the expectations of those implicated in the course, but could not possibly deal with the causes of their perceived inadequacies. As one member of the faculty at Illinois wrote to the University Senate Committee on Student English in 1955: "The present system of a Senate Committee on Student English is to blame. It perpetuates the problem by serving as a scapegoat, and thus encourages faculty irresponsibility" ("Background" 8). Instrumentality made freshman English a kind of tar baby; the more it was grappled with, the more inescapable the problem seemed to become.

Priority

FRESHMAN ENGLISH, THE IN-
STRUMENT OF TRAINING IN LITERACY within the academy, occupied a
problematic position during the postwar era. It was the prerequisite
that every student had to fulfill, yet it stood at the margin of all academic discourses. Virtually every discipline had to surrender its students
to freshman English for a semester or two, but this universally required
course had no power to generate its own disciplinary status. It included
everyone, but by that very function could not contain anything. In
"Derrida, Deconstruction, and Our Scene of Teaching," Sharon Crowley explains the relationship between freshman English and the academic disciplines:

> Instruction in expository writing is the fallen other—marginalized,
> bracketed off—which authorizes, literally underwrites, the authen-
> ticity . . . of mainstream academic work. Thus, if Michael Ryan is
> correct when he argues that "all knowledge operates through acts
> of exclusion and marginalization," we are provided an explanation
> for the continued maintenance of the huge institutional enterprise

which is composition instruction (140) [reference is to Ryan's book]. Composition programs are the margins, the blank spaces which surround and highlight the real texts produced in the academy. (179)

Crowley's interpretation of the status of composition programs in the 1980s applies to freshman English in the postwar era, as well. During both periods, the required composition course stood at the boundary of academic discourse; it was a nondiscourse, a discourse of what must come before the formation of discourse proper within the boundaries of a discipline.

Discussing the content of English A, the freshman English course at Northwestern, Harrison Hayford provides an example of the problematic position of freshman English. The Department of English had considered making English A into an introductory literature class. The majority of the incoming freshmen at a selective institution like Northwestern were thought to need no further instruction in grammar, syntax, and vocabulary, and it would have pleased the English faculty to be able to teach material that they enjoyed and that they believed could transmit moral and social value. But they had to consider their function within the university. In 1956, three years after he had directed a revision of English A, Hayford wrote: "The 1300 students in the basic course are not just the Liberal Arts freshmen but all the freshmen in the University, from the schools of Commerce, Journalism, Education, Technology, Music, and Speech, as well as the Liberal Arts. Neither their proficiency in composition and reading, nor the purposes for which their separate schools require them to take the basic course would justify us in subordinating composition and centering the course upon great literature" ("Literature" 45). Certainly there is no inherent obstacle to the course being based solely on literature.[1] Even those who still insisted on teaching prescriptive grammar and usage—and at Northwestern, they were few—had plenty of time to spend on literature; moreover, there was no mandatory, vital content that would be displaced. But Hayford and other members of the English department knew they could not justify the choice of content to their colleagues in the other disciplines that English A was expected to serve. As a result, those responsible for English A decided to "use literature," but to "emphasize composition because we think it is what the students most obviously need and what focuses the educative processes germane to the area most usefully for them and for us as their teachers" (45).

Hayford's experience at Northwestern illustrates the inescapable paradox of a course held responsible for the literacy of the entire academy. As a universal instrument it could not favor any particular content, yet given its charge of great responsibility the course had to represent itself as containing that which is fundamental and most important. Hayford named that content "composition"; Illinois called it "rhetoric," and Wheaton, "writing." In all cases, these names were supposed to identify an ideal entity that the discourses of actual disciplines reflected only partially or imperfectly. In "Accidental Institution: On the Origin of Modern Language Study," Wallace Douglas explains the process by which the "mental discipline" associated with the classics was transferred to modern language study in general, and to English studies in particular. He cites E. H. Babbitt, of Columbia, for example, who claimed "that a certain amount of work properly done by a certain faculty of the mind will give about the same increase in strength and readiness, whether the work be done in ancient or modern languages" (52). Like the mother department that gave it birth, freshman English could not exist unless there were posited certain basic capacities, mental faculties, or (most commonly) "basic skills" that defined the boundaries of literacy. Those responsible for the first-year course had to put aside the historical facts concerning the arbitrary establishment of English as a discipline in the late nineteenth century (the "accidental institution" that Douglas refers to). They had to take it for granted that basic skills existed a priori. During the postwar era, one of the foundational tenets of freshman English reveals itself through the ongoing attempt to identify these "priorities," in the sense of determining that which must come before all other discourse, as well as in reference to establishing the major goals of the course. Once they had identified such "priorities," postwar teachers and administrators believed that they could then invent pedagogies to transmit specific values and develop them within their students.

ONE METAPHOR SURFACES again and again in documents that relate to the practice of freshman English in the postwar era—the writer as a "craftsman." Like the craftsman, the writer—if he or she hopes to succeed —must attend well to preparations: searching for the best materials, obtaining and maintaining the proper tools. Once prepared, both craftsman and writer must develop and adhere to a suitable plan, and refine the product until it has assumed a form that pleases both the creator and the customer. One vivid example of this metaphor can be found in *Standards in Freshman Rhetoric at the University of Illinois.* The University Senate Committee on Student English published this booklet in 1956, primarily for distribution to secondary school teachers, administrators, and students. After describing the Rhetoric program at Illinois, it presents five compositions written by students for the Rhetoric 101 placement test, including a grade and comments for each. The one essay judged worthy of a superior grade (B+ or A), Sheila Bittman's "The Writer as Craftsman," had also appeared in the May 1954 issue of the University of Illinois freshman English journal, the *Green Caldron*. It represents a paragon of what was desired in the course during the postwar era.

"The Writer as Craftsman" provides examples of the priorities of the course. First, a writer must have an "adequate background," which the author identifies as an "idea . . . developed by studying other examples of his craft, and often just nature itself." Such an idea is the expression of an individual's unique perceptions of the world. "This idea can come only from an active mind which is constantly perceptive of the activities about it" (8). Before all else, students and teachers alike expected that writers had to examine their own experience in order to select something worth expressing. As Bittman writes, "Whether one is a carpenter, a composer, a writer, or a painter, all work is the result of thought" (8).

The second priority of freshman English was the acquisition and care of "tools," the proper use of which results in "style." "Just as the craftsman cares for his saw, hammer, and chisel, and views them with pride, so too must the writer establish and value his tools. He soon acquires a knowledge of grammar, punctuation, and spelling, and is constantly building up his vocabulary. With these, his basic tools, the writer can proceed to develop an individual style in which he can better express to others his own feelings. Faulty tools will always result in faulty craftsmanship" (8). The authors of textbooks used at that time often identified certain types of knowledge as tools necessary to academic writing. The most popular college handbook in the postwar era, also used at Illinois, was John C. Hodges's *Harbrace College Handbook.* The third edition, published in 1951, begins with chapters on grammar, mechanics, punctuation, spelling, and diction, then presents a chapter titled "Effectiveness in The Sentence." Only in the thirty-second of thirty-five chapters does it address "Planning and Writing The Whole Composition." *Inquiry and Expression,* a reader edited by Harold C. Martin and Richard M. Ohmann, was used at Illinois as well. They divide their textbook into two sections: "The Processes of Inquiry" (the gathering of ideas) and "The Means and Modes of Expression" (the deployment of the resources of the language in order to express one's ideas). In the first chapter of the second section, "The Writer's Words," they comment: "The writer's life is a life of words . . . and he takes care to know and respect his materials as do good craftsmen of every kind" (437). Martin and Ohmann identify words as "materials," whereas Bittman identifies them as "tools"; but all of them, as well as Hodges, consider the technical aspects of language a priority of freshman English, something to be acquired and practiced before the student actually engages in discourse.

The next priority that Bittman identifies is organization and development: "Once equipped with tools and an idea, the carpenter plans his project according to its purpose. . . . So too must the writer base his plan of development upon the purpose of his idea" (9). An essay begins as a kind of mental blueprint, an outline of its final shape, which then must be filled in with the materials that have been prepared. The final priority Bittman identifies is "polishing." "After the project has been planned and executed there results a rough product, which must then be polished. . . . In a similar manner the writer must revise" (9). Writing, then, for the author of "The Writer as Craftsman" consists in idealized steps or functions that can be learned in the abstract within the classroom, to be deployed later in the specific instances students will face throughout their academic careers and in later life. These steps—thinking, acquiring tools and style, planning, and polishing—constitute the content of freshman English.

The freshman English programs at Northwestern, Wheaton, and Illinois differed in many ways during the postwar era, but all exhibit these same priorities. The 1951 syllabus for English A at Northwestern, for example, contains four objectives (not the same four as stated by the author of "The Writer as Craftsman") concerning writing: first, students were expected "to develop a good working knowledge of the mechanics of the language." The second objective was that students "discover the qualities of contemporary informal style" by reading and discussing selections from anthologies. Third, they were to learn "to write clear and idiomatic English"—that is, they must observe common grammatical conventions and their work must have "a style and organization appropriate to themselves, their audience, and their subject." The final objective was that students "should learn to make use in their papers of their own resources of thought and experience" ("Freshman Composition" 16). All four of these objectives are based on a presumption that writing can be learned in the abstract by assimilating a body of component skills, such as correctness, awareness of style, organization, and original thinking.

This syllabus also includes objectives for reading, but these are directed not to reading in general but specifically toward literature: "to increase the range and intensity of the students' response to literature," and to expose them to "relatively sophisticated examples of literature . . . so that they can develop 'a full and appropriate response to what deserves to be called "literature"'" (17). The syllabus does make one bow toward the service function of the course in its statement that students should learn to enjoy their reading by being shown its "humane values." The author of this description, Ernest Samuels, justifies these priorities in light of the position of English A within the university: "Since ours is a service course, receiving students from a half dozen professional schools as well as the College of Liberal Arts, the needs of the classes will vary greatly as will their preparation" ("Freshman Composition" 15). The English department took its mandate for service seriously. Annual reports to the Dean of the College of Liberal Arts always included a section devoted to the issues of the freshman course. In his 12 June 1961 report to Dean Simeon Leland, Jean Hagstrum comments: "The highest use of language . . . represents the activity of the mind on its newest frontiers and is inextricably related to the entire educational process. A good university ought not to abandon compulsory exposition as its students get better but ought instead to lift the course to their level and beyond—and give everyone an opportunity of taking it" (3).

Wheaton College resembled Northwestern in its ability as a private school to admit only those students who met its high academic standards, but differed in that as a small liberal arts college it would not face a diversity of professional aspirations among its students. In addition, nearly all students at Wheaton came from the same social class and subscribed to a uniform set of moral and ethical standards, codified in a doctrinal statement contained in its catalog and to which faculty had to subscribe. This statement was first published in 1927 as a response to the controversy between those who took a fundamentalist approach to scripture and the theological modernists, who used the principles of historical and literary criticism in ways unacceptable to Fundamentalists. The first point addresses this controversy directly: "We believe in the Scriptures of the Old and New Testaments as verbally inspired by God and inerrant in the original writing, and that they are of supreme and final authority in faith and life." Its second through ninth points list belief in the trinity; in the birth, death, and resurrection of Christ; in the fallen nature of human beings that requires redemption; in justification through faith; and in "'that blessed hope,' the personal, premillenial, and imminent return of our Lord and Savior, Jesus Christ" (Bechtel 94–95).

Northwestern invoked "humane values," whereas Wheaton invoked religious values. Nevertheless, both schools invoked identical "priorities" in their freshman English programs. The minutes of departmental meetings and annual reports from this time reflect nearly constant discussion of Writing 111 and 112, and the problems these courses raised for the faculty. Professor Paul Bechtel, who began teaching at Wheaton in 1946 and in the 1960s became department chair, comments: "A great part of the department's energies were spent on that particular part of the program. . . . Literature was left to find its own way" (telephone interview, 9 August 1988). Minutes from faculty meetings reveal the issues on which the department spent its energies. In Writing 111 students were to perfect their skills in grammar, mechanics, sentence structure, diction, and spelling. They also composed short essays. Writing 112 included the writing of longer essays and "effectiveness."

The "Wheaton College Style Book," published by a faculty committee in 1949 and used through the 1950s, includes a section on "The Fundamental Characteristics of Acceptable Written Material." The style book describes six characteristics. The first is "unity," meaning that a single topic should govern the selection of material, which should then be organized logically so that an essay would "maintain throughout . . . unity of thought and unity in form and style" (n.p.). The second is "accuracy," meaning freedom from factual or grammatical error. The third, "writing ethics," concerns the responsibility for honesty that a Christian student must accept. This honesty meant the correspondence between one's inner self and one's written words (a correspondence enjoined just as strongly at schools like Illinois and Northwestern under academic, rather than religious principles). The fourth, "attractiveness," refers to the need for the writer to submit neatly prepared copy, and the fifth, "good form," to the requirement that all papers follow the conventions of academic writing as the placement of name and title, proper pagination, and adherence to standard bibliographic form. Finally, "promptness" is self-explanatory. These guidelines indicate that Writing 111 and 112 were concerned primarily with the same priorities as did English A—correctness, style, organization, and originality.

UNLIKE WHEATON AND Northwestern, where freshman English was taught for the most part by regular faculty, nearly all of the sections of Rhetoric 100, 101, and 102 at the University of Illinois at Urbana were taught by graduate students who often lacked any prior experience. To guide his staff, the director of the Division of Rhetoric, Charles Roberts, published a yearly *Freshman Rhetoric Manual and Calendar*. This booklet included the objectives and regulations for all Rhetoric courses, day-by-day assignments, and a lengthy list of books from which required readings were to be selected. According to the *Manual and Calendar* for 1949, students in Rhetoric 101 were expected to meet four objectives:

1. to express easily, accurately, and effectively the ideas and problems that arise in your own experience;

2. to read with understanding and pleasure,

3. to listen to others and understand the purpose, direction, and detail of what they are saying; and

4. to speak effectively and without embarrassment. (28)

Northwestern specifically excluded the "oral" aspects of English as embodied in objectives (3) and (4) because they had been assigned to the College of Speech, and Wheaton makes no mention of teaching listening and speaking skills; however, objectives (1) and (2) are identical to those for English A and for Writing 111 and 112.

These four basic objectives—writing, reading, listening, and speaking—are typical of the many postwar courses organized according to communications theory. They name the "basic skills" of literacy. In "The Writer as Craftsman," Sheila Bittman identified the content of these skills. The writer (and "writer as craftsman" just as easily could have been named "reader," "speaker," or "listener") learns his or her craft by mastering still more discrete subskills including thinking, knowing the rules of mechanics and style, planning, and polishing. In freshman English, literacy acts of all types became the sum total of a sequence of more and more finely defined skills that had to be learned prior to the students' participation in specific disciplines and discourses during their academic and postacademic careers. These "basic skills," although generally perceived as specific identifiable actions, recede one behind the other until ultimately they assume the status of ideal essences, more real than the actual practices in which they are embodied.

The history of freshman English reveals a continuous search for better ways to achieve these "basic skills." In "Literature in the Composition Course" (1958), John A. Hart, Robert C. Slack, and Neal Woodruff, Jr., sketch freshman English as it existed just before and after World War II. In the prewar curriculum, exercises from a grammar handbook and passages from an anthology provided the opportunity for stylistic analysis and written response. The second semester of this course might add a nineteenth-century novel to the readings. Following the war, Hart and the others find a welter of experiments through which teachers attempted to resuscitate "a dying course." Among these experiments, they mention the development of anthologies based on issues "presumably vital in the freshman's restricted world, pieces . . . which would make a lively claim upon his personal experience." Or, anthologies were replaced with "casebooks," collections of historical or current research materials that students might analyze or comment upon. Besides the creation of new textbooks, Hart, et al. also mention other new approaches to the course. "Emphasis has shifted to semantics and communications; or to logic, to 'thinking before you write!' Most recently, the teacher has been advised to reeducate his students in English grammar by using the findings of structural linguistics. Each of these expedients has its use and value, but none of them, used to organize the full course, gets it out of the doldrums" (236). Hart, Slack, and Woodruff suggest replacing ineffective content with something they were sure would fill the emptiness at the center of the course—literature.

Other observers documented the incredible array of pedagogies that had been tried in freshman English. In "Freshman English in America," Martin Steinmann mentions "speeded reading, panel discussions, mass media of communication, great ideas, sociology, general semantics, life-adjustment, vocational guidance, spiritual values, the humane tradition, and psychotherapy" (394). In addition to these, Robert Gorrell notes that the course had included orientation to college life and discussion of the common social problems students face as they begin their experience on campus, usage drills, logic, the history of the English language, study skills like using the dictionary or the library, and correspondence (93). In *Themes, Theories, and Therapy*, Albert Kitzhaber identifies "a great many alleged panaceas for teaching writing . . . suggested in the . . . past seventy-five years," including memorizing the "Laws of Discourse" in order to discipline the mental faculties, writing "daily themes," teaching the "paragraph as the composition in miniature," teaching writing via the study of belletristic literature, prescriptive grammar, general semantics, and communications. From his vantage point in the early 1960s, Kitzhaber saw that the latest innovations included attempts to streamline the delivery system of freshman English via team-teaching, lay readers, audio-visual technologies like closed-circuit television, and programmed learning books and machines (73–75).[2] He found all of these techniques ineffective, but thought they had failed because of "a vast uncertainty about aims, about content, about methods" (99). Kitzhaber fully expected that the pedagogical innovations being implemented in the wake of Sputnik would address the confusion of freshman English, if college people were wise enough not to turn a blind eye on them. From the perspective of the early 2000s, however, we can see that the incessant innovation continues. There can be no panacea for the problem of freshman English, because it occupies a paradoxically problematic position. The course is given priority by the rest of the academy because of the belief that literacy is an a priori need for all academic discourses, yet by virtue of such priority both literacy and the course—its instrument —are also inescapably marginalized. The more attention given to freshman English as a priority, the stronger it grows in its function as, in Sharon Crowley's terms, "the blank spaces which surround and highlight the real texts produced in the academy" ("Derrida" 179).

Unlike other disciplines, freshman English could not name that which was *not* properly part of its domain. No area of academic discourse could be excluded from freshman English. The course was required to prepare students of every interest and intention, even to the extent of being offered in specialized contexts, such as sections for students in Commerce at DePaul and in Engineering at Illinois; at Northwestern Jean Hagstrum was asked to set up a freshman English course for the College of Dentistry. David Russell describes the situation at the University of Michigan, where the College of Engineering had its own freshman English faculty that taught specialized courses in engineering, as well as in dentistry, pharmacology, and architecture (122). Confined to the margins of the acknowledged discourses of the academy and unable to establish itself as a discipline by excluding any knowledge as not-freshman English, the course was trapped in a paradoxical position. Like any other course, freshman English needed a proper content, but the search for its proper content became an endless pursuit of anything that might be considered logically anterior to itself. In freshman English, students were to become academically literate, but "literacy" could not be achieved without mastering certain skills, especially grammar. Grammar in turn had to be based on a subject, such as linguistics, which had to find its basis in another field of inquiry, like deep psychological structures. This type of search for origins in turn led into cognitive psychology, neurology, and the chemistry of the brain.

Martin and Ohmann seem to have realized the problem of infinite regress that freshman English cannot escape. In the introduction to *Inquiry and Expression* they acknowledge that their text makes an artificial distinction between "ideas" and "style" (between "thought" and "expression"), but they see no way to teach the course without doing so. "Certainly le style est l'homme même but, just as certainly, one improves by piecemeal learning rather than by sudden and total transformation. To divide the various jobs connected with teaching students to write well is, then, nothing more than to do what must be done in fact, whatever theory says to the contrary" (vi). Even though Martin and Ohmann recognized the trap into which they were venturing, they felt that they had to "do what must be done." Freshman English comprised a collection of such imperatives: students must learn to write, the academy must be responsible for literacy, democracy must have literate citizens.

The problem of freshman English lay not in its failure to achieve its goals, but in its inescapable marginality. Martin and Ohmann's decision to "do what must be done in fact" might seem to offer escape from an epistemological vortex; but the network of a discursive practice cannot be eluded by willing that it disappear.

Efficiency

Two surveys of freshman English appeared at the end of the postwar era: Albert Kitzhaber's *Themes, Theories, and Therapy* (1963); and Robert Gorrell's chapter, "Freshman Composition," in *The College Teaching of English* (1965), published by the National Council of Teachers of English. Both described a hodgepodge of differing pedagogies, with different emphases, course contents, and requirements from one college to the next, even from one classroom to another within the same institution. Kitzhaber and Gorrell called for reorganization of the freshman course to make it more consistent in content and to reflect advances in scholarship, especially in linguistics. They called for the long-overdue replacement of prescriptive grammar with language study based on scientific principles, and for the revival of rhetoric as a replacement for the study of the modes of discourse and methods of paragraph development.

They thought this kind of overhaul was especially urgent, given the return to academic rigor they saw in secondary schools in the wake of Sputnik. Gorrell noted: "Many high schools are making imaginative revisions of the curriculum and imposing higher standards, especially in connection with advanced placement and other devices for encouraging the good student. Some traditional freshman English courses obviously take the student from one of the better high schools a step backward" (103). They foresaw an influx of well-prepared students who would respond with disdain or discouragement to the chaos of freshman English as it then existed in college. Although Kitzhaber and Gorrell did not envision a new millennium of literacy on the horizon, they were convinced that the momentum begun in the secondary schools could lead to a more effective freshman English curriculum.

Kitzhaber admitted that "no one should expect a particular device or method or kind of subject matter in the English course to transform what must always be a slow and difficult process into one that is quick, easy, and unfailingly successful" (7). He realized that students learn to accommodate themselves to the rigors of academic literacy through the cumulative effect of many experiences, but he did not doubt that the first and most important of those experiences should occur in an introductory course early in a student's college career—something very much like the freshman English courses that he and Robert Gorrell had critiqued.

Observers such as Kitzhaber and Gorrell, as well as those involved with freshman English programs at Wheaton, Northwestern, and Illinois, believed that the course had the potential to be a more efficient cause of academic literacy. The practice of freshman English during the postwar era was permeated with a belief that the course needed to be modified, and that those modifications would allow it to operate in ways closer to its true purpose. What I call "efficiency" should not be confused with other uses of the term. For example, in *The Emergence of the American University*, Laurence R. Veysey devotes a section of one chapter to "Social Efficiency as a Yardstick of Value." This term, popularized via a speech by Charles W. Eliot to school superintendents in 1888, suggests a union of the scientific with the practical. "Efficiency (or 'social efficiency') names a desire for collective effort and organization, and perhaps 'a vigorous liberation from dead traditions'" (117). Veysey points out that the phrase came to mean a variety of things to a great variety of people, disintegrating into a catchphrase devoid of meaning.

Raymond Callahan, in *Education and the Cult of Efficiency*, discusses the attempts to apply principles of industrial scientific management in schools. Perhaps the most notable influence of this sort was Frederick

W. Taylor's movement of industrial efficiency in the late teens and twenties. James Berlin notes how these influences came to bear in the teaching of composition, primarily in the form of qualitative evaluation scales that teachers could use to streamline their burden of paper grading (*Rhetoric and Reality* 53–54).

I use the term neither in the sense of Eliot's "social efficiency" nor in the sense of Taylor's industrial efficiency. What I have named "efficiency" resembles a phenomenon Mike Rose has called "the myth of transience." In "The Language of Exclusion," he writes: "The belief persists in the American university that if we can just do *x* or *y*, the problem will be solved—in five years, ten years, or a generation—and higher education will be able to return to its real work" (355). David Russell cites the "myth of transience" as the source of "the many solutions proposed over the years [that] tended to marginalize writing instruction . . . by masking the complexities of the task" (*Writing in the Academic Disciplines* 7). I use the term "efficiency" instead of "transience" because the former term conveys a dual meaning. "Efficient" can be taken both in a pragmatic sense (more streamlined, more productive) as well as in a philosophical sense (that which brings something about). The consequences of the changes made as a function of this belief reveal the problematic nature of "efficiency."

Those engaged in freshman English at Wheaton, Northwestern, and Illinois believed that by fine-tuning their curricula more students would achieve the standards of literacy expected at their particular institutions, and the course would become what it was destined to be. The changes they proposed—clarifying expectations to the students and modifying pedagogical strategies—left the programs largely as they had been. Not until the late 1960s were more drastic changes made, for example, abolishing English A at Northwestern or dropping the English Qualifying Examination at Illinois. No one expected that their tinkering with the course could effect what Kitzhaber called a "panacea," but they were convinced that drastic change was not needed.

The Department of English at Wheaton College prided itself in its maintenance of high standards in all areas, including freshman English. It attracted students from the upper third of their graduating classes; as Roger Shuy, who taught at Wheaton from 1957 to 1964, has put it, "Our students actually wrote pretty well when they arrived and wrote pretty well when they left" (personal letter, 15 August 1988). Given the generally high level of performance among both incoming freshmen and graduates, surface-level errors were particularly galling for the Wheaton faculty. Minutes of department meetings contain accounts of frequent discussions over how to deal with egregious errors, especially in spelling. During one such exchange (20 May 1955), the department discussed "What is the minimum beyond which we will not budge?" They decided to allow one misspelling per 300 to 500-word paper. Two misspellings would cause the grade to be lowered by one mark, and three or more would cause any grade to be reduced to an F. Given the supposedly competent students in freshman English, the most efficient way of addressing this particular flaw in their academic literacy was simply to forbid it.

This solution proved ineffective, as the English faculty frequently called the strict standard into question. At a meeting the following September, the department discussed whether students should be able to make up grades lowered due to misspellings. It decided not to allow this make-up work. In the words of one department member, Dr. Hone, "They will produce if you make them, so the fewer the qualifications the better." To qualify the expectation of precision in spelling would be a step away from the true purpose of the course. To maintain their efficiency as instruments of academic literacy, Writing 111 and 112 could not be adulterated.

The spelling penalty was dropped in 1960, but not because the department found it ineffective. The minutes of 29 November 1960 note: "No one questions the need for continued attention to students' spelling, but our present rule seems to make spelling THE crucial matter, seeming to distort some other values, as some other gross errors should be penalized." In their tinkering with freshman English, the faculty at Wheaton could justify dropping the spelling rule not because it failed to produce correct spellers, but because it was seen as an obstacle to greater efficiency.

At Northwestern, we also find traces of the constant tinkering that signals the quest for efficiency. In his description of the Northwestern freshman English course in the *Illinois English Bulletin* (1951), Ernest Samuels comments: "The semantic and linguistic approach reflected in many textbooks surely indicates the steady drift toward the stress upon function and the wholeness of the writing experience, and toward more rigorous analysis of texts, whether expository or imaginative" ("Freshman Composition" 15–16). This "drift" is apparent in the catalog descriptions of Northwestern's freshman offering, "English A: English Composition and Literature." English A included three quarter-length courses. The first introduced students to academic literacy in general. The second and third were devoted to the reading and interpretation of literature. The first emphasized writing; the second, short fiction; and the third, poetry and drama. Between 1947 and 1964, the catalog description changed three times. In 1947 the first quarter was described as "the fundamentals of grammar; essentials of simple expository writing; practice in careful and exact reading" (40–41). In 1948 the description was changed to "the basic writing process with review of fundamentals of grammar. Practice in careful and exact reading of short prose selections" (47). In 1955 the course was renumbered as English A10 and was described as "the basic writing process. Practice and exercises in expository writing. Practice in careful and exact reading of short prose selections" (55). It retained this description until the 1964 catalog, which began to list only course titles; after 1968, English A10 disappeared altogether.

Albert Kitzhaber points out the perils of relying on published accounts for information about actual classroom practices. In a letter to Wallace Douglas (13 March 1961), he writes: "As a former member of the breed, I would be the first to say that you should never believe what a composition director says in correspondence about his own program. The ideal and reality are often far apart." Moreover, part of the problem of freshman English is the remarkable tenacity of classroom practices in the face of calls for change or revisions of course descriptions. Richard Miller uses David Tyack and Larry Cuban's phrase, "the basic grammar of schooling" to name "the remarkable stability of educational institutions" (*Learning* 22). Keeping those caveats in mind, we see that the public description of English A was changed from a course based upon a theory of literacy as adherence to a set of rules, to one based upon a theory of literacy as growth in a natural process. "The fundamentals of grammar" and "essentials of simple expository writing" became "the basic writing process" and "practice and exercises in expository writing," with an intermediary stage in which "process" and "fundamentals" coexisted uncomfortably for a few years. If a single overriding pedagogical issue captivated teachers of freshman English during the early 1950s, it was the debate over the need to replace prescriptive grammar with more "natural" approaches to language, at first with general semantics, and later with structural linguistics.[1] The changes in Northwestern's course descriptions reflect that general movement from the teaching of "fundamentals" and "essentials" to "process" and "practice and exercises." The choice of the word "process" to describe what was considered fundamental in writing suggests how this need for change was part of a larger cultural phenomenon. "Process" echoes the organic concept of textuality basic to New Critical theory (a connection to be discussed in a later chapter, "Correspondence"), the scientific methodology of structural linguistics, and the self-reflexive quality of modernist writers, who made the process of writing the focus of literature itself.

Whether description of its content was couched in more progressive terminology or not, English A still remained Northwestern's instrument by which students were prepared to engage in the significant academic discourse they would face in the future. The changes in approach suggested by these catalog descriptions reflect an attempt to increase its efficiency, not reconstitute its essence.

Records of the University Senate Committee on Student English (Urbana) document almost constant attempts to allow the assumed efficient causality of freshman English to emerge. Those in charge of freshman English considered the course to have an ideal form and innate potential. They assumed that academic literacy would come about if only its agent, the freshman course, were allowed to operate according to its true design, free of the modifications imposed by myopic administrators. Often, the changes brought about to increase efficiency involved adding or deleting noncredit or remedial courses for students who performed poorly on placement tests or in Rhetoric classes. Between 1927 and 1956, the university instituted then abandoned Rhetoric 0 (later numbered Rhetoric 100) four times.

Two years before the launch of Sputnik provoked a national debate over deplorably lax standards in public education, the board of trustees publicly declared that in its own best interest as well as in the interests of taxpayers and students, the University of Illinois would no longer continue offering a course that repeated what should have been learned in high school. This penultimate episode in the cycle of remedial Rhetoric at Illinois (Rhetoric 100 was reinstated during the early 1970s, and still is offered today) provides a detailed example of how curricular change was thought to effect greater efficiency.[2]

In 1956 the board announced that, beginning in 1960, the University of Illinois would no longer offer Rhetoric 100. This change was justified partly for financial reasons. The number of sections had been increasing, causing the university to spend, in the words of Harris Wilson, "between thirty-five and forty thousand dollars each year on a course that is not a college course at all" ("Illinois vs. Illiteracy" 71). Moreover, the university's records indicated that 80 percent of those students who had taken Rhetoric 100 left the university due to academic deficiencies within three semesters. Remedial Rhetoric seemed to be an expensive way of helping only a few students.

The greater benefit claimed for this decision, however, was not financial. Charles Roberts, discussing the decision in *College Composition and Communication,* claimed that American education had been "suffering through a period dominated by educational nonsense" that was "responsible for the hordes of unprepared students dumped on our doorstep annually" ("Unprepared Student" 97). The decision was hailed by educators all across Illinois, and it received favorable coverage in Chicago newspapers as well as in national magazines including *Time* and *Saturday Review.* Roberts and many others who agreed with him saw this action as the first step in realigning the theory and practice of education in the United States. In 1955, when he first proposed to the University Senate Committee on Student English that Rhetoric 100 be eliminated, Roberts wrote: "I have not seen a more opportune time than the present in which to straighten out the lines of responsibility in English instruction in the entire public school system. The good sense of public school administrators and teachers is beginning to reassert itself" ("Unprepared Student" 97). Roberts viewed the educational system at that moment as crippled by inefficiency. If the "lines of responsibility" could be straightened out, "the good sense" of those enmeshed in this tangle of conflicting efforts would be able to "reassert itself." The problem of illiteracy (Harris Wilson's article on the same topic is entitled "Illinois vs. Illiteracy") lay in the inefficient deployment of resources. Elements within the system had been allowed to go awry, but its underlying integrity remained. The "good sense" of secondary school administrators and teachers would allow the system to regain its efficiency (Roberts, as did Kitzhaber and Gorrell seven years later, saw the impetus for educational reform coming from the schools, not from the universities). Roberts's colleague, Harris Wilson, noted that this decision would allow high school administrators, teachers, students, and their parents to realize that "English must be given more time and attention and that reasonable standards of written expression must be attained before the student is certified as a high-school graduate and be a qualified aspirant for a higher degree" (73). It would seem from Roberts's and Wilson's contentions that the only thing keeping the entire establishment of English education from operating efficiently had been the assumption that students would always have a last chance to make up their deficiencies at the University of Illinois.

The symbolic value of a gesture by a large, nationally known institution and the motivational purposes it could serve cannot be denied. But the actual change needed, according to Charles Roberts, was quite modest indeed. He commented: "If the one recommendation [by the Illinois Association of Teachers of English, in 1955] of a theme a week throughout the four years of high school were generally accepted, our remedial problems, at the college level, would vanish" ("Unprepared Student" 97). As with the problems of spelling at Wheaton, the infractions against academic literacy committed by "remedial" writers were thought to surface because inefficiencies within the system allowed them. If the system of academic literacy was properly adjusted, it would operate according to its true design.

One more event from the files of the University Senate Committee on Student English reveals the problematic nature of the search for efficiency. When the university announced the end of remedial freshman English, it conducted an intensive information campaign, especially with secondary schools. To every high school in the state the university sent a copy of *Standards in Freshman Rhetoric at the University of Illinois*. It also sent copies of the placement essays and grades its graduates had received in Rhetoric classes to each school from which students had come to Urbana. Due to the four-year lead time between the inauguration of this campaign and the end of Rhetoric 100, Roberts and Wilson predicted that when the course had been phased out there would be no appreciable adverse effect on the performance of students in Rhetoric 101. They expected that by 1960, the high schools would be able to produce students who no longer needed Rhetoric 100.

One set of figures in the Committee's records ("Results of the Qualifying Examination in English, 1944–1967") allows a comparison between the Rhetoric program's performance before Rhetoric 100 was discontinued, and after. Students who earned less than a "B" in Rhetoric 102 had to take the English Qualifying Examination during their junior year. Presumably, those students who had been enrolled in Rhetoric 100 would be among those subject to this examination. In the 1955–1956 academic year, when the impending abolition of Rhetoric 100 was announced, 34.3 percent of students who received a C or D in Rhetoric 102 failed the English Qualifying Examination. This figure is typical of performance on the exams during the early 1950s; between 1950 and 1956, the failure rate ranged from a low of 21.2 percent to a high of 37 percent. In 1960 Rhetoric 100 was dropped. In 1963 students who had entered the university under the revised Rhetoric program, which no longer included Rhetoric 100, began to take the English Qualifying Exam. In that year, 51.4 percent failed. Between 1956, when the abolition of Rhetoric 100 was first announced, and 1966, the last year in which those who failed the English Qualifying Exam were required to enroll in a remedial Rhetoric course, failures ranged between 42.4 percent and 55.4 percent. These figures show an average increase of almost 15 percent. Clearly, Roberts and Wilson erred in expecting that abolishing Rhetoric 100 would bring about a more efficient freshman English program. These figures demonstrate neither that offering Rhetoric 100 decreased the failure rate, nor that eliminating Rhetoric 100 increased it. In the mid-1960s, an unexpected decline in student test scores began across all of academia, confounding the optimistic expectations that we find from those at Illinois, as well as from those who took a larger view, including Kitzhaber and Gorrell. These failure rates do provide evidence of the problematic nature of freshman English. It would seem to make "good sense" to streamline the system of academic literacy, to ensure that those students who wanted to enroll at the university received proper preparation. The changes made for the sake of efficiency, however, only resulted in making the system all the more inefficient.

THE CRASH OF STUDENT test scores is a complex phenomenon, undoubtedly caused by many different factors. It is not due solely to abolishing any one course, or to modifications in the curriculum such as abandoning the teaching of prescriptive grammar or dropping spelling penalties. The unexpected decline of students' performance, however, does illustrate the paradoxical belief in efficiency. Despite their faith that students would attain greater competence in academic literacy if the course were improved, teachers of freshman English continued to encounter the same or worse problems. In the face of adversity, however, those involved with freshman English never seemed to lose faith in the possibilities for the course. In the University Senate Committee's "Background Material for the Study of Faculty Cooperation in the Improvement of Student English," Jessie Howard summarizes the almost naive expectation of progress in this fashion: "As one thumbs through old Minutes and other Committee papers, one gets the feeling that former Committees always seemed to approach the problem with a rather easy optimism; if only the right letter to the deans were written, the more searching study to be made, or the more attractive booklet distributed— then results would follow!" (6).

The one change not considered—indeed, considered irresponsible —was that which would undermine the instrumentality of freshman English. Charles Roberts railed particularly against what he called the "educational nonsense" of R. H. Lauchner, of the National Association of Secondary School Principals, who suggested that mandatory literacy in the junior high school was a counterproductive educational policy. He also disagreed vehemently when the National Council of Teachers of English attacked the establishment of objective standards for promoting students from one grade level to another ("Unprepared Student" 97–98). He conveyed his notions about so-called progress in an address to the graduates of the Onarga (Illinois) Military School in 1954. Roberts told the cadets, "I am beginning to suspect that something must have happened in this old universe. . . . My guess is that the earth got a bit too close to the moon." He described some of the "lunatic ideas on education" that had arisen, including ignoring poor spelling and putting only positive comments on students' themes. He then noted that many public schools "have wisely rejected . . . the absurd theories and practices which have caused so much trouble" ("Roberts 'Just Marking Time'" 8). Perhaps the proposals of Lauchner and the NCTE may have left unchanged, or even may have worsened the problem of what Roberts calls "the unprepared student" in the university; but he does not judge them on their impracticality. These proposals invoke his sarcasm and wrath because they are "absurd" or "nonsense" or "lunatic"—they call into question the very logic and legitimacy of mandatory graded instruction in literacy. Without the need for instruments of literacy, freshman English would not exist at all.

Roberts's successors continued to tinker with freshman English, changing textbooks, adding and deleting requirements, introducing new approaches such as transformational grammar, searching for the ultimate efficiency that must be hidden within the next innovative pedagogy. The experience with freshman English at Wheaton, Northwestern, and Illinois during the postwar era suggests that the problem does not lie in certain flawed components of the course. So long as it has been considered an instrument of academic literacy, it has been found wanting— and so, ironically, open to further attempts to make it more efficient and effective.

Individuality

I
N "PERSONAL WRITING AS-
SIGNMENTS," ROBERT CONNORS contrasts the insignificance of
self-expression in classical rhetoric with its importance in late-
nineteenth-century American schools. "The classical tradition in
rhetoric . . . was essentially unconcerned with personal expression of
personal experience. There was no branch of ancient learning that
meant to teach students how to 'express themselves' in any personal
way; the very idea of teaching such a thing was alien to the ancients"
(168). Self-expression entered writing instruction through "Romantic
rhetoric," a term James Berlin uses. He explains, "The material world
is looked upon as being informed with an ideal element, an underlying
reality that is discovered only through an act of interpretation brought
to experience by the observer" (*Writing Instruction* 10).

In *The Methodical Memory*, Sharon Crowley locates the origins of
current-traditional pedagogy in the tenets of British new rhetoric. She
explains how such school rhetoric includes Romantic notions of an individual author: "The allegiance of eighteenth-century discourse theory
to psychology and logic permitted two relatively new features to emerge

within rhetorical theory: the privileging of a single authorial mind, rather than community wisdom, as the source of invention and the concomitant privileging of texts as reflections of the workings of this sovereign authorial mind" (12). Crowley explains the theoretical origins of the notion that rhetoric deals with ideas and texts as the products of individual minds. Connors, however, explains the practical needs that made personal writing assignments both attractive and necessary to American schools. Before the last half of the nineteenth century, students were expected to "invent" compositions based upon material in their commonplace books or upon knowledge gleaned from their classical reading background. After the Civil War, however, students attending the university lacked classical backgrounds and so were assigned topics based on their own personal experience, especially after Alexander Bain's modal system, in which students began by writing narration and description, became a standard method of writing instruction.[1]

Even though students were expected to mine their own experience for material upon which to base their compositions—an essentially romantic notion—Connors notes a tension between classroom writing assignments and "real work"—what he calls "writing that gets the world's work done" (*Composition-Rhetoric* 327). Crowley notes this same contradiction in current-traditional pedagogy:

> Even though it placed responsibility for the quality of invention squarely in an individual author's mind, introspective invention was never a paean to Romantic notions about individual creativity or originality. Rather, it insisted that the quality of any discourse could be measured by its adherence to a rigorous set of standards derived from psychology and logic. All reasonable persons were expected to be capable of uttering the "natural" forms taken by this discourse, regardless of the fact that on an empirical model of the mind, each person was regarded as having different experiences that might, conceivably, endow her mind with fairly idiosyncratic contents. (53)

What I call "individuality," then, names this problematic position that an individual must assume as a student (or teacher) of freshman English. The student is expected to display an original, honest self, yet at the same time conform to rigid (and usually tacit) notions of the qualities that an original honest self must display in academic discourse.

Individuality can be readily detected in a complete spectrum of practices common to freshman English: statements of purpose by authors, committees, and individual teachers; the structure of freshman English programs; textbooks and other materials; classroom practices; the topics that students chose or were assigned for their compositions; standards for and techniques of evaluation. The unacknowledged ubiquity of individuality in freshman English emerges in particular practices, as well as in the wider discussion of the course, evidenced in the proceedings of professional conferences and articles in journals. During the postwar decade, it was impossible to engage in freshman English without reference to the unique individuals whose personal thoughts, feelings, and experiences constituted the proper locus of every aspect of the course. It was also impossible to escape a tension between the rhetoric of individuality and the stated purposes and conscious practices of freshman English, as well as between the rhetoric of individuality and the subtle conformity that freshman English imposed.

The paninstitutional context of freshman English, reflected in articles from *College Composition and Communication* and in proceedings of workshops from the yearly Conference on College Composition and Communication, contains frequent references to individuality. For example, Kenneth Oliver's "The One-Legged, Wingless Bird of Freshman English" (1950) argues against the attempts of specialists, especially structural linguists, general semanticists, and communicationists, to direct the course toward their particular interests. Oliver seeks to articulate the assumptions of the mainstream freshman English teacher; the fact that neither Illinois nor Wheaton nor Northwestern chose to implement any of the newer techniques against which Oliver argues suggests that he speaks for those schools as well. "To assume that there is no general need for the teaching of expression of personal experiences and convictions to college students in the only course required of them where such teaching might reasonably be done, is to deny the importance of man as an individual capable of his own response to his total environment" (5). The value and purpose of the course, Oliver claims, lie in the fundamental importance of each person as an individual, and in the obligation of the instructor to teach students to discover and to express their innate self-worth and uniqueness. These basic assumptions were also articulated in the proceedings of a workshop, "Materials,

Devices, Attitudes in the Composition Course," held at the Conference of College Composition and Communication in 1950.[2] Among those attitudes deemed "favorable" for composition instructors, the participants agreed on the following: "Recognizing that . . . individuals must be worked with as individuals, that adaptation of ready-made plans should be made to allow for individual differences. . . . Desiring to know all that can be known about the student. . . . Realizing that the course should be organized so that the student teaches himself" (3). These "favorable attitudes" bespeak a valuing of the individual as unique, interesting, potentially self-sufficient. As the actual practices at Illinois, Wheaton, and Northwestern exemplify, these attitudes permeated every aspect of the course. Such invocations, however, ignore the complications that ensue when individuality is claimed as the basis of a mandatory course used in a variety of ways—to confirm the individual's fitness to be a member of the academy, to hold a baccalaureate degree, to be a competent citizen. Freshman English embraces a paradox. Students were expected to display themselves as individuals—persons who have discovered their own uniqueness and are capable of evaluating and judging according to their singular points of view. Those responsible for the design and deployment of freshman English assumed that their course fostered this individuality. Nevertheless, the individuality that students were expected to contain and that their teachers expected them to display was limited within boundaries that were definite yet never explicitly described.

The tension between individuality and the acknowledged purposes of freshman English appears in statements concerning the relationship between the freshman course, the individual, and democratic ideals. In a personal interview (27 July 1988), Martin Steinmann, who directed the undergraduate composition program at the University of Minnesota from 1949 to 1964, spoke about the basic assumptions of the freshman English course. He described these assumptions as peculiarly American: "Not only do we expect everyone to go to college, but in addition we expect everyone to write well." According to Steinmann, American schools operate under these assumptions for two reasons: first, the country is rich enough to devote the resources necessary for such mass education; second, Americans assume that each individual can aspire to whatever he or she chooses. A corollary of this assumption is that every individual has not only the ability but the right and corresponding duty to such aspirations.

Steinmann's observation that the individual's presumed potential for academic literacy has assumed the status of an obligation in the United States explains the curiously contradictory desire that individuals must express themselves, yet by so doing also must conform to and so advance the national political agenda. Statements made by Charles Roberts also illustrate how individuality necessitates an obligation to conform to the ideology of capitalistic democracy. In "The Unprepared Student at the University of Illinois," Roberts argues against the "educational nonsense" that schools should excuse any students from the responsibility of developing their own literacy. He cites approvingly a 1954 statement of the Illinois Association of Teachers of English: "'Be it resolved that the primary job of the teacher of English is to teach all students to read and write so that each and every one of them may become an informed, thoughtful, and articulate member of our democratic society.' There you find [Roberts comments] an admirable statement of our American democratic ideal of a sound education for all" (98). This passage acknowledges individuality ("each and every one"), but emphasizes the political agenda of freshman English ("a sound education" equals training in the roles expected of those in "our democratic society"). Individuality proclaims "the importance of man as an individual capable of his own response," but the rights and obligations of literacy dictate the content and form of an acceptable response. In "Competing Theories of Process," Lester Faigley questions the curious nature of freshman English. He asks "why [are] college writing courses . . . prevalent in the United States and rare in the rest of the world?" (539). The paradoxical function of individuality within the discursive practice of freshman English, which calls simultaneously for recognition of each person as a unique individual and for conformity to a particular social and political role, offers an answer to Faigley's question. In American higher education, freshman English (and perhaps the rest of the mandatory educational apparatus) has been invented to contain these contradictory desires.[3]

The tension between individuality and the "standard model" of writing instruction does not show up only in broadly stated impressions of the course like those of Oliver and Roberts. It also emerges, albeit more subtly, in handbooks and course syllabi from Illinois and Wheaton. The objectives of the course, as defined for both instructors and students, state what seem to be straightforward goals. "A Proposed Syllabus for Rhetoric 101 and 102" from the University of Illinois at Navy Pier[4] lists two "General Objectives" for Rhetoric 101: (1) the elimination of gross errors in mechanics; and (2) improvement in organization and expression in a student's writing. The "Wheaton College Style Book," a mimeographed handbook produced by a faculty committee in 1949, states in a section entitled "Purpose" that "a Christian Writer, even though he be but a college freshman, should maintain the uniform modes of expression and the high quality of work that is characteristic of the scholar." The open reference to "a Christian Writer" in a clear context of current-traditional teaching suggests interesting parallels between the religious and the pedagogical belief systems.

In *Rhetoric and Reality,* James Berlin discusses the origins of current-traditional rhetoric in the "new elective university." He sees that this rhetoric "denied the role of the writer, reader, and language in arriving at meaning, that [it] instead placed truth in the external world, existing prior to the individual's perception of it" (36). Extending the model of the nineteenth-century application of the scientific method to all facets of experience—including aesthetics, politics, and ethics—the newly minted professional class of the postwar era developed a "naive faith . . . that economic and political arrangements that benefited them were indeed in the nature of things." Berlin finds that in the postwar milieu the new professional members of the middle class "used current-traditional rhetoric to justify their privileged status in society" (37).

Faith in the power of the scientific method as it devolved to current-traditional rhetoric bears strong parallels to the Fundamentalist Christian system of belief that underlies an institution like Wheaton College. According to Martin Lloyd-Jones, "For us [Fundamentalist Christians] . . . there is no real choice. On the one hand, trusting to human ability and understanding, everything is flux and change, uncertain and insecure, ever liable to collapse. On the other, there is not only 'the impregnable Rock of Holy Scripture' but there is the Light of the world, the Word of God, the Truth itself" (cited in Dunstan 202). The surety that current-traditional rhetoric provides in a turbulent intellectual milieu corresponds strongly to the surety that Fundamentalist Christianity provides to its believers. Just as current-traditional rhetoric proved compatible to the economic and political ideology of the postwar middle class, so it also proved compatible to the belief system of postwar evangelicals.

Since 1927, Wheaton College has required its students and faculty to subscribe to its "Standards of Faith and Doctrinal Platform." (The nine points of this platform are discussed in "Priority.") This platform had been written in response to "the tendency, in modern times, to explain away the historic faith of Protestantism by discrediting or giving unnatural meanings to the words of Christ and the doctrines of the Scriptures." It was printed in the college catalog, and within the "Appointment Questionnaire" that all new faculty had to fill out. Peter Veltman, for example, who taught in the English department from 1948 to 1959, answered queries such as these:

- Do you accept the doctrinal platform . . . of Wheaton College?
- Will you endeavor to the best of your ability through the enablement of God's grace so to teach and so to live your entire life as to give consistent testimony and hearty support to the standards of faith and life printed on page 4 of this questionnaire?

Teaching at Wheaton required a person to profess an individuality that set him apart from those who could not answer yes to these questions; yet this same profession acknowledged his willingness to conform to the tenets of orthodox evangelical belief, and to construe his identity as a teacher as "testimony . . . to [such] standards of faith and life." The qualities that underwrite Veltman's identity as a Christian teacher and the students' identity as Christian writers resemble those assumed within the "General Objectives" for students in Rhetoric 101 at Navy Pier. Both had to eliminate error and to express themselves within acceptable norms of style. Charles Roberts's use of freshman English to promote American democratic ideals and Wheaton's use of freshman English to promote orthodox Protestant Christian ideals reveal how in current-traditional ideology the promotion of "individuality" masks a demand for conformity to tacit ideologies.

The *Stylebook of English,* prepared by the University Senate Committee on Student English at Urbana in 1951,[5] also reveals the tension between individuality and conformity. In its introduction the *Stylebook* states that "good English, spoken and written, will be expected of you as a college graduate. . . . To assure your preparation for the future, the University requires you to express yourself in clear, concise English" (1). On the one hand, this statement repeats the same injunction as the Navy Pier and Wheaton documents: to write correctly and with a polished style. On the other hand, the words "express yourself" suggest a hidden requirement. The handbook enjoins students not only to produce "good English," but to "express themselves." But only one sort of self-expression is allowed, that which is "clear and concise" (i.e., correct and stylistically sophisticated). The phrase "express yourself" seems innocuous, even necessary for describing what students had to do in order to learn to write.[6] However, other documents reveal these words as the sign of a common tension in freshman English. Writing assignments and instructors' responses to them reveal the pervasive importance—and conflict—that "express yourself" has imposed upon freshman English.

The Wheaton archives contain few papers that students had written during this period, but the minutes of one department meeting (26 April 1960) reveal what "express yourself" meant for students. The Freshman Writing Committee had presented a report on the status of Writing 111 and 112, the two required freshman courses. From the ensuing discussion, several points of agreement emerged regarding the purpose and importance of the course. Among them was this exhortation: "Re-state the validity of the writing experience: it is more than putting words on paper. . . . It should be a major means of making an impact on one's time and generation. Finally, the importance of selecting the right word, of committing one's innermost self to paper." In order to confess or reveal the essence of the individual as a thinking, feeling being, one must select the "right word." Even though the Wheaton faculty believed, as did many of their colleagues at Illinois and Northwestern, that the proper expression of "one's innermost self" could have profound social impact, the effectiveness of this expression depended upon correct presentation, in the preferred style. The instructor in freshman English had to encourage the deepest, most powerful self-expression, yet also require that the self be expressed in officially sanctioned words. The student somehow had to infer that what was wanted was not just self-revelation, but revelation according to a tacit formula. The department's need to reaffirm "the validity of the writing experience" implies that, according to some, the teaching and learning of writing must have degenerated.

THE ARCHIVES AT Illinois (both Urbana and Navy Pier) and Northwestern contain many documents—examinations, textbooks, personal memoirs, student papers, and lecture notes—that illustrate the tension between individuality and classroom practices in freshman English.

The major project of the University Senate Committee on Student English at Urbana—administration of the English Qualifying Examination—exemplifies this problematic tension. The three-hour test included a multiple-choice battery concerning grammar and usage, as well as twenty to twenty-five writing prompts from which students could select. In "Invention and Assignments," a chapter of *Composition-Rhetoric,* Robert Connors explains the origin of such topics. In the post–Civil War era, schools faced an influx of students whose only common body of knowledge was "a little readin', a little writin', and a little 'rithmetic" (308). College writing instructors could no longer presume a uniform body of knowledge from their incoming students. They had to switch from *accretive* methods of invention (gathering together non-personal information about a topic) to *selective* methods through which writers had "to choose something" from their personal fund of knowledge and experience, "narrow it to a workable theme topic, and [then] develop it in some way" (313). Topics taken from English Qualifying Exams given in 1951, 1953, and 1960 reflect this selective method of invention. They include a curious admixture of current events ("Hard Times for Liberals"), popular culture ("TV—The Electronic 'Pied Piper'"), sports ("The Yanks Again"), college life ("The ROTC"), career choices ("The Value of Mathematics to the Engineer"), personal morality ("My Father's—or Mother's—Religion"), gender issues in academics ("A College Curriculum for Women"), foreign relations ("Why the Asiatics Hate the U.S.A."), economics ("Trade, not aid, is best for the U.S. farmer"), and some that defy classification ("Nylon, Orlon, Dacron"). The one common ground for all of these prompts is the student as self—their experiences, feelings, ideas, values. Some openly request students to use themselves as the basis for their papers: "My

College Education Thus Far," or "Advice (What was the best or worst advice you ever received from an elder? Why was it good or bad? What have been its consequences? What have you done about it? Exactly, what is advice?)."

One prompt, a quotation attributed to Henry Seidel Canby, a former member of the Department of English at Yale University and one of the founding editors of the *Saturday Review,* expresses the unstated assumption that seems to have influenced the concoction of all of these topics: "Writing is like pulling the trigger of a gun; if you are not loaded, nothing happens." These topics require students to confess what they are "loaded" with. This load, however, is made up of more than personal experience. It also includes the particular formulae by which students were expected to express themselves. Moreover, students were never provided with an explicit explanation of how their essays would be evaluated. The criteria for grading the exam reveal no acknowledgment of the paradoxical context within which these topics are located, the inescapable tension between the idiosyncratic possibilities they evoke and the rigid requirements within which students had to operate and upon which their literacy was evaluated. Directions for the 1951 examination state: "This examination has been designed primarily to determine (1) whether your writing is reasonably free of faults and errors in spelling, punctuation, paragraphing, grammar, sentence structure, and diction; and (2) whether your writing is clear, accurate, unambiguous, coherent, and properly planned with respect to relationships among details, organization of paragraphs, and development of a well-defined theses [*sic*]." These standards for evaluation echo the purposes stated in the Navy Pier and Wheaton course descriptions. No doubt the persons who composed this examination believed that having students write a three-page paper on just about any topic imaginable would allow them to demonstrate their ability to write correct, polished prose. But the design of the examination makes it a test not only of correctness and style, but of a student's ability to invent a self that can simultaneously confess intimate thoughts, actions, feelings, and values yet remain within the boundaries of academic discourse. Students must find themselves sufficiently "loaded," as well as able to discharge that load in a predictable, formulaic pattern in order to impress the examiners sufficiently and so earn certification of competence.

One essay, written on 29 November 1951, illustrates how a student could be caught between his own notions of how to express his individuality and the tacit expectations of his examiners. From a list that included (among others) "Winter sports in Illinois," "The river," "Taft's tactics," "A farmer's life for me," "My idea of heaven," "I go to church," "Naming the baby," and "An engineering problem," he chose "My troubles." He titled his essay "My Troubles—Bitter Words." The "troubles" to which he narrowed his topic concerned a rhetoric teacher who, according to the author, evaluated him on the basis of his political beliefs rather than what he had been told would indicate success in the course—correctness and style.

The author begins with a challenge to his audience, who he obviously presumes are implicated in the system that has wronged him. He understands that their sympathies will not be with him as a student, but argues that he does not intend to play by the rules of petty politics; he portrays himself as a person of thoughtful integrity, not mere emotion. "Any 'competant' [sic] politician would squirm at what I am about to say, because the politician—using the popular connotation of the word—has as a basic axiom for success: 'never antagonize, never belittle, never be completely affirmative, always feint compromise and appeasement [sic].' I refuse to compromise and I stand by the dogma I put down here as rational thought rather than peevishness with selfish motives." He goes on to explain his reasons for entering the university in 1948 after his discharge from the army, presumably after service during World War II. He admits that he enrolled for reasons that were "primarily mercenary," but also argues that his education has come at a personal cost—a "sacrifice . . . [of] time and money." He demands "recognition for what [he has] given up in order to obtain an education" and "fairness."

Having established his ethos, the author goes on to describe his "troubles": "an unfair and descriminatory [sic] act on the part of an instructor at the University of Illinois who placed the propagation of his own political ideals above those of free thought or oppinion [sic]." Before marshalling his evidence, he makes one more attempt to win the sympathy of the hostile audience he imagines: "The facts are boring and, without doubt, pretty trivial to the individual scanning this paper for its rhetorical worth." He cannot contain his true emotion, however, and continues, "but they offer a gratifying release to pent-up rage." This army veteran who no doubt had lived through boredom and danger on a far grander scale than what he found in a Rhetoric 102 classroom makes his case:

> The gentleman was a socialist. I am not a socialist. He preached socialism. Very few self-respecting students of any great character hold any profound interest in being preached to, especialy [sic] by a wispy pedantic almost completely lost in his world of erudition and daydreams. Let a man who has calouses [sic] on his hands tell me what it is to labor; let a man who has the proud scars of war tell me what combat is; but take away that fellow with his head in the clouds who with great fascist gusto will attempt to tell me how to think.

Keep in mind that this student had to take the English Qualifying Examination because he did not get a B in Rhetoric 102. He claims that this instructor graded him down because of his personal opinions. He points out that he had earned a B+ average on his themes and on his final examination and notes that "in the instructor's own words, my class discussion was 'fully worth the same' as the above grades." One of the four graders who looked at this paper underlined "fully worth the same" and wrote in the margin: "If he said this, he's guilty"—presumably referring to the author's attempt to evade the reason for his grade. The author has tried to accuse the "wispy pedantic" socialist instructor of subjectivity, but the evaluator took the accusation as self-incrimination. Perhaps the author intuited that he had made a tactical error here, so he pointed out that he had taken other "advanced rhetoric courses" and earned B grades in them. In his summary and peroration, he appeals to his readers' higher values:

> This, to me, is proof enough that the very fact that I am here this evening filling in little circles [he earned 77 percent on the objective section of the test] and writing bitter words is a gross injustice. These facts, combined with the others offered above, which I am able to support with documents, give pretty solid reasoning for my contention that political descrimination [sic] exists in a department of the University where politics should remain a topic of interst [sic] rather than prime importance—a department where tolerance and liberal thought and integrity should be considered paramount.

Perhaps he sensed that he could overcome his mechanical errors and his thin evidence only by means of his rhetorical skills. He wrote one last sentence, an appeal to his audience's sense of humor and pity: "My ulcers feel better." His calculated risk paid off. One grader passed this essay; a second wrote, "Consult. But if another theme isn't better, put him in 200." A third grader commented, "Let him write one when his ulcers are not so active." It appears that the final say was left to the head of the department, because "C Roberts" wrote "Pass," and the paper was bundled in the archives with other "pass" exams from 1951.

Although the author of "My Troubles—Bitter Words" misspells frequently, makes some factual errors (How could a socialist act with "fascist gusto"?), and lacks evidence for his case, he clearly has a sophisticated vocabulary, understands how to organize an effective argument, and can turn a stylish phrase. It would seem that some evaluators responded negatively not because he failed to meet the stated criteria, but because he violated the implicit requirement that he adopt the kind of individuality freshman English instructors expected but did not articulate.

A document of the University Senate Committee on Student English, "The Qualifying Examination in English: Background" (1962), states: "In the final grade most weight is given to theme quality" (4). And what constitutes theme quality? This background study indicates that "today we expect the student only to produce simple, basic English. We do not grade for 'straight thinking,' originality, or style, for example" (3). Yet, this same document admits the impossibility of evaluating a paper solely on a student's ability to produce "simple, basic English." In discussing the steady decline in scores on the exam, Jessie Howard states: "The estimation of theme quality is of course a subjective process" (5). Students in Rhetoric 200 (and in the Writing Clinic, which will be discussed later) were told that, in order to succeed, they needed only to produce correct texts. Indeed, the instructors in Rhetoric 200 and the graders of the English Qualifying Examination believed that they were operating only according to a standard of correctness. But, as "My Troubles—Bitter Words" clearly shows, it is impossible for students to write, or for teachers to evaluate, this type of work outside the context in which both groups were operating, a context deeply implicated in the expectations and requirements of individuality.

Other sources contain the same types of assignments. The required anthology for Rhetoric 101 and 102 at Navy Pier in 1960 was *Pro and Con,* edited by Myron Matlaw and James B. Stronks. Stronks, a faculty member at Navy Pier, taught rhetoric courses. *Pro and Con* doubly illustrates the teaching practices at Chicago's Undergraduate Division—the book reflects what Stronks was doing in his classroom, and the classes in turn began to use his assignments. I have examined a copy of this text annotated by Mary Sidney, who began teaching at Navy Pier in the late 1950s. She had assigned topics like these:

> An old adage says: "The style is the man." Do you consider your essay style to be "the outward and visible symbol" of yourself? If so, how? If not, why? (7)[7]
>
> If you consider yourself a liberal, show how Mill's philosophy is in accord with your stand on some important contemporary issues. If you consider yourself a conservative, explain how your stand on contemporary issues contradicts Mill's theories. (330)

Even more overtly than the prompts from the English Qualifying Examination, these topics require revelation of a student's self-concept and political views. Not only do the topics require the confession (or, perhaps, the fabrication) of intimate details, they require the justification of those values and beliefs. The first topic is offered as a response to H. L. Mencken's "Literature and the Schoolma'm," a diatribe against backward teachers who believe that style can be taught as a set of rules. Even though it may seem that the first-year writer was allowed to argue against "style is the man," he or she would not be likely to do so after being browbeaten into submission by the Mencken essay, chock-full of statements such as: "American high-school students . . . write badly because they cannot think clearly . . . because they lack brains" (quoted in Matlaw 4). Students, having read Mencken as their first taste of college-level prose (the essay is the first in the book), would very likely take "If not, why?" as an interrogation of their own failure to display a correspondence between self and style in their classroom writing.

The spring 1962 issue of the *Pier Glass,* Navy Pier's journal of freshman English, contains an essay that addresses the topic from *Pro and Con.* In "The Role of Mechanics in Writing," Helen Berkhout describes how her own primary and secondary education had been compromised by "zealous pedagogues" who valued "the mechanics of writing," vocabulary development, and grammar over "a child's development of his own style" (14). She completely avoids the issue of whether her style is "the outward and visible symbol" of herself; instead, she adopts Mencken's judgmental tone to criticize the very teachers who had taught her to write with the clear, effective prose she uses to accuse them. She concludes:

> It would seem that Mencken is correct in his belief that many teachers are wasting their own time and the students' time and money on a fruitless search for something that cannot be acquired—the ability to think logically and thereby be able to write enduring literature. This talent was given only to a chosen few, probably one-eighth of one per cent of the human race, as Mencken suggests. The rest of the world's population would do better to concentrate their efforts elsewhere. The pedagogues are doing little good and much harm. (15)

Seemingly cowed by the sample essay's forceful style, Berkhout does not dare use herself as an example of a clear-thinking American student who confounds Mencken's generalization. Instead, she adopts an antagonistic identity, one that seems to come not from within herself, but from the essay to which she is responding.

The topic based on Mill's philosophy also seems to allow an opening for students to question the categories of political thought by its use of the conditional "if." The topic, however, effectively blocks the probability of inquiry by forcing students to make an either/or decision, rather than considering political thought as a continuum or even as an open field of possibilities. Using either of these prompts, particularly self-possessed students could find grounds for calling the topics themselves into question; however, the statements clearly attempt to limit discussion within the established political domain. Matlaw and Stronks as well as the teachers who used these assignments meant to allow students to discuss significant issues. Nevertheless, in effect they restricted the field of discussion to those issues deemed safe or compatible with prevailing intellectual and political values. These topics reveal how what was done under the rubric "freshman English" was bound up completely with the belief that the student enters into academic discourse via "expression of personal experience," by revealing "all that can be known," by "committing one's innermost self to paper," but only so far as this kind of self-revelation conforms to unstated but ubiquitous expectations.

In the early 1950s at Northwestern, instructors in English A used the anthology *Readings for College English,* edited by John C. Bushman and Ernst G. Mathews. This textbook contains a wide range of nonfictional and fictional short prose passages, arranged according to the topics "Personal Experience and Observation," "Toward Education," and three more sections on exposition, criticism, and personal narrative. The editors justify their choice and arrangement of material by appealing to the variety of individual interests students bring to the course, and to their need to express themselves. Bushman and Mathews write: "The unusual number and variety of personal-experience selections should provide especially useful models for the young writer; they give him the opportunity to begin where he easily can—with what he has seen and experienced" (v). In his copy of Bushman and Mathews, Walter Schillinger, a Northwestern alumnus who received his BA in 1953, checked off essay topics he had been assigned. These topics demand the same sort of confessional writing as did those from *Pro and Con.* For example, he was requested to respond to assignments like these: "Write an account of an experience in adapting yourself to a new job or other new activity such as a sport, dramatics, or military life" (14). "Write a theme showing the characteristics of life in the community in which you grew up. . . . Your account can, of course, be either favorable or unfavorable to your community" (65). As do the other writing assignments examined in this chapter, these two seem to request that the student display and judge personal experiences, and they presume that the student will benefit from having done so. Like the topics from Navy Pier or Urbana, however, they limit the student to fields that allow only a particular "self" to be revealed. The former assignment requests accounts of self-adaptation and suggests that the adaptation be to socially sanctioned activities. The latter seems to present an opportunity to question the topic itself ("either favorable or unfavorable"), but the topic requires the student to locate himself within the community in order to make his choice.

Although Nathan Freedman did not write "A Door Was Opened" in response to the topic in Bushman and Mathews, his essay does show how a student who used their topic might assume the kind of individuality expected in freshman English. Freedman's essay, written for a Rhetoric

101 class at Navy Pier, was published in the fall 1959 issue of the *Pier Glass*. He describes two adaptations: the first is from civilian to military life; the second from the military to academic life. The details, the metaphorical language, and the careful tone of "A Door Was Opened" suggest a writer not so much recalling personal experience as reconstructing it to fit an academic model.

The essay begins by describing the hustle and bustle of Midway Airport in Chicago, where Freedman waited to be shipped out for basic training: "The dancing neon of Caffarello's Restaurant . . . the staccato report of high heels on the concrete floor . . . stewardesses in tailored blue suits with white silk headscarves." "Under different circumstances," he notes, "I too would have shared the feeling, but for me, pleasure and gratification were four years away" (8).

After this evocative opening, he describes the conditions at Chanute Air Force Base: "Wooden barracks whose walls had long ceased to be impervious to nature's elements. . . . Coal dust was inescapable. . . . Sanitation was at a minimum." As he evaluates the experience, his diction becomes more distant and abstract: "The training would have been more enjoyable and would have resulted in a higher percentage of graduates if someone had investigated these grievances and made the necessary adjustments" (8). He uses similar diction to describe the honky tonks of North Africa where he was stationed ("The Airmen's Club . . . closely approached the atmosphere of a Clark Street dive."), his loneliness among rough companions ("There are moments in the military when humiliation and reproach become intolerable."), and his anxiety at leaving the financial security of the Air Force ("After four years of financial independence, would I be content with the government subsistence?") (8–9).

After his discharge, Freedman describes the difficulty of beginning college at Navy Pier. "I seemed to take immediate offense at negative criticism. . . . Uncertain and disconsolate, I could neither enjoy nor assimilate my studies" (9). Two mentors helped him through that difficult adaptation: "a wonderful girl and a teacher" (9). He describes them with the same careful, dispassionate tone with which he has recounted his basic training at Chanute, his service in North Africa, and his return to civilian life. "Jo Ann was like that. A smile, given as directly as any ribboned gift, a few words of praise, a joke, a tale of personal experience—

she always seemed to sense my need and to respond accordingly" (10). "In order for a teacher to create such an atmosphere [one of expectation and enjoyment], he must display not only a high degree of professional skill, but also a warmth in personality without effusiveness. Such a man was my Speech 101 instructor" (10).

Freedman's essay recounts the changes in his life clearly and poignantly; it displays his vocabulary, his ability to create images, and his syntactical skill. That the Rhetoric department chose to publish his essay reveals that the teachers deemed this kind of writing exemplary. But the "adaptation" that Freedman describes fits within safe boundaries; it reveals little of his own idiosyncrasies. Perhaps it shows best how he had adapted himself to the rational, careful, socially acceptable self that freshman English valued most. As Connors states in "Personal Writing Assignments," to be trained in rhetoric was to learn to express "the personal feelings, experiences, thoughts, and appreciations of the writer" (170); but Connors's elucidation does not acknowledge "the writer" to be a rhetorical construction too.

In the fall quarter of 1956, Jean Hagstrum—later to head the Department of English at Northwestern—taught a section of English A10 (English courses had been renumbered in 1955). His notes reveal how thoroughly individuality permeated his teaching. He expected three types of writing—formal themes of 500 words or more; class themes and exams, and short papers. In his directions for the short papers, he commented, "limber up; tell me about your problems." Some of the problems he invited his students to share with him emerge through several of the topics he used during the quarter. The first assignment requested "analysis of present abilities in writing or reading." Later assignments included: "A former teacher: personal experience"; "Effect of environment on someone you know . . . parents . . . home life: brother or sister . . . econ[omic?] conditions: father's work or status"; "Personal experience . . . change of mind . . . [or] choice of vocation." Hagstrum's outline for English A10-2, the second of the three required freshman courses, notes that the second theme was to be based on "something you know first hand. . . . If you can try to get some things you've wanted to say something about: urge to express something."

Yet, the course descriptions indicate that the writing component would include "the basic writing process. . . . Practice and exercises in expository writing." A10-2 is to include "expository writing of a more advanced sort." Hagstrum's notes reveal how he translated the catalog descriptions into practice. The criteria he used to evaluate papers included adequate development, unity within paragraphs, use of vivid detail, and spelling. The papers he liked were, in his words, "vivacious, sharp in detail." For Hagstrum, freshman writing amounted to accurate accounts of personal experience composed correctly and in an acceptable style. Students and teachers at Northwestern seem to have been engaged in the same sorts of classroom practices and topics as those at Wheaton or Illinois. They wrote papers, either after having read a provocative text or drawing upon their personal fund of knowledge and experience. The assigned topics [no evidence suggests that students were allowed to generate their own topics] did not require students to display mastery of any particular content. Ostensibly, teachers read these papers to evaluate their students' mastery of mechanics, syntax, and organization.

A pattern of practices emerges from this brief account of the writing that was done at these three schools. The course required the instructor and the student to elicit and to produce written texts that conformed to academic expectations. To meet these expectations, students had to "express themselves," but self-expression had to be correct, coherent, and clear. The self to be expressed had to conform to a certain academic model. Those responsible for the course were convinced that they empowered students to bring their uniqueness to bear upon the world about them. But the mandatory nature of freshman English ensured, paradoxically, that students had to invent their own uniqueness within the bounds of a particular ethical and political model. Not only did the stated goals of correctness and style mask the unstated goal of personal expression, but the goal of personal expression concealed still another —that of constructing a rhetorical self according to the ideology of the academy.

The Harrison Hayford papers at the Northwestern University archives contain an essay that exemplifies how these hidden requirements of freshman English emerged in a student's writing. The author of "The Evaluation of My Paragraphs" attempts to critique the work he had done in one of Hayford's A10 sections in 1959. The student writer begins, "In looking over my past three papers, I have become rather disappointed with myself." He continues to cite two main self-criticisms: failure to develop paragraphs adequately, and failure to provide adequate transitions between paragraphs. He develops the two paragraphs that describe his feelings of self-disappointment by inventing original metaphors for his two failures. In the first, he describes a reader of his paragraphs as a stranger at a party who cannot figure out how to join in the conversation, feels out of place, and eventually leaves. In the second, he surmises that a reader not supplied with adequate transitions must feel like a traveler who has fallen asleep in a moving automobile. Upon awakening, the traveler feels disoriented because he can recall where he had been and can describe where he is now, but cannot account for the change. This author acknowledges that his writing is supposed to create a close bond with a reader not only by supplying immediate and personal details ("making the reader feel as though he was actually there"), but also by conforming to the conventions of academic writing as commonly presented in freshman English handbooks (well-developed paragraphs clearly arranged in some logical order).

The organization of this paper reveals how he has accommodated his writing to the academic model. It contains two principal paragraphs, each of which is developed with an extended metaphor. The opening sentence ("In looking over my past three papers . . .") clearly states the topic of the paper and the second paragraph opens with a transitional phrase ("In addition to the development of my paragraphs"). The paper concludes with a one-sentence summary ("These are the two main criticizisms [sic] that I have against my papers, and in the future, I will certainly try to improve my writing to a point where the reader doesn't feel like leaving.").

More than anything else, the content and style of this paper provide evidence of the author's desire to display certain rhetorical features and so prove his "mastery" of (or self-accommodation to) academic prose. More subtly, the paper also displays the author's sense that he must somehow reveal himself in his papers—his disappointment with "himself," not with his writing, and his almost poignant desire to ensure that he maintain a personal relationship with his reader (certainly, Hayford himself) so that the reader would not "feel like leaving." In confessing and describing his self-criticisms in an academic style (something he was assigned to do), this paper exemplifies how a successful freshman English writer must conform to the subtle requirements of individuality.

The earnestness of those who shaped freshman English emerges in Hans Guth's summary of the respective roles of teacher and student. In "Rhetoric and the Quest for Certainty," he writes: "The teacher in freshman English must convince the student that writing means recording one's own observations, pinning down one's own reactions, interpreting one's own experience, formulating one's own judgments, questioning one's own premises and making one's own mistakes. In short, the writer must realize that the mind he must put in gear is his own" (134). From the perspective of several decades' critical distance, we can see what Guth (and others who were engaged in the practice of freshman English at that time) could not. Perhaps the teacher in freshman English had to convince himself that his successful students were putting their own minds in gear. However, all the individual qualities cited in Guth's passage—reactions, experience, judgments, premises, even mistakes—had to be constructed according to the prevailing institutional model. To interpret Guth's last sentence in light of individuality, the writer must remake himself or herself according to the specifications of the prevailing ideology—which was never made explicit—and then put *that* "mind" in gear.

A LAST AND MOST REVEALING trace of individuality can be found in the statements and practices having to do with evaluation from the postwar era. These practices, as did course design and writing assignments, operated in an obscure way. Students were told how to succeed in freshman English largely by being told what to avoid. First and foremost, students were told to avoid plagiarism. Connors has found that the issue of plagiarism in composition classes arose with the advent of personal writing topics. Before 1870, he notes, the whole concept of a paper based on outside sources would have been moot—all papers would have been "research papers" in some guise, as students' writing was to reflect their understanding of collective knowledge and wisdom, not their own ideas. Yet in the post–Civil War era of personal writing topics, using easily found secondary sources became a way of avoiding personal writing; hence injunctions against plagiarism (*Composition-Rhetoric* 321, and n. 8).

Teachers may not have been clear on what constituted self-expression, but they were undeniably certain about what it was not. Students who passed off another's work as their own surely were not expressing themselves. Of all the injunctions of freshman English, only those against plagiarism are ubiquitous and unequivocal. Hagstrum's notes indicate that the one thing he chose to stress during his introductory lecture was plagiarism. The University Senate Committee's *Stylebook of English* contains the following advice: "Honesty is necessary; it is a factor in an instructor's grading. The borrowing of significant ideas, plans, and phrasing from another—a fellow student, teacher, lecturer, or author —must be acknowledged in your text or in a footnote" (2). Handouts at Wheaton College in 1960, two full pages entitled "Plagiarism" and "Plagiarism and Other Dishonest Practices," state explicitly the taboo of presenting something other than original material as one's own. The former document, a reprint from the university bulletin of UCLA, recounts the experience of a Professor Bone, who detected plagiarism in the work of ten of his students. As a result, they were assigned failing grades and were reprimanded by the UCLA Faculty-Administration Committee on Student Conduct. The committee commented that "the student's role in education is an active one, and he alone bears the responsibility for the work he does. Whoever refuses this responsibility is unworthy of a university education." The student had to present himself and himself alone, without the camouflage of others' words or ideas; whoever could not or would not conform to this standard did not deserve to be part of the academic community. The latter of the two Wheaton documents begins with an etymology of the word "plagiarism": "Plagiarism is passing off the words and ideas of others as your own. The word is derived from the Greek plagios, meaning 'crooked, oblique'; hence, 'underhanded, not straightforward.' It is a vicious practice, but eventually the keen edge of conscience is dulled and the 'borrowings' tend to become more and more frequent."[8]

The *Freshman Rhetoric Manual and Calendar* (1949) from the University of Illinois at Urbana contains a mechanism by which students were constantly reminded of plagiarism and its consequences. For each paper submitted in their rhetoric courses, students were required to sign a pledge, which stated, "I understand the Rhetoric Manual statement regarding honesty in written work. I pledge that this entire composition is an honest example of my own work" (4). In a section entitled, "Honesty in Written Work," the *Manual and Calendar* describes this pledge as "designed to keep you out of trouble and to remind you of the importance of honesty and originality in your work" (5).[9] These injunctions against plagiarism indicate the powerful value ascribed to individuality. Not only were individuality and all its consequences to be fostered; lack of individuality was proscribed. Plagiarism indicates not only a misunderstanding of directions or laziness, but also unfitness and turpitude.

Plagiarism reveals the paradox of a demand for individuality and accounts for the vehemence with which it was enjoined. Teachers could tolerate the kinds of flaws that fall *within* the bounds of individuality—the clumsiness or even outright illiteracy of the beginning freshman trying to "get his mind in gear." Such bumbling elicits solicitude from the best, sarcasm from the worst; but it does not result in expulsion. Plagiarists, however, refuse to engage in the discourse at all. Instead of playing the game, groping their way toward an accommodation of self to the institutional pattern, plagiarists brazenly adopt someone else's pattern as a mask, preserving an unaccommodated self behind it. In a way, plagiarists remain individual; whether by design or by accident, they do not allow their "innermost selves" to be expressed at all. A true expression of one's innermost self on paper, with all its randomness and disconnectedness, would never be accepted into the discourse of freshman English.[10] To accommodate one's self to that discourse is to become the correct, coherent, clear self desired by the academy and by democracy.

The plagiarist was considered beyond redemption. Students who committed the forgivable, venial sins of incoherence, blandness, or (most commonly) incorrectness could take their problems to the "Writing Clinic." At the University of Illinois, this type of clinic was set up to nurse along those students preparing for the English Qualifying Examination. Like a medical facility, the clinic "aids [any student with a writing problem] to diagnose his writing difficulties and their causes, discusses these problems with him, outlines a program of work for him, directs practice exercises and checks on the progress made. All work is done in individual conferences" (University Senate Committee, "Maintenance" 5). Failure in freshman English was deemed a disease, to be cured through proper diagnosis and regular therapy. Even classroom instruction was construed in this fashion. The 1949 *Manual and Calendar* uses the language of the medical clinic to describe the goals of writing instruction: "If you submit papers which are not genuine evidence of your own ability, you are thwarting your instructor's efforts to diagnose your writing ailments and to cure them" (5). The classroom instructor may have had the power to cure writing ailments, but the clinic was not empowered to do more than show an individual his or her own problems and how to correct them. In fact, students in freshman English were specifically enjoined to accept specific suggestions from no one but their instructors. The 1949 *Manual and Calendar* states, "Do not allow anyone other than your instructor to correct or revise your papers at any stage in their composition. Bring this warning to the attention of scholarship advisors and others who may offer to 'help' you" (5). If students desired long-term tutoring or proofreading, the regulations of the writing clinic stated that they must hire "individuals who are available for such professional work" outside the university ("Maintenance" 5).

Within the university, this overt help was considered an act of collaboration.[11] Like plagiarism, collaboration involved the appropriation of someone else's words instead of one's own, providing an illicit escape from the individuality that freshman English required. In *The Wadsworth Manual*, Hans Guth cites Indiana University's "Manual for Elementary Composition" concerning "Collaboration, Plagiarism, and Insufficient Documentation."

> The only way to learn to write is by writing, and writing is hard work. It is understandable, therefore, that occasionally you should want to ask someone to help you with your writing. Sometimes this help is permissible; the Writing Clinic is organized to assist you with your writing, and you may legitimately receive similar help from other sources. But too much help is both unethical and unprofitable. If you are to learn to write, and if your instructor's comment on your writing is to be useful to you, you yourself must do the hard work of writing. (96)

The adjectives applied in this and in the Wheaton documents to plagiarists and collaborators bespeak the high value placed on individuality: "unworthy," "vicious," "unethical," "unprofitable." Individuality provides the only licit context for avoiding error and improving one's style;

lack of individuality cries out for punishment, for therapy, for a kind of redemption.

Less heinous, but also a sin against individuality, was the simple lack of originality. The Bushman and Mathews textbook contains a set of criteria by which students could evaluate their own writing. Under the heading "Self-Criticism," the editors suggest that writers ask themselves, "Is my work original in content or interpretation or feeling?" (xiii). *Standards in Freshman Rhetoric at the University of Illinois* lists as the first criterion for an "A" paper "originality of thought in stating and developing a central idea" (3). The pledge of honesty required with all written assignments at Urbana was designed not only to thwart plagiarism, but also to "remind you of the importance of honesty and originality in your work." The "Wheaton College Style Book" offered the following suggestion under the heading "Writing Ethics": "We will be as honest in our writing as we would wish to be in every other aspect of life. . . . What we represent ourselves as feeling, that we must really feel or have felt. . . . What we represent ourselves as believing, that we must really believe" (quoted in Thomas 10). In these specifications, "originality" (in the Wheaton document, "honesty") indicates a correspondence between one's own deepest beliefs and values and one's written expression. In *An Index to English,* a popular textbook in the 1950s used at Navy Pier, Wheaton, and at Northwestern, Porter Perrin comments on originality: "When a style deserving the label 'original' appears, it is usually the byproduct of an active and independent mind, not the result of trying to be different" (432). Perrin, as well as instructors from Northwestern, Wheaton, and Illinois, read "originality" as "that which comes from the source," and that source was the unique individuality of each student.

Instructors and textbook authors may have stated their belief that originality derived from independence, from an honest correspondence between a student's inner self and outer expression, but they expected writers to limit themselves to carefully constructed self-expression. Any teacher of freshman composition has had the experience of receiving texts that display deeply felt beliefs (often on issues of personal morality), or highly idiosyncratic styles that bend or ignore the standard conventions of mechanics, usage, or form. These sorts of papers usually receive kind but firm comments regarding what is "acceptable" in an academic essay. Originality, like individuality, requires writers to infer the tacit ideology within which they may operate; it is a confirmation not of the uniqueness of the individual, but of conformity to the desired type of discourse. Moreover, it is an explicit marker of what is included in the center of academic discourse, and what is marginal. Lack of originality indicates not worthlessness, but marginality and ineptitude. Therefore, students who lack "originality of thought" will not merit distinction, but neither will they incur the violent sanctions invoked against plagiarism.

The handbook used with freshman English courses at the University of Minnesota in 1962[12] states clearly the connection between originality and individuality: "[A good theme] communicates to the reader a fresh, clear impression of an individual and original person, a person with a mind and emotions of his (or her) own who has something to say that is thoughtful and genuinely felt, and who is drawing on a recognizable experience of life in order to say it" (Barker vi). It is not difficult to imagine a text that would meet all of these criteria for a good theme, yet still receive a failing grade. That is exactly what seems to have happened to a young man who took the English Qualifying Exam on 13 April 1961. He had scored 74 percent on the objective section of the test, enough to earn a passing grade unless his essay was of less than marginal quality. In "The Qualifying Examination in English: Background" (1962), Jessie Howard notes: "In the final grade most weight is given to theme quality . . . usually an objective score of at least seventy-five is required for a border-line theme to be passed" (4). He chose the topic "My special day" and produced a three-page essay that described two events in his life that had occurred on the same date—15 April. Writing just two days before that date, he also projected what it would mean in his immediate future.

The student begins: "April 15, just another day in the year to many people, is a very special day in my life." The first time the day achieved significance for him occurred "several years ago, three to be exact, while I was still a junior. . . . I was sitting in Physics class . . . when an announcement came over the loud speaker saying that I had just been elected President of the Student Council. My heart leapt for joy, and I keep hearing the announcement over and over again, just as if a record was stuck and no one was there to turn it off." At a victory celebration that evening, he struck up a conversation with a girl he had not known previously. He asked whether he could walk her home. "I wasn't sure she could accept;" he wrote, "but when she did, my head began to spin all over again."

After he graduated and went off to the University of Illinois, their "letters became more and more serious, and before long we were talking of marriage." Just as in *Romeo and Juliet,* the parents objected, so the couple decided to elope on his first day of spring break: "You see, Good Friday and April 15 fell on the same day." He continues, describing the happiness he and his young wife share, even as she lives at home with his parents and cares for their nine-week-old son while he studies at the university. He concludes by looking forward two days to "this Saturday, April 15 . . . our first, and as many people say, our most important wedding anniversary." He concludes, "I am sure that this day will continue to be the most important day in my life."

"April 15, My Special Day" is written simply yet clearly with few spelling or mechanical errors. According to *Standards in Freshman Rhetoric at the University of Illinois* (1956), a passable theme has "a central idea organized clearly enough to convey its purpose to the reader." Although it may lack "vigor of thought or expression," it avoids errors in grammar, spelling, punctuation, sentence structure, paragraphing, and penmanship that would lower it to a D or an E (failing) grade (3). "April 15—My Special Day" seems to meet those criteria. So why did the graders fail this essay? They made no marks on the paper, but in light of what I have presented in this chapter, I would argue that this author did not construct the kind of individuality that freshman English called for. His account of his experiences is indeed heartfelt and personal, but it is also formulaic. He mistook "originality of thought" to mean honesty or straightforwardness. His evaluators expected subtlety and verbal inventiveness. An "original" writer does not merely tap some well of raw emotion and experience. An "original" writer must express himself in a style that appears thoughtful and genuine, but must conform to unstated stylistic norms. In other words, an "original" writer must construct an expected, prescribed version of "self."

five Transcription

*H*AVING TAKEN FRESHMAN
ENGLISH, STUDENTS WERE EXPECTED to speak with poise and force,
write correct and stylish prose, and understand the content as well as
the nuances of what they had heard or read. The scope of the course,
however, did not stop there. Literate students would manifest certain
attitudes or beliefs as well, such as thinking logically and critically, appreciating the kinds of literature generally considered part of the canon,
valuing the accomplishments of human reason, and believing in the
innate worth and potential of human beings. Through their training in
reading, writing, speaking, and listening, students were expected to absorb an indoctrination into a humane value system.

Writing in 1962, Hans Guth uses a biological metaphor to describe
the connection between the teaching of freshman English and the attitudes it was expected to inculcate: "It is sometimes said that critical thinking and sensitivity to values cannot be taught, that they are 'catching.' This
would seem to be an excellent argument for exposing the student to the
work of writers who are known to be carriers of infection" ("Rhetoric
and the Quest for Certainty" 133). Guth supposes that students would

pick up the desired qualities as if by exposure to some agent of contagion. Words such as "infection" or "contagion," however, suggest a negative influence, the opposite of what was expected or desired. The word "inoculation" comes close to describing this particular function of the freshman course, but is not totally satisfactory because it suggests a purposeful action to ward off an evil. These overtones resonated in the postwar course, but they do not capture the full sense that archival evidence of actual classroom practices conveys.

"Transmit" suggests the communication of a power or quality from one source to another by unseen yet effective means. Laurence Perrine uses this metaphor in his introduction to *Sound and Sense:* "The act of communication involved in reading poetry is like the act of communication involved in receiving a message by radio. Two factors are involved: a transmitting station and a receiving set. The completeness of the communication depends on both the power and clarity of the transmitter and the sensitivity of the receiver (and on whether it is tuned to the proper wavelength)" (10). In Perrine's analogy, a text resembles a transmitter that emits a constant stream of electromagnetic waves. Despite time and distance, they invisibly register themselves on receivers. Freshman English was thought to convey the humane value system via such "transmission." A teacher had to get students "turned on" and "tuned in" so that they could receive what the texts chosen for the course were transmitting. Like the passage of radio waves, the transmission from text to student is invisible, mysterious, ineffable. Unlike a radio receiver, however, the student was expected to do far more than merely convert the signal to some analogous medium (mere summary, an indication that she or he had not received all that the text had to offer). Not only were the students to repeat what they had read, they were to be changed, converted by the power of the text.

Both David Russell and James Berlin, using Laurence R. Veysey's term, "liberal culture," have discussed at length the function of literature in freshman English courses. Citing an author from the 1890s, Charles F. Thwig, Russell explains the motivation of those who would base the introductory course on literature and the values that it could transmit: "Advocates of liberal culture tended to see themselves as embattled humanists in an age of Babbitry and resisted the encroachments of scientific and professional fields as middle-class barbarisms, which thwarted the Arnoldian ideal of the 'well-rounded man,' a person with 'a wide vision of the best things which man has done or aspired after'" (168). Transmission is congruent with this Arnoldian notion of English as a discipline, the perception that culture—the best that has been thought and said—transforms its initiates. In *Culture and Anarchy*, Matthew Arnold presents "men of culture" as "apostles of equality . . . carrying from one end of society to the other, the best knowledge, the best ideas of their time" (113).[1]

In *Rhetoric and Reality*, Berlin discusses what he calls "the rhetoric of liberal culture," prominent in the first two decades of the twentieth century. In contrast to Arnold's perception of culture as promoting equality, Berlin characterizes such "liberal culture" as "aristocratic and openly distrustful of democracy" (45). Nevertheless, the elitism he sees in the early part of the century was transformed in the postwar era. In James Murphy's *A Short History of Writing Instruction*, Berlin claims: "The distinguishing feature of the fifties in considering the relations of literature to composition is that . . . college professors were in large numbers insisting that the best way to teach composition is through reading literature and writing about it" (203).[2] As I pointed out in my earlier chapter, "Instrumentality," freshman English was seen as an important tool in promoting democratic values. Berlin explains how the elitist notion of liberal culture could be enlisted in the name of democracy. "Literature preserved the integrity of the individual against the tyranny of the mob. . . . College is to prepare the leaders of a democratic society, and literature is the best means for doing so" (204).

"The Color of Red" by Mark Johnson illustrates how the literature selections in freshman English served to promote individualism in the name of advancing democratic values. Johnson had read Shakespeare's *Tempest* and Huxley's *Brave New World* for his Rhetoric 101 class at Urbana. He begins by commenting on the bloody connotation of the word "dictator" at the time he was writing (1961), after the world had witnessed the effects of Hitler, Mussolini, Franco, and Stalin. Johnson notes: "We point to democracy, especially that of our own country, as a system that insures justice and equality. But this term also may be misleading. Red-blooded democracy and blood-red dictatorship . . . will always be in direct contrast. But conceivably the added connotations of good and evil could be reversed" (11). Johnson then contrasts the benign "supernatural" dictatorship of Prospero with the hellish "scientific democracy" of Mustapha Mond. He draws this conclusion: "A common fallacy in our present society is the idea that a *Brave New World* can only be the product of a dictator's mind. With a little thought and effort we can certainly keep a democratic government, such as ours, strong and stable." He concludes with an admonition that a democracy might easily descend to the level of Mond's new world, if people do not exercise independent thought. "But can we avoid slipping into a world such as Huxley describes, a civilized inferno of science in which 'human beings are to be made the means'? O *Brave New World* that has such helpless people in it" (12). The *Green Caldron* published Johnson's essay as an example of a book review; the syllabus for Rhetoric 101 required students to read and respond to three supplementary books. Later in this chapter, I will explain further the function of assignments like Johnson's within freshman English. Although Johnson was not assigned supplementary reading to advance an explicit political agenda, he seems to have understood that the literature he read for his class served to preserve "the integrity of the individual against the tyranny of the mob."

Reflecting Berlin's characterization of freshman English during the 1950s, the practices in freshman English classes at Illinois, Wheaton, and Northwestern exemplified many features of liberal culture. Proponents and practitioners stressed the value of canonical literature, especially in contrast to the popular writing of comic books, dime-store novels, and newspapers. Students were expected to internalize such value, thereby achieving a better, more enlightened view of their experiences. In turn, their writing—in terms of content and style—would improve. What Berlin calls "Brahminical romanticism" (*Rhetoric and Reality* 44), a resistance to the utilitarian focus that the rest of the academy seemed to expect from the first-year course, suffused their teaching.

In "Captive Audiences: Composition Pedagogy, the Liberal Arts Curriculum, and the Rise of Mass Higher Education," John Heyda alleges, "The role of English has long been taken up, to a far greater extent than teachers of other subjects might imagine, with the 'character building' elements in the curriculum" (25). Freshman English, as the agent of academic literacy, was believed not only to confer the "skills" of reading, writing, speaking, and listening, but also to confirm students' personal integrity and validate their status as humanists. To have succeeded in freshman English, then, indicates the achievement not only of higher moral status, but higher status in academic society as well.

As humanists, students were expected to recognize the inherent inferiority of certain categories of literacy, especially those associated with mass cultures. Heyda cites Margaret Mathieson's observation that in the early twentieth century British educators conceived of the study of English literature as a prophylactic to the pernicious influence of the popular press, especially the corruptive, vulgar power of the "penny-dreadfuls" (135). During the postwar era, freshman English retained this valuation of canonical over noncanonical literature. Having completed freshman English, students were expected to prefer belletristic over utilitarian or popular texts. In the *Green Caldron,* two essays by Ronald Carver—"The Need for the Study of the Great Books" (May 1950) and "The Menace of Television" (October 1950)—exemplify the humanism freshman English was thought to transmit. Carver's essays also reveal other forces at work in the discourse of freshman English: the promotion of democracy, the validation of middle-class values, and the emphasis on expressing one's unique individuality.

In the first, Carver maintains "there is a vital need for the study of the world's great books . . . [to reverse] the decline of popular taste in literature" (1). He sets up unattractive images of popular culture, against which he contrasts the "cultivated tastes" that the great books convey. He describes the blue-collar worker who relaxes by "flop[ping] into his easy chair and . . . switch[ing] on the radio or pick[ing] up his funny-book, or go[ing] down to the corner tap to guzzle beer and chin pointlessly with his cronies" (1). He speaks of the diversions of working-class women with equal disdain: "The slickly contrived 'How to . . .' articles of the 'Digests' and 'Women's Magazine,' or the flow of books, offering tailor-made philosophies for $3.50 and two evenings of one's time" (3). In contrast, he extols the great books because they encourage readers to "develop themselves . . . to be aware of what is going on in the world, and what has gone on in the world . . . to set off a trend against inferior tastes . . . to look more carefully into the nature of things, and to avoid flinging himself into the whirlpool of unworthy mass trends" (2). Carver accuses purveyors of cheap entertainment of disrespecting a reader's natural intelligence by their eagerness to "foist off on him their own ideas and thoughts without regard to his own intellectual powers" (3). By way of contrast, the study of great books "aids the individual to be his own arbiter in matters of judgment and taste . . . and . . . be able finally to reverse the decline in popular tastes in literature and in other important things" (3).

Carver considers television more insidious than other forms of popular entertainment because he sees no way to counter its influence. "The Menace of Television" (a title that echoes the "Red Menace" of communism so feared in the 1950s) accuses the new medium of undermining "the contemplative life." Even "doctors, lawyers, scientists, teachers, and other such supposedly culturally advanced members of our society are just as liable to fall before the television menace as the man who drives the fruit truck" (31). He minces no words: "Television is evil" because it "destroys ideals . . . increases the worship of the vulgar . . . idealizes men such as Milton Berle, who offer nothing worthwhile" (31). Unlike the weak forces that the great books can easily fling aside—comic books, radio programs, barroom conversation, self-help books, and women's magazines—nothing can oppose the "menacing rise" of television. Pessimistically, Carver fears that "the thought processes of men cannot at one moment entertain great thoughts and take in the offerings from the television screen" (31).

An anecdote from the archives of Wheaton College illustrates how the expectation that freshman English would convert students from vulgar to loftier tastes played out in an overtly religious milieu. Since Jonathan Blanchard's administration in the 1860s, "the Wheaton program of studies was the essence of a liberal arts education" (Bechtel 23). A statement in the 1886 catalog exemplifies what that term meant to the administration and faculty: "Wheaton College has never yielded to the clamor for short courses leading to cheap degrees which only serve to inflate the vanity of the possessors; but it has afforded its students courses of study valuable not only for the information acquired but also for the mental discipline to be gained by pursuing them" (Bechtel 54). The same philosophy of education extended into the postwar era. The English department rejected the allure of "vanity" and embraced "mental discipline" when it came to a decision concerning a possible connection between their writing program and a commercial publishing house.

Scripture Press, a publisher of religious tracts, proposed to relocate onto the Wheaton campus. The presence of this specialty press could have provided students in Wheaton's writing major an opportunity for practical experience, but the department decided against this relationship. The minutes from a discussion on 7 November 1955 contain this statement: "Our [writing] major is not vocational, but intended to give a liberal education with an appreciation of good techniques; not to sell, primarily. . . . Our emphasis is different, and better." "Vocational" education is not considered evil (the notes later say, "This does not mean teaching a student to write a novel which will NOT sell"), but it is inferior to the "liberal arts." Like Matthew Arnold, the Wheaton faculty did not despise the practical, but rather saw it as a good on a lesser plane than the liberal arts, which are something "different, and better."

Arnoldian ideology suffuses the commentary on freshman English from professional journals during the postwar era. In 1958 Robert Saalbach contributed his ideas on "The Status of the Composition Teacher" to the "Staff Room Interchange" of *College Composition and Communication:* "Our emphasis . . . should be shifted to training persons who are primarily interested in creating a more literate public because they sincerely believe that the cultural values of our great literary heritage are the property of all who can understand and that they will greatly enrich the lives of the ordinary men and women who take no more than a year or two of college work" (30). Saalbach does not employ Arnold's evangelical language, but there seems to be little difference between his teachers of composition and Matthew Arnold's "apostles of equality," working to improve the lives of those who have not yet had the advantage of exposure to academic instruction in English, and so have transferred to them the values of the "best knowledge, the best ideas of their time."[3] The key word in Saalbach's description of the role of the composition instructor is "believe." The ultimate effect of what teachers of English do is a matter of faith, faith in the beliefs and values upon which academic literacy depends for its special power.

Toward the end of the postwar era, Hans Guth recasts in psychological terminology the Arnoldian articles of faith in the uplifting power of literacy. In "Rhetoric and the Quest for Certainty" (1962), he equates success in freshman English (which implies satisfying the expectation of academic literacy) with achieving psychological maturity. He describes the liberal arts as a means of students' self-fulfillment, and the teacher as the facilitator of their growth and development. The teacher of freshman English is responsible for "complex psychological variables . . . informed awareness of language at work . . . sensitive, responsible, informed critical thought . . . emotional literacy. . . . Freshman English, which at its least inspiring dwindles into a service course, can be a crucial part of the students' liberal education" (136). For Guth, freshman English transmits "emotional literacy," a kind of personal accommodation to the enlightened psychological state that academic literacy has the power to confer. Arnold calls it "best knowledge"; the Wheaton faculty call it something "different, and better" than mere vocational training; Saalbach calls it "cultural values." All speak, however, of a belief in the power of English as a school subject (in particular, literature) to raise up the students. Teachers of English function as agents of the uplifting that occurs via *contact* with the material in the English course. The transfer itself, the "mission" of the English course, is something ineffable, something beyond mere technique or rules. Robert Connors describes this "mission" as an almost magical transfer that was presumed to occur through the study of English. In his discussion of stylistics in the context of the freshman composition course, he comments, "The low-level 'physical basis' that books covered in their discussions of triteness, commas, and grammar and the large terms offered by static abstractions [e.g., "unity," "coherence," or "emphasis"] were all that was available to composition students of the 'aesthetic mystery': the rest had to be absorbed some other way—through reading, perhaps, or more likely through magical thinking" (*Composition-Rhetoric* 281). Guth, Arnold, the Wheaton faculty, and Saalbach profess a faith in English as more than a set of skills. It is not enough to view freshman English as a mere service that renders students competent in speaking and writing the language of academia. Transmission makes the course into the point of contact between the beginning university student and the realm of the liberal arts, a place of higher knowledge, greater values, even psychological equilibrium.

Transmission appears as part of the paradoxical or problematic nature of freshman English when these ethical claims are measured against the actual conduct of the course. Producing liberally educated persons by means of one or two semesters' worth of study constitutes one of what Robert Gorrell has called the "major miracles" expected of freshman English. In the face of such a formidable—if not impossible—task, many teachers of freshman English lapsed into what Gorrell calls "unconscious hypocrisy. . . . Recognizing the impossibility of doing all that is expected and turning to whatever happens to interest [them] most, on the theory that it will help the student as much as anything else," they filled the hours of teaching with reading and discussion of literary examples, and writing on "topics" (98). They did not choose such content because of conscious subscription to theoretical statements like those of Arnold or Guth, but because of the institutional nature of English itself. Instructors, almost all of them English majors, considered themselves academically literate; they had reached that condition, so it would seem, by means of their specialized studies. Faced with a limited amount of instructional time and numerous lofty expectations on the part of the rest of the department and of the university as a whole, they did what they supposed had been effective for them. Sharon Crowley explains this "unconscious hypocrisy" in terms of the teachers' blindness to a possible theory of rhetoric and composition:

> Composition belonged to the English Department, and . . . English teachers seemed unable to comprehend that writing instruction might involve anything other than literary study, on the one hand, and drill in grammar, usage, and formal fluency, on the other. They understood required composition instruction to be an exercise in the improvement of character and good taste. . . . In the absence of a viable rhetoric or theory of composition, these teachers simply could not imagine composition as an independent discursive or pedagogical practice. (*Composition in the University* 102–3)

Crowley and other historians, such as James Berlin and Gerald Graff, perceive the history of freshman English in terms of "the fallen other against which literature measures its own superiority" (Crowley 11). I would argue, however, that the problematic context for teaching composition as a required course is more subtle and complex than that. The problem and strength of this course lie not only in the imagination (or lack of imagination) of teachers, but in the interplay of forces that together constitute the discursive practice of freshman English.

Dudley Bailey provides evidence of the prevalence of this pattern of the teaching of freshman English via extensive yet random reading and writing assignments. In 1958 he wrote, "The most common observation I have made as I have talked with hundreds of students from my own and other institutions is that they never know what they 'had' in Freshman English. And there is a clear note of disgust or contempt when they tell me that they 'read some stories' and they 'wrote some more stories'" (234). The students with whom Bailey had spoken recognized that whatever they did in freshman English did not change their own self-image as readers and writers. A significant aspect of how the presumption of transmission works is the hiddenness of what is supposed to happen as a result of the course. Perhaps the students Bailey interviewed had become academically literate after having taken freshman English; but they did not realize what was expected of them beyond performing a few required tasks in reading and writing.

Transmission, then, means more than the use of belletristic literature in the attempt to teach reading and writing on a college level. Rather, this term names the tacit belief that the encounter between students and selected texts—whether excerpts in handbooks and anthologies or complete novels, plays, or poems—would produce transformations in the students' attitudes and values. Apart from showing students how to place themselves in proximity to a text via close reading, teachers of freshman English did not identify any particular mechanism by which texts could exercise such power. They identified no particular patterns or features of the texts that might produce such effects, nor did their methodology—apart from the vague notion of "exposure"—account for them. Transmission is problematic in that it is implicit and unstated. The value placed on individuality prohibits the purposeful manipulation of students, especially of their interior lives. Even at Wheaton, students were never forced to accept the doctrinal statement that the college officially endorsed and included in its catalog. Rather, transmission names the supposedly automatic and natural production of humanistic values associated with instruction in literacy.

TRACES OF THE operation of transmission within freshman English can be found in the readers and handbooks commonly used as texts, and in the teaching practices as evidenced by the course descriptions and syllabi. In *Themes, Theories, and Therapy*, Albert Kitzhaber has pointed out the ubiquity of the "reader" as a textbook in freshman English courses: "The books of readings, used presumably for analysis and imitation but actually serving more often than not merely as springboards for discussions of things in general, are a phenomenon peculiar to freshman English" (16). Kitzhaber notes the incredible variety of these books (he found fifty-seven different readers used in the seventy-six institutions he surveyed), but despite the huge number of different editions, they share a common instructional strategy. All follow the same format —collections of short selections, usually arranged according to thematic topics, followed by questions intended to provoke a closer examination of the readings themselves and topics for writing in response to the reading and class discussion.[4] This common format itself suggests the tacit understanding that motivates the use of these textbooks in a freshman English course. Via their contact with these selections, students were to absorb ideas they did not previously have, to discover thoughts that had lain hidden or dormant within them, to adopt new modes of expression. These purposes show how transmission worked within freshman English. Students were to reach higher planes of thought and expression by exposure to what Myron Matlaw and James Stronks, editors of *Pro and Con,* called "good literature [that] . . . challenges thought, requires discriminating responses and complicated, responsible moral choices—as does life itself" (xv). For Matlaw and Stronks, literature itself "requires" the responses and choices, serving as a surrogate life experience. Literature was placed in a curious category through such a statement; it became something not part of life, yet more real than life. Reading (and writing in response, as this textbook and all other "readers" required) became the vehicle for learning how to live a thoughtful, responsive, morally responsible life.

The reading selections were expected to produce humane persons; more important, they also were thought to produce good writers. John Bushman and Ernst Mathews, editors of *Readings for College English,* suggest that students use the reading selections as models by asking a series of parallel analytical questions about their own writing and about that in the selections.

> Ask these questions [an extensive list is provided] after you have accomplished the major task of enjoying, understanding, evaluating.
>
> Do not hesitate to accept the writers as stimuli and as models. Imitating them will teach you many tricks of expression. (xiii)

This passage reflects the belletristic bias of the editors, a bias shared by many who taught freshman English. The "major task" for Bushman and Mathews is reading the selections they have provided. Writing, then, must remain a lesser activity. Reading brings about important outcomes: "enjoying, understanding, evaluating." As far as style is concerned, ironically, students could be expected to absorb from the texts they had read only superficial ornament: "tricks of expression." The way Bushman and Mathews present the interrelated functions of reading and writing illustrates how transmission operated. The selections in the textbook contained beliefs, values, and the means of transmitting them that together comprised academic literacy. Reading produced automatic transmission. Any reader (who read properly) received humanistic beliefs, values, and abilities by means of his or her contact with the source materials. To become literate meant to be able to produce texts of one's own that reflected the same sensibilities, ethical choices, and stylistic niceties as exhibited by the selections in the textbook.

Editors of the readers used in freshman English often affirmed the value that the reading selections could transmit by contrasting "good" and "bad" literature. Matlaw and Stronks contrast desirable with undesirable literacy in this fashion: "A person who reads only comic books . . . is immature and unwilling or unable to face reality; he is escaping into triviality or into juvenile fantasies where he is never required to come to grips with life as it really is. Similarly, the 'pulp' and 'slick' magazine stories, and most drugstore best-sellers, offer only time-passing entertainment that permits the indolent mind to slide along the surface of things" (xv). Not all editors spoke their minds quite as openly as Matlaw and Stronks, but the frank elitism of this passage is reflected in the kinds of selections that college readers of the 1950s often included. Freshman English was expected to produce mature, industrious, serious students. Those who taught the course sought to accomplish this by weaning students from the "trivial," the "juvenile," the "indolent" kinds of things that one might lapse into unless properly guided toward "good literature" and skillful writing. Sharon Crowley cites several examples from professional journals of the 1950s that echo these sentiments. Perhaps most salient to the discussion here is a statement written by Gerald Thorson in 1956: "As teachers of English we are concerned not only with the teaching of skills; we are also interested in the transmission of values" (*Composition in the University* 105–6).

Skillful writing derives partly from mastery of grammar and mechanics, but most college instructors deemed such things the province of elementary and secondary education. What made college writing different from the writing students should have been capable of at earlier stages of their education emerges precisely through transmission. Matlaw and Stronks write, "As we see how experienced writers express themselves, we can learn to make our own writing more effective and increase the power and satisfaction that come with skill in writing" (xiii). Skill comes not from following certain methods of invention or from following certain rules of composition, but from "see[ing] how experienced writers express themselves." That privileged vision was deemed sufficient to bring about the maturity and style that sets the academically literate apart from the masses who read comic books and drugstore novels, and who presumably don't write anything at all.

Grammar handbooks also reflect an ideology of transmission.[5] John C. Hodges's *Harbrace College Handbook* was the most popular during the postwar era. According to Debra Hawhee, it "still stands as *the textbook* used by more composition instructors and students than any other" (505). Hodges comments in his introduction to the fifth edition (1962), "In your reading you should observe the practice of good writers so that you may eventually gain the confidence that comes from first-hand knowledge of what good writing is" (viii). The format of his handbook bears out this injunction. The various sections contain rules, followed by examples (usually chosen from professional writing and accomplished student essays) of their proper use. Then follow various exercises that allow students to demonstrate their knowledge of the rules, usually by correcting sentences that violate them. Just as passages in the reading textbooks reputedly contain the qualities that would be transmitted to students, so handbook rules, examples, and exercises offer the correctness and style students needed to succeed as writers. To teach, then, was to put students in proximity to the sources of academic literacy; to learn was to allow the desirable qualities of the sources to penetrate oneself.

Passages in the course descriptions for freshman English at Illinois (both Urbana and Navy Pier), Northwestern, and Wheaton reflect the integral function of transmission. The 1960 Rhetoric 101 syllabus from

Navy Pier, which had remained largely unchanged since the mid-1950s, contains this statement: "Students should learn that we are concerned not only with the ideas in an essay but chiefly with how a good essay is put together and how they might employ (to the improvement of their own work) some of the methods and devices good writers use." Implicit in this statement of purpose is a model of writing in which a text ("a good essay") contains some sort of natural structure that the students have somehow appropriated for themselves. The fact that *Pro and Con* was one of the required texts for Rhetoric 101 suggests how students were expected to discover and employ the "methods and devices" of "good writers." Moreover, the list of "Supplementary Paperback Orders" for the Rhetoric staff in 1960 comprises twenty-two different literary titles, including novels, collections of poetry and short stories, and drama.

At Urbana, the *Manual and Calendar* for 1949 lists as one of the four objectives for Rhetoric 101 "to read with understanding and pleasure" (28). The actual syllabus gives precise directions for every class meeting of the fifteen-week semester, but includes no assignments geared specifically toward achieving this objective except for occasional class discussions of essays from the *Green Caldron* and, as mentioned earlier in this chapter, three book reports to be completed "in accordance with plans announced by your instructor" (7). The thirty-three-page reading list at the end of the *Manual and Calendar* contains the titles of a variety of nonfiction, novels, collections of short stories and poems, and drama. If the samples published in the *Green Caldron* can be taken as representative, the students' tastes tended toward modern novels for these reports. During the decade from 1953 to 1963, reports appeared on *The Catcher in the Rye; Look Homeward, Angel; Brave New World; Babbitt; Light in August; Darkness at Noon; All the King's Men; The Grapes of Wrath;* and *The Screwtape Letters.* The same issues in this span of years also printed essays on a handful of nineteenth-century novels (*The Red Badge of Courage, Wuthering Heights, Crime and Punishment*), two short stories ("Paul's Case" and "The Secret Life of Walter Mitty"), two nonfiction selections (*Walden* and Plato's *Republic*), and one epic poem (Homer's *Odyssey*).

Howard Siegel's "First Impressions" conveys the attitude with which students approached the reading assignment. Siegel had read *The Odyssey.* His first impressions reflected what often happens when a student selects a work labeled "good," but has no context for his reading experience: "I was struck by my failure to react with any genuine enthusiasm to such a highly acclaimed piece of literature" (8). Curiously enough, he holds his own extensive reading background the cause of his finding Homer inaccessible and dull:

> Homer's plots . . . do not excite the imagination as do those of Maugham or Hemingway. Odysseus's character . . . when compared to that of Holden Caulfield, stimulates the reader about as much as melba toast or yogurt stimulates the gourmet. The exploration of ideology appears ridiculously shallow after one has read the political science fiction of George Orwell or Dostoievski's *Crime and Punishment.* Homer's humor in comparison to George S. Kaufman's or James Thurber's is as pitiable a mismatch as Abbott and Costello opposing Charlie Chaplin. [Here Siegel reveals, as did Ron Carver, how he has bought into the values of liberal culture.] Homer displays none of the warmth of Saroyan, none of the insight of Chayevsky, and none of the allegory of Miller or Williams. (8)

As his essay continues, Siegel simultaneously displays his erudition yet criticizes his undeveloped taste by claiming that at first he found Mozart childish compared to "romantics and moderns" such as Tchaikovsky, Rachmaninoff, Beethoven, Franck, Saint-Saëns, Debussy, and Chopin; but he relates that he has come to "love Mozart" because his works are "so uncontaminated by sophistication" (8). So, despite his considerable musical and literary experience, Siegel concludes that he somehow is lacking: "I need only to increase my exposure to Homer, to discover new elements and standards, in order to have mastered another master" (9). As I will explain further in chapter 8 ("The Student"), freshman English required a student, no matter how accomplished, to acknowledge his own flaws and his ability to improve.

Ernest Samuels describes the 1951 syllabus for English A at Northwestern as including objectives for both reading and writing, objectives that assume the absorption of literary qualities through contact with models. The writing objectives state that students "should discover the qualities of contemporary informal style" by means of their reading and discussion. Then, "on the basis of this relatively factual knowledge, they should learn to write clear and idiomatic English." Samuels's description does not explain how reading and discussion effect this discovery, nor in what way "the qualities of contemporary informal style" can be reduced to a system of facts. The syllabus continues with this statement on the reading objectives: "The purpose of reading literature in English A is to increase the range and intensity of the students' response to literature; to give them some relatively sophisticated examples of literature to work on, so that they can develop a full and appropriate response to what deserves to be called 'literature'" ("Freshman Composition" 16–17). Like the writing objectives, these suggest that a complex response, both in terms of determining what deserves to be called "literature" as well as in terms of formulating a response that is "full and appropriate," will follow automatically from mere exposure to the texts chosen for the course.

The teaching notes of Jean Hagstrum for English A10 (fall 1956) reveal how one teacher and his students sought to meet these objectives. From the handbook (Porter Perrin's *Index to English*), Hagstrum assigned only the sections on plagiarism and outlining. He required three informal and four formal themes on a variety of personal topics. The bulk of the class time, however, was spent on the discussion of literature—thirteen different short stories, fourteen expository essays, and four poems.

At Wheaton, the "Proposals for Writing 111 and 112" of 1957 include nine different suggestions. One of them is "that a number of pieces of good literature suitable both in style and subject be introduced into the course and made largely the source of papers written by students."

All of these examples document the degree to which freshman English was devoted to what John Heyda calls "'character building' elements of the curriculum." Under this guise, the course served as an instrument of academic literacy, but literacy for a particular purpose—to allow students to absorb the humane qualities that were supposed to inhere in belletristic literature, whether established works from the literary canon or essays produced by accomplished students. The very acts of reading and writing—at a level presumed to be qualitatively better than that of mass culture—were presumed to cause the readers or writers to be "infected," in Guth's words, with the qualities, beliefs, and values of humanistic culture such as reason, order, a certain type of aesthetics, and the innate, superior value and beauty of the human spirit.

Like instrumentality, efficiency, and individuality, transmission was so much a part of the way those in the academy operated that it assumed the status of a naturally occurring element. Mere contact with "good literature," for example, was supposed to effect certain kinds of changes in the students. When that did not happen—and for students such as those whom Dudley Bailey interviewed, it did not—the fault may have been assigned to the students' poor preparation in high school; the inexperience, fatigue, or incompetence of the teaching staff; or the students' own laziness, intransigence, or, in Laurence Perrine's words, being "not properly tuned" (10). Nevertheless, the failure of students to achieve or maintain the desired literacy may have originated in unexamined suppositions about the relationship between text and reader. If students were not "infected" by the things they read, perhaps the texts did not contain the power to infect.

Another problematic aspect of the presumptions of freshman English, including transmission, rises from the difference between what teachers and students assumed they were doing and what actually was happening. Commentators such as Robert Saalbach assumed that the course was communicating "cultural values"; Hans Guth assigned it the task of producing "emotional literacy." Both assumed an Arnoldian perspective, that the discipline of English has the power to enlighten, to raise students from a lesser to a higher mode of existence. From some historical distance, however, we can see that "enlightenment" came at the price of teaching students to devalue the culture that they had brought to the university, and to adapt themselves to another preferred by the academy. Some students, such as Ron Carver or Howard Siegel, seem to have achieved such "enlightenment." Others, such as those whom Dudley Bailey interviewed, may have failed to achieve this goal not so much due to their own psychological or cognitive deficiencies, or because of the lack of proper technique or materials on the part of the teaching staff, but out of a natural resistance to give up the familiar and useful for the unknown. Perhaps students who failed to change were rejecting the haughty pronouncements that dictated that "literature" was literary because it contained inherently superior qualities. Perhaps they sensed but could not express their intuition that its superiority derived not from intrinsic quality but from being more highly valued by those in power at the university.

Correspondence

CRITICAL THEORY DOES NOT SO MUCH PROVIDE A MEANS FOR interpreting the texts to which it turns its glance, as it attempts to describe at a given moment what a text is, and how readers read it. At any moment in history the principles of the dominant critical theory provide insight into the basic educational issues of that time—what counts as a text, how to read, write, and think, who one must become in order to participate in discursive practices.

Powerful influences from the outside affected the academy just after World War II—a sudden, huge increase in enrollment, bringing many "nontraditional" students to campus; the broadening of the professoriat to include persons from social, religious, or ethnic groups that had been largely absent from academic life; changing national political, economic, and social agendas. Robert Connors believes that three huge shifts changed the face of composition as a discipline: (1) the communications movement, which brought together composition and speech scholars; (2) the general move away from historical or philological methodologies and toward a more populist New Critical way of reading; (3) the change in the socioculture of the professoriat in the wake of the influx of "'new men' (and women) . . . from lower-middle-class backgrounds" (*Composition-Rhetoric* 203–4). Of these changes, none had a greater impact on the practices in freshman English classrooms than did New Criticism. Arthur Applebee cites two leading figures of the new critical movement in order to document the sharp difference between pre- and postwar departments: "[Cleanth] Brooks could write in 1943 that the New Critics 'have next to no influence in the universities,' [but] by 1953 [René] Wellek was observing that such interests completely dominated the younger staff members" (163).[1]

In my questioning of twenty staff members who had been active in the teaching of writing at Urbana, Navy Pier, Northwestern, and Wheaton, virtually all mentioned how much New Critical principles had been part of their teaching. Given that freshman English was always left to the newest members of the department or to graduate students who with few exceptions had entered the profession because of their interest in literature, it would be reasonable to expect that those responsible for freshman English were operating according to this set of critical principles, and therefore informed their teaching with them. As W. Ross Winterowd has put it, "Since composition is embedded in English departments, and since English departments are, for all intents and purposes, departments of literature, literary doctrine and practice get translated into the teaching of writing" ("Post-Structuralism and Composition" 79).[2]

In her dissertation, "New Critical Rhetoric and Composition" (University of Southern California, 1987), Colleen Kay Aycock examines the connections between New Critical literary doctrine and writing pedagogy.[3] She maintains that the influence of New Criticism went far beyond the interpretation of literature: it informed a school of rhetoric that "continued to influence the teaching of freshman composition until the sixties when it became absorbed by interests in classical rhetoric and the development of newer composition theories" (1).

Because New Criticism exercised pervasive influence during the postwar era, it seems inescapable that, in Aycock's words, "virtually all of us who have traveled through freshman and sophomore English, as teachers or students in the second half of this century, have been affected by it" (1). During its hegemony, neither teachers nor students could escape being informed by New Critical theory.[4] One of the constituent forces within freshman English during the postwar era was a marked correspondence between the tenets of New Criticism, including its notions of the self, and of what constituted the teaching and learning of academic literacy.

The most powerful of these correspondences was based on the New Critical concept of a text. Under a New Critical reading, a text becomes an "organic construct of interdependent meaning" (Aycock 32). As something with its own organic unity, a text takes on a life of its own, the interrelationship of every word, phrase, or sentence to be teased out via "close reading." In describing "The Idea of the Freshman Composition Course" (1955), Herman Bowersox explains the place of close reading in freshman English: "The rhetorical analysis of a prose passage operates on the assumption that a well-written discourse is a structure of articulate elements. . . . Its purpose is to exhibit the various elements in discourse as interlocking parts in a complex whole" (39). Given that a text was seen as constituted of organic parts, subtly related within a complex whole, close reading enforced certain values. "New Critics valued unconventional or novel insights; rich verbal texture of organic interrelationships among structure and meaning; the concrete, presentational over the abstract; and metaphor as the fundamental language principle" (Aycock 35). Under this theory, the mind becomes "an unlimited source of symbolizing activity" (137), endlessly inventing connections and patterns within the inchoate world around it. Referring to the turbulent economic, political, and social environment of the twenties and thirties during which New Criticism arose, Aycock comments: "Where form did not exist in life, one could create it in art. One could, through form, shape one's way out of chaos" (40). To read meant to discover a principle of order within what could appear to be random; to write meant to discover the connections between the multifarious concrete impressions and experiences of which life was constituted.

In freshman English, students were required to learn to read and to write (and in some cases, to listen and to speak as well) according to the standards expected within the academy. These activities were commonly taken to be composed of a priori "skills," such as forming ideas, deploying style, or organizing arguments. Course syllabi refer to such "skills" in fixed, absolute terms. Northwestern's (1951) states: "Students in English A . . . should discover the qualities of contemporary informal style. . . . On the basis of this *relatively factual knowledge* [emphasis in original] they should learn to write clear and idiomatic English" ("Freshman Composition" 16). Style and the subsequent texts to be produced as a result of having employed it were thought to be expressions of autonomous, timeless standards.

The syllabus for Rhetoric 101 at Navy Pier makes direct reference to "close reading," stating that as a result of having scrutinized their writing, students should discover "how they might employ (to the improvement of their own work) some of the methods and devices good writers use." Neither of these syllabi acknowledges the possibility that close reading does not cause a text to reveal the principles of style or ideas that lie hidden within it, but actively constructs those principles and ideas according to the organic model that the theory imposes upon it.

Not only does close reading construct the text, it also constructs *the readers* according to the theory by which they are reading, and *the teachers* according to the standards by which the readers/writers are to be judged. Aycock comments: "What the student does learn to value in the writing process is discrimination, subtlety, precision, conciseness, and wit. What the teacher learns to value is clear, coherent, graceful, and interesting prose—but above all—well-formed, well-disciplined prose in which no word is idle" (156). Just as students were expected to display not their own version of their individuality, but one constructed to fit the model sanctioned by the academy, so they were expected to become readers and writers corresponding to the model presumed by New Critical theory.

The textbooks used in freshman English courses provide examples of this correspondence between the New Critical organic model of a text and the methods by which students were expected to construct themselves as readers and writers. *Reader and Writer,* published in 1954 by Harrison Hayford, of Northwestern University, and Howard P. Vincent, of the Illinois Institute of Technology, claimed to attempt "more openly than has been done before to bring together the major language problems as such—the problems of reading, writing, and thinking—with the literary and ideational interests of teachers and students" (vi). The chapters of *Reader and Writer,* as the title suggests, take students through the issues of who a person is, first, as a reader, then as a writer—particularly one who seeks to express his or her individual experience—then as a thinker, and finally as a user of language, especially in the context of mass communications.

Hayford and Vincent define a reader by describing various kinds of reading, arranged on a scale of importance. Most fundamental is "subsistence reading," the kind required to decode advertisements, labels, and simple instructions. Higher is "technological" reading, by which one acquires information, ideas, or opinions. This "technological" reading is said to enable a reader "to grasp another's central meaning in proper relation to its parts, and thus to have a view of the whole" (1), a description that echoes the organic quality that New Critical reading assumes texts exhibit. The highest form of reading, according to Hayford and Vincent, is done for the pleasure of the act itself, an enjoyment based upon the "precision and sensitivity" in words, the appreciation of word structures, the "nobility of the English sentence," the "comfort and pleasure" of books (2). The pleasures Hayford and Vincent speak of can only come about as the result of a close reading of a text.

Reader and Writer explains to students who they ought to be as writers, an identity tied to the reader they must first become. Echoing the requirement for individuality,[5] which has already been noted in chapter 4 as an identifying feature of freshman English, Hayford and Vincent advise students: "You have things to say . . . that will be of interest to others, and you can interest them best by being your honest and natural unassuming self" (88). The construction of self as a writer can be seen in their further advice concerning how to judge writing: "Good writing . . . is packed; it is continually saying something. Every sentence and every word adds to the thought and the experience. And much thought goes into it which does not necessarily appear on the surface—like an iceberg, which is nine-tenths out of view" (88). Students would know that they had succeeded as writers when they were able to produce the kinds of texts that could be read for the organic interrelation, the subtle texture, the submerged yet powerful metaphor that proponents of the New Criticism desired.

Hayford and Vincent do not stop at informing students about who they ought to be as readers and writers. The power of New Critical theory can be seen in their logical extensions of literacy. The third chapter in *Reader and Writer,* "The Arch of Experience," illustrates how all aspects of an individual's life—"your family, and your feelings about them; your school experiences, in class and out; playmates and classmates; the teachers who terrorize, inspire or bore you . . . your roommate, your last night's date, the heavy snow that fell this morning, the tedium of a laboratory on a spring day, or the excitement of a laboratory when you finally identify the unknown" (208)—find value and meaning as a result of their construction in writing according to New Critical principles. The fourth chapter, "The Ways of Thought," reconstructs mental activity in terms of New Criticism. By examining critically the structure of what he reads and writes, a student "is well on the way to greater mastery and control of himself and his world" (296). That control takes on massive dimensions in the last chapter of the book, "The Mobilized Word," which attempts to have students consider how New Critical values can show them the way to evaluate and change for the better the immensely powerful modern mass media. Having read closely the selections in this chapter, students are told that their reading "may help [them] do [their] part toward raising the standards of a nation" (506). Hayford and Vincent intend that everything in students' lives—not only their reading and writing but their immediate experiences, their thought, their entire culture—be made to correspond to New Critical theory. An examination of the critical theory that informs this freshman English textbook, then, illustrates how a particular way of reading and writing does not merely provide a key to unlock the secrets of the texts that students will encounter in their academic life and after. It reveals the type of student they had to become in order to participate in academic literacy, and how they were shown to make their entire experience correspond to a critical model.

The "self" students had to construct in order to participate in literacy as it is modeled in *Reader and Writer* suggests another connection between freshman English and New Criticism. For Hayford and Vincent, acts of reading and writing are ahistorical. To be a reader does not require any particular prior fund of information, but a kind of insight whereby an individual can discern and appreciate the subtle interplay of connections from which a text derives its value. Freshman English writers were not required to convey any particular body or category of knowledge, but to express their own experiences and insights, carefully chosen and arranged. "Reading" and "writing" exist as a priori skills, developed from within the individual.

One of the appeals of a pedagogy based upon the New Criticism was its freedom from historical or philological prerequisites. In "The University and the Prevention of Culture," Gerald Graff explains the rapid spread of a New Critical approach in postwar American colleges and universities. Even though the original proponents of New Criticism such as T. S. Eliot and I. A. Richards "were not mere explicators but engaged critics of culture" (67), after the war the academy's influx of "nontraditional" students and faculty led to a very different kind of reading:

> Tailored to the needs of the fifteen-page article or the fifty-minute class session, the cultural context of first-generation New Criticism fell away. . . . In the new mass-education conditions after the war neither students nor faculty could be depended upon to presuppose a common history or a language in which historical differences could be compared. . . . The expedient thing in these circumstances was to isolate and mass-produce the New Critical technique of reading, which did sharpen a student's powers of critical attention. . . . In order to ape the old scholarship one had had at least to find out some information, whereas to do a fair impersonation of a New Critic one required no prior knowledge of any kind. (68–69)

New Critical reading and writing easily became elements among the "priorities" that freshman English was expected to provide.

Another text, *Pro and Con*, by Myron Matlaw of Hunter College and James B. Stronks of the University of Illinois Chicago Undergraduate Division, begins with an essay that illustrates the commonly accepted notion of how literacy and the individual relate to one another. This selection, H. L. Mencken's "Literature and the Schoolma'm," also illustrates the subtle forces of correspondence at work.

Mencken concocts a tirade against what he considers the evils of misguided teaching. The "schoolma'm" is the type of teacher who attempts to foster style in his or her students by invoking systems of rules. Mencken rails against this kind of well-intended ineptitude. He writes: "For the essence of a sound style is that it cannot be reduced to rules—that it is a living and breathing thing . . . that it fits its proprietor tightly and yet ever so loosely, as his skin fits him. It is, in fact, quite as securely an integral part of him as that skin is. . . . In brief, a style is always the outward and visible symbol of a man, and it cannot be anything else" (3–4). Using Mencken as their authority, Matlaw and Stronks attempt to persuade students that style is the outward expression of their interior condition, the presentation to the world of their inherent wholeness and complexity. But qualities of organic unity, subtlety, complexity—those that Mencken claims cannot be reduced to a system of rules in a handbook—are the very qualities in the texts that the New Critics sought with their close reading. This lesson on style amounts to the injunction that students construct their inner selves according to a model provided by critical theory.

Aycock claims that another textbook, *Essays and Essay Writing,* by Bernard L. Jefferson of the University of Illinois at Urbana, provides a clear explanation of the prose form "most suitable for studying and producing prose in light of New Critical values" (142)—the friendly essay. Jefferson discusses the reflective, detached essays of writers like Lamb, Franklin, Emerson, and Lowell, men whose rhetoric made "use of the pleasant fireside conversation instead of the contentious public forum" (Aycock 143). According to Aycock, the style of these essays accounted for their appeal to those who would teach writing according to New Critical principles. "Thus style reflects not only content but also the dramatic character of the observer/writer. The text provides a 'characterization' of the author. The ethos of the writer, Jefferson says, is one of certainty; the writer is direct and assertive, yet is not a strenuous advocate of reform. The writer is guided by curiosity, not alarm or precaution, and is genuinely warm and human" (144). The writer of the friendly essay must adopt a particular ethos and must correspond to a specific set of values congruent with New Critical theory. This is not to claim that Lamb, Franklin, Emerson, or Lowell subscribed to the New Criticism, but only explains why the friendly essay form proved suitable to New Critical pedagogy.

It is curious, however, what happens to such material when it becomes part of freshman English. One of Jefferson's students, Louise E. Rorabacher, edited *Assignments in Exposition* (1946), a textbook used for some time in Rhetoric 101 at Urbana.[6] Although she had moved on to Purdue, in her acknowledgments Rorabacher mentions Jefferson and Charles Roberts, the head of the Division of Rhetoric at Urbana. *Assignments in Exposition* also contained sample essays from the *Green Caldron,* the magazine of freshman English at Urbana. Rorabacher's textbook presents practical advice on the types of assignments commonly taught in freshman English courses, such as description, narration, argumentation, process, comparison and contrast, classification, partition, and definition. It also includes chapters on some types of texts common to academia, including the summary, outline, research paper, critical paper, character sketch, familiar essay, examination, business letter, and social letter. These contents are not unusual for a freshman English textbook of the postwar era, and none (except for the familiar essay) seems at first glance to reflect New Critical theory. Rorabacher, however, introduces these chapters with the claim that her book "presents common logical patterns, or 'brainpaths' which the mind must follow in order to be understood by other minds" (1). A later chapter, on description, provides some evidence for what she means by a "brainpath." She advises her readers that description requires concrete detail and bases this suggestion on the operations of the mind itself: "The human mind must often deal with the abstract. . . . Yet the mind still more dearly loves the specific" (27). According to Rorabacher, a writer employs concrete detail not because readers expect to find it when they read description, but because the mind somehow has a predilection for this kind of detail. A "brainpath" seems to be a pattern in a text that corresponds to the general structure of minds. According to Rorabacher, the text takes its form from an inescapable natural structure.

A curious series of steps seems to have been taken in order to make the claim that the friendly essay, for example, represents a "brainpath," or that the need for specific detail in a description corresponds to the structure of the mind. Initially, certain authors within a particular historical context invent a certain style of essay. Then teachers who subscribe to New Critical theory choose specific essays typical of that style because they are particularly amenable to close reading and because they provide a useful model for the kinds of texts they would like their students to produce. Finally, one student (Louise Rorabacher) who herself has been educated under the New Criticism, and who has presumably constructed herself as a reader and writer so as to correspond to the theory, sets down what she has learned in a handbook. And in this handbook, the correspondences she has formed according to critical theory become part of the natural order.

This curious pattern illustrates how the presumption of correspondence functioned in freshman English. Just as with the problem of individuality, students are presented with "facts" that are claimed to be unambiguously and inescapably part of the natural order of things—an essay consists in an open and honest sharing of one's "true self"; a text has a subtle, organic texture that can be unlocked only via close reading; in order to work well, writing must be invested with a wealth of detail, cleverly and subtly interrelated by principles of organic unity that derive from not only the structure of language but also the structure of one's own mind. Although these critical tenets are taken as immutable "facts," they derive from the hypotheses of a particular critical method, not from the laws of nature.

One final piece of evidence reveals how New Critical theory had become so embedded in the practice of freshman English that it had itself achieved transparency, and its beliefs and values had become part of the presumed natural order of things. Hans Guth wrote authoritatively about freshman English during the postwar years. In the early 1960s, he, with others such as Robert Gorrell, Albert Kitzhaber, or Richard Braddock, wanted to create an effective pedagogy of writing suitable for the college classroom. He saw that those who taught freshman English had either minimal academic experience (as in the case of graduate assistants) or experience unconnected to or even inimical to the teaching of writing (as in the case of many new assistant professors of literature who taught the course only until they achieved tenure). One of Guth's attempts to advance the cause of freshman English was *The Wadsworth Manual: A Guide for Teachers of Composition* (1965). Through this little manual, he hoped to begin to reach a consensus concerning the "shape and purposes of the composition course," to propose a "clear sense of purpose" for a course that took many different forms, and to offer assistance to those who wanted practical advice. Chapters of *The Wadsworth Manual* offer definitions of the course, discuss the substance and structure of freshman English, give practical advice about conducting a course and grading papers, and present what were then current developments in the field. In many ways, Guth's booklet is a time capsule of freshman English at the end of the postwar era.

Guth never mentions New Criticism by name, but its ideology surfaces throughout the book. For example, he advises novice teachers of writing, *"The teacher's work is successful to the extent that the student succeeds in becoming his own critic"* (emphasis in original) (48). What does Guth mean by a student "becoming his own critic"? He indicates that the students must learn to apply the principles of close reading to their own work and judge it accordingly. "To make instruction in writing effective, teachers of English must counteract two equally unfortunate tendencies. Work focused on composition is often too mechanical, designed to drill into students patterns they should instead develop organically through much reading and writing. Work focused on language and literature is often considered a holiday from the grind of trying to improve the student's written work" (48). He is invoking the same connection between reading and writing seen in Hayford and Vincent's textbook. Reading supplies an organic pattern, which then will inform the students' own writing. The subtle unity that they discover through close reading of the canonical texts provides the standard by which they should learn to judge their own essays.

"The Teaching of Composition" presents an emphasis quite different from what one might expect, given the purposes that Guth claims for his manual. In this chapter, he devotes nine pages to methods for conducting class discussions on assigned readings. He devotes only a page and a half to actual composition pedagogy, and the two strategies he suggests (free writing and using the class itself as an audience) explain nothing about how to advise students in their composition of actual essays. He spends two pages on how to make a writing assignment, three and a half on evaluation of papers, two and a half on conducting class discussions of student papers, and four and a half on practical tips for classroom management. If Guth's manual reflects the pedagogy of freshman English—an enlightened pedagogy, at that—what it reveals is a classroom devoted mostly to discussion of reading assignments. Some class time may have been applied to brief inventional strategies or discussion of the students' own texts, but clearly the students were expected, from their close reading and discussion of literature, to assimilate what constituted an acceptable text and what their roles were as writers.

W. Ross Winterowd points out the influences we may expect in contemporary composition classrooms as a result of the rise of theories that, as he sees them, are marked by skepticism in their reliance on notions of indeterminacy. "The incisive debate of the New Criticism will be replaced by a long, drawn-out, enigmatic shrug of the shoulders" (90). However, to examine critical theory in order to determine its relationship to composition pedagogy is more than merely deciding which will offer more interesting or more measurable results. Theory is inescapable; it is not a costume that readers or writers put on to present themselves in one fashion or another. It is the model or set of principles by which we function at a given historical moment. As Sharon Crowley puts it, "Reading and writing pedagogies are inevitably grounded in theory, whether these theories are consciously subscribed to or not" (*A Teacher's Introduction to Deconstruction* 28). The lesson of New Criticism, with its influence on freshman English in the postwar era, is not one of having followed a true path or a false one. It is that acts of literacy are not absolute; they are constructed so as to correspond to a system of beliefs and values. Pedagogy, then, is not so much *influenced* by critical theory as it constitutes critical theory in action.

part two

The Practice of

Freshman English

The Course

seven

IN THE PREVIOUS SIX CHAPTERS I HAVE ATTEMPTED TO DESCRIBE freshman English as a particular discursive practice; that is, a system of presumptions, both acknowledged and unacknowledged, manifested in the set of practices that constituted the first-year composition course at Wheaton, Illinois, and Northwestern during the postwar era. From archival evidence, a portrait with distinctive features emerges. Just as a face is more than the sum total of particulars regarding nose, chin, lips, teeth, forehead, eyes, ears, and hair, each of the presumptions of freshman English—instrumentality, priority, efficiency, individuality, transmission, and correspondence—works in relationship to the others within the discursive practice.

At the behest of the institution (not from the impetus of a particular discipline) freshman English served as the instrument of literacy for the entire academy. Sharon Crowley notes that its primary function has always been "the instrumental service ethic . . . to make student writing available for surveillance until it can be certified to conform to whatever standards are deemed to mark it, and its authors as suitable for admission to the discourses of the academy" (*Composition in the University*

253). Freshman English had no disciplinary boundaries, making its content open to the search for the knowledge or skills that students needed to establish prior to achieving academic literacy. Those who taught freshman English, frustrated by the multifarious methods used in postwar classrooms yet confident of finding the means of accomplishing their instrumental goal, always sought better ways of achieving effectiveness and efficiency. The humanistically oriented faculty who taught the course presumed that instruction in writing would liberate their students' true selves. But, as Sharon Crowley states succinctly, "The course is meant to shape students to behave, think, write, and speak as students rather than as the people they are, people who have differing histories and traditions and languages and ideologies" (*Composition in the University* 9). Those same teachers, themselves steeped in liberal culture, presumed that one important function of the course was to facilitate their students' self-liberation by allowing (or more accurately, *requiring*) them to assimilate the humane values that canonical literature could transmit. Finally, the dominant critical orientation the era, New Criticism, pervaded the postwar milieu of reading and writing. New Critical notions of text, reader, and writer corresponded closely to the instrumental nature of the course.

The next three chapters will outline how these six presumptions functioned in an interrelated fashion within the discursive practice of freshman English during the postwar era. As a practice, most apparent is the interaction of three principal elements—the course itself, including its content, the benefits it was thought to provide, and the ways in which it changed; the students, including both how they were assumed to be and how they actually had to construct themselves in order to succeed in the course; and the teachers, including both what was expected of them, and what they became as a result of their teaching freshman English.

In researching *Writing in the Academic Disciplines, 1870–1990*, David Russell investigated many college English programs, including those at Colgate, the University of California at Berkeley, Iowa State, Harvard, Columbia, Kansas, Missouri, Michigan, Minnesota, Ohio State, Central College, MIT, Radcliffe, and the University of Chicago. In my introduction, I cited his comment that his examination of curricula in writing across the curriculum and in general education did not reveal a "typical" freshman English program, given the diversity among American institutions of higher learning (personal correspondence, September 1988). As Russell found in his research, the three schools upon which this study is based differ markedly from one another in the types of students they attract, the size and diversity of their academic programs, the teaching staff and course plans for freshman English, and the relationship between freshman English and graduation requirements. As private institutions, Wheaton and Northwestern select their students according to relatively exclusive academic standards (and in Wheaton's case, doctrinal standards as well); Illinois, a state university, enrolls a clientele with greater cultural and intellectual diversity. Illinois and Northwestern, both large universities, enroll thousands of undergraduates in numerous academic and professional specializations; Wheaton, a small liberal arts college, enrolls a much smaller, more homogeneous group of students. At Wheaton and Northwestern, for the most part regular faculty taught freshman English, whereas graduate assistants taught over 90 percent of all sections within the Division of Rhetoric at Illinois. The curricula at Wheaton and Illinois were quite similar—both required two semesters of freshman English, made extensive use of handbooks, progressed through the various "modes of discourse" culminating in the documented research paper, and required a proficiency examination in English during the junior year as a prerequisite for graduation. Northwestern, on the other hand, divided freshman English into three quarter-length courses, deemed as unnecessary the handbook exercises so prominent at Wheaton and Illinois, emphasized the process of writing (which meant, for the most part, students learning to externalize their individual thoughts and perceptions) rather than the modes of discourse, and focused attention on reading and writing about literature during the second and third quarters. Although Northwestern's catalog included a regulation by which a student could be denied graduation due to "poor English," it seems never to have been invoked. Despite these differences in size, in sources of funding, in selectivity in enrollment, in staffing, and in curriculum, an examination of freshman English at Wheaton, Northwestern, and Illinois reveals a common discursive practice.

Robert Connors, among others, has pointed out that freshman English came into being "by social fiat," rather than by emerging from a tradition of scholarship. Because of its abrupt birth, "teachers were invited to invent course content to fill the culturally mandated shell"

("Rhetorical History" 233). As I argued in "Priority," this invention of content was limited to areas outside the boundaries of other academic disciplines. Freshman English consisted in furnishing students with the prerequisites for academic, professional, and personal success. In 1955 Herman Bowersox (of Roosevelt University in Chicago) argued that the purpose of the course was "to provide the student with skill in the production of the kind of discourse, chiefly exposition and argument, that he needs in his other classes and in later life" (39).[1] The "skills" with which students were provided, the texts they read and analyzed, the papers they wrote all served as practice for subsequent, more important realities. Success in freshman English did not indicate mastery of a particular body of knowledge, but the attainment of a readiness to assume a productive and respectable position within the academy, the economy, and democratic society. Lynn Z. Bloom, commenting on the values that undergird the contemporary first-year course, makes an observation that was true in the postwar era as well. In "Freshman Composition as a Middle-Class Enterprise," she describes the course as an indoctrination into the Franklinesque virtues that characterize the American middle class: "Freshman composition, in philosophy and pedagogy, reinforces the values and virtues embodied not only in the very existence of America's vast middle class, but in its general well-being —read promotion of the ability to think critically and responsibly, and the maintenance of safety, order, cleanliness, efficiency" (655). Students succeeded when they showed that they had realized their unique individuality by expressing it in their writing; however, this uniqueness came not from some previously untapped inner source, but from conformity with the tenets of freshman English. Lester Faigley has described what was expected of students as the construction of "a unified, reflective, rational self that can interpret past experience in relation to the present self" ("Study of Writing" 253).

The first-year courses at Illinois, Wheaton, and Northwestern used similar methods to bring about their students' self-reconstruction. All three programs assumed that students were empty (or only partially filled) receptacles ready to be infused with the skills considered necessary for serious academic work. They used literary texts of one sort or another for a variety of purposes—as examples of style, as starting-points for discussion and writing, as sources of information. All were based on what Susan Miller calls "an intransitive vision of writing" (97) that required students to "express themselves."

At all three schools, the skill considered prerequisite to all others was the ability to compose correct prose in a suitable style. The syllabus from the *Freshman Rhetoric Manual and Calendar* (1949) at the University of Illinois devotes seventeen of forty-four class meetings to chapters from the *Harbrace College Handbook,* covering headings such as sentence form and correctness, paragraph structure, spelling,[2] punctuation, agreement, and diction. A 1946 letter from Ernst Mathews, Executive Secretary of the University Senate Committee on Student English to H. W. Bailey, dean of the Chicago Undergraduate Division, confirms the priority given to correctness within the rhetoric courses at Illinois. Mathews details the procedures for administering and evaluating the English Qualifying Examination; concerning scoring, he notes, "To pass, a paper should be equal to a strong D paper in Rhetoric 2 [later renumbered as 102]. We mark as failures those which show great weakness in sentence structure, grammar, the important marks of punctuation, paragraphing, and organization." Correctness was the fundamental quality of acceptable writing, the basis upon which more sophisticated structures could be built.

Previous chapters have shown that the Department of English at Wheaton devoted considerable time to discussing how to ensure that students in Writing 111 and 112, as well as in all disciplines throughout the campus, meet minimum standards of correctness. Independent studies of Wheaton College, like those in Morris Keeton and Conrad Hilberry's *Struggle and Promise: A Future for Colleges,* have noted the high caliber of students that Wheaton attracted, an observation confirmed by those who taught freshman English there in the 1950s; even so, the department assigned first priority to establishing and ensuring proficiency in basic skills. A document from as late as 1968, "Guidelines for Grading Compositions," reflects the continuing emphasis upon standards nearly identical to those expected at Illinois.[3] Of the six "classifications of grading considerations" listed, four have to do with sentence structure, punctuation and mechanics, diction, and organization of sentences and paragraphs.

Northwestern devoted less classroom time to basic skills, but English A was still expected to certify the students' competence in them. In 1951 the chair of the English A committee, Ernest Samuels wrote: "Not much time is spent upon grammar in the abstract. Commonly several class meetings early in the course will review the essentials of grammar and correct usage and punctuation. . . . Thereafter we are concerned with the more troublesome questions of unity, coherence, emphasis, style, and choice of words" ("Freshman Composition Courses" 16). In "Style Theory and Static Abstractions," a chapter in *Composition-Rhetoric,* Robert Connors traces the history of terms such as "unity, coherence, and emphasis." He notes in particular that after 1910, "learning style inductively through readings was the only choice that writing teachers had after individualist and Crocean ideas won wide acceptance" (284). It is logical then, that at Northwestern, the school with a composition program most solidly wedded to literature, the old method of static abstractions had the most influence. Northwestern concerned itself more with style than with correctness, but just as at Illinois and at Wheaton, their freshman course was the instrument whereby students' writing would be given a certain "shape." Later, these blank shapes could be filled with the various kinds of important content that the disciplines would impart.

The first priority of freshman English at all three schools, therefore, was the attempt to instill in students a code of correctness and style, adherence to which would ensure minimal competence in all areas of academic and nonacademic discourse. Although some instructors proceeded straight through handbooks like *Harbrace,* or Perrin's *Index to English,* students' adherence to such a code was not judged by their ability to complete workbook-style assignments or to answer questions concerning grammar, punctuation, and spelling on tests. All three schools required weekly papers, and the evidence suggests that students generally did them. These papers were not read as attempts to convey or construct knowledge, but as proof that they had internalized the code. Part of the content of freshman English, then, was the production of texts that would demonstrate the degree to which students had learned standards of correctness and rudiments of academic style.

A second part of the content of freshman English was the reading and discussion of literature. Various documents from all three schools, covering the period between 1947 and 1960, mention nine different textbooks devoted partly or entirely to supplying short selections of professionally written prose, with occasional short fiction or poems included as well. The four different handbooks also used included shorter—usually paragraph-length—samples. All three schools also required supplementary works such as biographies, novels, and plays. Harrison Hayford, coeditor of one of the most successful freshman English texts of that era, *Reader and Writer,* claimed that English faculty always held differing opinions whether freshmen should be offered excerpts from classic essayists such as Johnson or Addison; or whether they should be reading more current, "journalistic" samples (personal interview, 2 March 1989). His own textbook reveals that tension; a section entitled "Reading as Pleasure and Work" juxtaposes an essay by Francis Bacon with the text of an advertisement from The Readers' Book Club. The heading "Some Precepts and Examples—Shaping Ideas" includes selections ranging from the notes of a student composing an essay about a deaf-mute to Thoreau's "Thoughts on Composition." The majority of the anthologies used at Wheaton, Illinois, or Northwestern reflect a compromise between "quality" and "relevance." Perhaps the strongest example of such a search for currency between the readings and the students' experiences can be found in the *Green Caldron* and *Pier Glass,* periodicals published by the Divisions of Rhetoric at Urbana and Chicago. These publications acknowledged superior writing that the faculty who served as editors selected from essays produced in their rhetoric classes. At the time, each of these journals received wide acclaim. Charles Roberts began the *Green Caldron* in 1931, and it was published biannually for forty years. The 1953 *Manual and Calendar* described it as "the oldest and one of the most distinguished publications of its kind" (15). The rhetoric faculty at Navy Pier borrowed the idea from their sister school in Urbana. *Pier Glass* was published for eight years, from 1955 to 1963. This journal achieved a certain notoriety beyond Navy Pier. In 1958 the winter issue carried two frontispieces. The first, in his own handwriting, was a message from Carl Sandburg: "Hurrah for The Pier Glass & all who look into it." The second bore this message:

> The dean of American literary critics writes:
> "Congratulations to *The Pier Glass.* It is a pleasure to encounter a college magazine that is so remote from the 'anything goes' school of English. Now that our language is spoken the world over, how important it is to write and speak well."
> Van Wyck Brooks

Teachers used examples from these magazines as required reading in Rhetoric 100, 101, and 102.

Textbooks such as Francis Connolly's *Rhetoric Case Book* or Louise Rorabacher's *Assignments in Exposition* presented readings as material for rhetorical analysis and imitation. They were organized according to rhetorical mode (exposition, narration, description, persuasion) or purpose (process, comparison and contrast, partition, analysis, definition). Others, including Hayford and Vincent's *Reader and Writer* or Matlaw and Stronks's *Pro and Con,* arranged their readings according to argumentative issues, for example, the purpose of education, the advantages and disadvantages of college life, the status of American culture, or the clarification of one's individual values. Even these books, however, included at the end a supplementary index listing its selections according to mode and purpose. *Reader and Writer* or *Pro and Con* are examples of a "thesis text," that is, a book that "announces that one powerful 'master idea' about writing should control the way students learn to write, and it gives precedence to this central thesis, subordinating all other theoretical material to it" (Connors, *Composition-Rhetoric* 250).

Connors cites Albert Kitzhaber's condemnation of the reduction of rhetoric to adherence to the "four forms" (narration, description, exposition, argumentation) or the "principles of composition" (unity, coherence, emphasis). Kitzhaber states, "These two items of theory encouraged writing by formula, writing as an academic exercise to illustrate certain abstract principles or fulfill certain specifications imposed neither by the needs of the student nor by the requirements of the subject or situation. It was writing in a social vacuum, with no motivation behind it except the necessity of handing in a theme" (*Rhetoric in American Colleges* 223). Richard Ohmann also has pointed out the triviality of the writing done in college composition courses—writing themes for the sake of writing themes, outside any real social, personal, or political value. In freshman English, he notes, students were "writing to measure," not writing from true impulses to "explain, exhort, justify, or criticize" (153).

In the conclusion to *Rhetoric in American Colleges, 1850–1900,* published originally in 1953, Kitzhaber states: "Most composition teaching today, in fact, is still being done in the shadow of rhetorical theory that came into prominence between 1885 and 1900" (226). His generalization certainly applies to the programs at Illinois, Wheaton, and Northwestern.

AUTHORS SUPPOSED THAT reading the kinds of selections included in their freshman English textbooks would facilitate each student's growth as a "unified, reflective, rational self" and their development of individual styles that reflected the students' unique personalities. For example, Francis Connolly claimed that the study of literature would lead students to personal freedom, "that still loftier harmony of thought and actions, feeling and imagination which is the achievement of the free and full personality" (*Rhetoric Case Book* 731). However, the reading practices common to freshman English could not escape the purposes for which the course existed. Teachers presumed that freshman English would liberate its students from the banality and mindlessness of the world outside academia; however, the kinds of reading and writing commonly done served not to liberate, but to elicit conformity. The claim that reading literature would open students to a world of thought and feeling that they had never before experienced masked a subtle yet powerful enforcement of an elitism that professed its values to be different than those of the mass culture, and better.

Moreover, the technique of reading commonly taught in freshman English contained an unacknowledged requirement of conformity. Careful observation and questioning of a text through New Critical close reading were supposed to allow students to perceive its natural structure and appreciate its unity. These qualities, however, came not from the text itself but from the readers who had learned to re-create what they read according to the image in which they had been led to create themselves—an image constructed according to the tenets of freshman English. As the academy's instrument, freshman English served to indoctrinate students with the presumptions concerning literacy that would bring them into conformity with academic culture.

Although language study and reading were major components of the content of freshman English, its foremost obligation was the development of the students' ability to compose acceptable academic prose. Within the practice of freshman English, however, composing took on a specific character. A student-written text was expected to indicate the degree to which its author had accommodated herself to the formulae of freshman English, established patterns of expression through which communication was thought to occur. The 1956 *Manual and Calendar* calls these patterns "the kinds of discourse" (exposition, narration, description, and argument). They themselves are assembled by a writer's deploying still more particular patterns of expression such as cause and effect, comparison and contrast, partition, classification, definition, or analogy. To make a writing assignment meant to give students the occasion to prove that they had mastered a certain function of discourse, evidenced by their ability to fit whatever experiences, thoughts, observations, or feelings they happened to have at a certain moment into these schematic patterns. In 1953 George D. Stout, of Washington University in St. Louis, described the function of writing assignments within the freshman English course. He commented that freshman composition should serve as "indoctrination of the student with the idea that language . . . is not an end in itself [but] a medium of communicating information, ideas, emotions, and images from the mind of the writer or speaker to the mind of the reader or hearer" ("Why and How for Freshman Composition" 26).

In the freshman English course, students were to learn the properties of the medium, the elements of which a communication is composed. The *content* of the message makes little difference, as Stout claims when he suggests that students be assigned "conventional and apparently trivial subjects" (26) in order to practice their writing and speaking. For Stout, as for most practitioners of freshman English, learning to communicate meant learning to arrange one's thoughts, feelings, and experiences according to universal patterns that could be applied within any context, and to any purpose.

Although he does not use the label, Stout is expressing the tenets of current-traditional rhetoric. In *The Methodical Memory*, Sharon Crowley explores the origins of this rhetoric in faculty and association psychology. Part of her discussion elaborates the basis for Stout's statement of the purposes of the course:

> Current traditional rhetoric . . . subscribes to the notion that "subjects" . . . are mental configurations whose existence is ontologically prior to their embodiment in discourse; it prefers the discursive movement from generalization to specification; it concentrates on expository discourse; it recommends that the inven-

tional scheme devised for exposition be used in any discursive situation; and it translates invention out of the originating mind and
onto the page. In other words, this rhetoric assumes that the
process of invention can be graphically displayed in discourse. (13)

In freshman English, the subject of a composition exists independently
of language, waiting to be expressed via one of the modes of discourse.
A writer's task is to find a way to fit whatever personal information he
or she may have accumulated into a particular "mode" so as to demonstrate mastery of that particular form, and mastery of the standards of
correctness.

Prompts supplied for the English Qualifying Exams at Illinois provide evidence of what Stout calls "conventional and apparently trivial
subjects." The June 1958 examination contains eighteen quotations or
topical commonplaces about a variety of familiar subjects. These topics
suggest that a successful freshman paper need not be about anything in
particular. Rather, they share the possibility of being treated in an expository essay, developed by one of the several formulaic patterns taught
in freshman English classes such as comparison and contrast ("Pure
vs. Applied Mathematics"), description ("The Tractor—'Jack-of-All-
Trades'"), cause and effect ("If we are to rear our daughters to be proud
that they are women, we must end our present peculiar habit of educat-
ing them as though they were men"), analogy ("A Great Athlete and a
Great Man"), or definition ("We have forgotten that the automobile is
supposed to be a vehicle of transportation and not a collection of gadg-
ets")—a topic that could also serve to illustrate classification.

In discussing one such pattern, partition, Louise Rorabacher comments that "you may be interested only in discovering of what pieces the
safety razor is made . . . [or] you may be searching for the elements which
constituted Washington's greatness. In either case, the process is logically
the same" (152). The breadth or narrowness, the triviality or profun-
dity of a paper made little difference, provided the students could display
how they had mastered the "basic skills" of communication. They wrote
to demonstrate how well they had accommodated themselves to the unacknowledged ideology of freshman English, an accommodation demonstrated by their display of academic values: correctness, rationality,
orderliness, subtlety, and dispassionate evenhandedness as reflected

in their ability to use prescribed methods of organization and development.

Students were expected to resign their participation in meaningful discourse for the sake of formal display even though tremendous events were transpiring around them. At Urbana, for example, several major issues rocked the campus during "The Ninth Decade, 1947–56," as Roger Ebert labels the postwar era in *An Illini Century: One Hundred Years of Campus Life*. During this period the campus newspaper, the *Daily Illini*, reported ferment over the Korean conflict; McCarthyism; a ban on political speakers at the campus; the indifference of the "Hollow Generation"; the threat of nuclear destruction; exploitive movies, music, and television; the integration of fraternities and sororities; discrimination against African Americans (at that time, referred to as "Negroes") by restaurants and barbershops; and anti-Semitism.

The University Senate Committee's files of the writing topics for the English Qualifying Exam constitute a time capsule of the world as viewed through the lens of freshman English. Each exam contained between fifteen and twenty-five prompts designed to provide a broad selection so that any test-taker could invent something connected to his or her experience. In 1951 the exam was given six times; a total of 140 topics were offered. Of these, only three addressed directly issues that the rest of the campus was debating: "Racial prejudice goes to college," "Movies and morals?" and "Optimism in the atomic age" (which, interestingly enough, suggests a positive spin to the possibility of nuclear annihilation). The one examination I found that dealt with one of these topics ("Racial prejudice goes to college") described an incident in which the author witnessed a young man being blackballed during a fraternity rush because the brothers thought he may have been Jewish. Three others touched somewhat on topics that Ebert found in the *Daily Illini*: "Defer the college kid," "What every young soldier should know," "The Korean War should be stopped." Another eleven asked students to address national or international issues; these included national elections ("Should Truman run in '52?"; "Eisenhower for president: pro and con"); political controversies ("MacArthur makes a speech," "Taft's Tactics"); international relations ("Republican foreign policy," "Are we world leaders?"); and the Communist menace ("The Chinese Puzzle," "Russians as propagandists," "The push-button war"). The remaining 128 topics ranged from the thought-provoking: "I want to know why____." "Science has run away with civilization?" or "An enlightened view of sex"; to the mundane: "How to plant a garden," "The college wardrobe"; to the trivial: "The ukelele [*sic*] player," "Hadacol and hair restorers," "Arthur Godfrey is twins." The range of topics makes sense, given that freshman English solicited writing to allow the author to display cleverness and technical mastery. Despite the stated expectations that students should learn to "express themselves," revealing their command of formal elements was paramount, not their entering into any real public forum in which they might articulate their personal beliefs and values.

Another example of the expectation that students' writing would display the extent to which certain rules or schemas had been internalized is the list of suggested essay topics in Francis Connolly's *Rhetoric Case Book* (1953). Following a set of chapters on "Basic Methods of Analysis" (definition, classification and division, example, comparison and contrast, cause and effect, and process) and another set on "Argument and Style in the Whole Composition" (exposition, argument, description, and narration), Connolly provides a list of topics that students could use to demonstrate their rhetorical proficiency. The list includes items that seem to require political or social acumen, for example, "The 1952 presidential campaign," "War in Indo-China," and "The Caste System in India," as well as everyday commonplaces: "Men's hats," "Headache remedies," and "Types of fountain pens" (270). Within the discursive practice of freshman English, these diverse topics can be considered equal because their purpose is not to give students the occasion to enter into social or political discourse, but to give them as much latitude as possible in choosing familiar ground upon which to demonstrate how well they had mastered the prescribed patterns of cause and effect, classification, or description.

Given the expectation—from teachers as well as from students—that a major function of writing was to demonstrate one's mastery of language as a "medium of communication," even assignments that might seem to call for active participation in academic discourse were reduced to the equivalent of finger exercises for a pianist. Northwestern's "Suggested Topics for A10 Themes" (1950) contains the following assignment: "Comparison of the Catholic Encyclopedia account of Henry VIII or Martin Luther with that in the Britannica. The purpose is to show students they should not believe everything in print, and to teach the importance of evidence" (n.p.). This assignment, if the students were encouraged to do so, may have invited questioning historical documents and may have suggested discussing their truth value. However, another Northwestern document from the same year, "A suggested outline for judging composition papers," reveals what instructors were looking for. Its major headings are "Organization of the whole composition," "Paragraph structure," "Development, or expansion of the paper" (including "a coherent skeleton" and "a body of relevant, supporting details"), "Sentence structure," and "Diction" (n.p.). The instructor who made this assignment and who used the suggested outline for judging the students' products would not have read the papers as attempts to enter into historiography, but as examples of their mastery of rhetorical techniques.

At Navy Pier, Marie Peters wrote on a similar topic. *Pier Glass* published "Mr. Pseudoscorpionida Shares His Knowledge" in fall 1956. Peters adopts a clever narrative style in which a bookworm, "Mr. Pseudoscorpionida," guides a student, "Bob," through an assignment: "to write a biography of a priest named Savonarola" (2). Bob believes he has found all that he needs in the *Encyclopedia Britannica*. He is about to leave the library when he hears a small voice that chides him, "Oh, you think you are just about finished? I think you have just started" (2).

The bookworm invites Bob to examine other sources, *The Catholic Encyclopedia,* and *Encyclopedia Americana.* Bob discovers differences in the coverage each of the three sources provides, and even finds some factual discrepancies. Surprised, he asks his little mentor, "Why is there such variation?" (4). The learned bookworm offers four reasons: "One . . . is the use of a human instrument for interpretation. Then, there's the amount of detail. . . . Details can be made subjective merely by the interpreter's . . . own purposes. . . . The point of view . . . is another important consideration. A fact may be an unchanging condition, but people can alter the unchangeable by slanting the interpretation. Let us consider coverage as a point, too. The purpose for the biography might dictate what aspect of the person's life will receive the greatest emphasis" (4). At this point, Peters has established a framework for discussing the subjectivity of the different authors, or the editorial purposes of the three encyclopedias. As the Northwestern topic suggests, she could have explored why she "should not believe everything in print," or she could have explored the rhetorical strategies that led to the sources' selection of evidence. However, she has Bob ask the question she chooses to pursue: "Bookworm, would you mind if I asked you a pretty subjective question? How would you say these particular versions differ in the points you just talked about?" (4). The question she asks—a question that reflects the current-traditional milieu in which she produced the paper—is not *why* the three sources differ, but *how*.

The bookworm provides answers that satisfy the requirements of Peters's freshman English teacher. Regarding the selection of detail, Bob's mentor points out that "these books seem to be roughly representative of their distinct categories," by which the worm means that *Britannica* has the most, *Americana* the least, with *Catholic Encyclopedia* falling somewhere between the two. Regarding point of view, Bob learns that *Britannica* is favorable to Savonarola, *Catholic Encyclopedia* unfavorable, and *Americana* is neutral. *Britannica* emphasizes political and religious aspects, *Americana* only the political, and *Catholic Encyclopedia* only the religious. Finally, Mr. Pseudoscorpionida points out that each of the three articles uses evidence from different sources. The paper concludes with Bob thanking his mentor: "This evening has been enlightening, and although we did not go over all the discrepancies, I am sure I shall have plenty of material to do a good job on my assignment" (4). Not going over "all the discrepancies" suggests that Peters noticed other problematic issues in her reading of the three articles about Savonarola, but she also knew that she had used up her 2000 words, and that she could do "good job on my assignment" (that is, get a good grade) without making her discussion needlessly complex.

I presume that the rhetoric faculty at Navy Pier printed "Mr. Pseudoscorpionida Shares His Knowledge" because they wanted other students to emulate her approach. Peters certainly shows that she has found and read the three sources, and that she can invent a clever form to present many of the facts she has unearthed. Her essay remains safely within the framework of expository display. She stands at the margin of deeper thinking; but pursuing the more subtle question—*why*—would have taken her out of freshman English and into historiography. Evidently neither she nor her teacher wanted her to go there.

For the Northwestern and the Navy Pier assignments—as well as for the examination topics from Illinois and those from *A Rhetoric Case Book*—students wrote neither to display the knowledge they had acquired nor to participate in the continuing formulation of knowledge in academic discourse, but to provide evidence that they had been properly indoctrinated into the system of values and beliefs prized in the academy.

In addition to sharing similar content, the systems of freshman English at Wheaton, Illinois, and Northwestern provided similar services for the students themselves, for the institutions, and for the entire society. Before all else, freshman English was supposed to benefit individual students. At the very least, the course left them with a sense of accomplishment; they could take pride in having completed something difficult yet necessary. Kitzhaber described the course as "one of those things like spinach and tetanus shots that young people put up with because their elders say they must" (*Themes, Theories, and Therapy* 1). Like children who have finally forced themselves to swallow unpalatable food or endure a dreaded medical procedure, students felt a curious mixture of repulsion and self-satisfaction.

Much of the vocabulary associated with the freshman English course echoes another experience familiar to students in the postwar era—military basic training. Textbooks and class meetings were filled with "drills," "exercises," and "practices" through which students were to "get in shape." Like soldiers preparing for combat, students had to endure tedious, repetitive tasks so they would be able to respond unhesitatingly and effectively when they faced the real challenges for which they had been preparing.[4] For example, *Standards in Freshman English at the University of Illinois* states: "Your instructor in Rhetoric 101 . . . will expect your final examination paper to demonstrate conclusively that you can, and will henceforth, write correctly and effectively even under pressure" (3). Also like basic training, freshman English often weeded out the unsuitable and the unfit; those "veteran" students who managed to finish looked back on their experience with a sense of relief, regret, and pride similar to that of Marines fresh from Camp Pendleton. Franklin Elder's "An Example Paragraph" conveys a student's view of the fearlessness that the course sought to impose: "No man is wholly fearless. Take me, for example. I do not ride a bus because it may be involved in an accident. I am afraid to take a shower because I might drown. Standing up straight frightens me because if I were to trip, I would have too far to fall. It scares me to stay in bed for fear that the walls may cave in, or a plane may crash into my bedroom. However, I am not entirely a coward. I hand in this paragraph to you, my rhetoric teacher, and that is something few men have the courage to do" (16).

Students also left freshman English with a vague yet real sense of intellectual accomplishment. In their preface to *Pro and Con,* Matlaw and Stronks called it "the power and satisfaction that come with skill in writing" (xiii). Of the schools in this study, only Illinois, in a 1965 study by Wilmer A. Lamar and Ruth E. McGugan, conducted a systematic investigation of students' opinions of their own experience in freshman English.[5] They found that over 90 percent of students taking Rhetoric 101 and 102 agreed that the courses should be required of all students and that it had been a useful preparation for their careers. Between 50 and 75 percent agreed that their training in these courses had made them more aware of the qualities of good writing and had led them to strive to improve their writing in all areas. However, the percentages ranged from 50 down to 30 for those who could identify specific areas of improvement in their work—reading comprehension, style, vocabulary and diction, grammar, spelling, library use, and positive impact on grades in other courses. These students felt that they had achieved something important, but could not connect it directly to the stated content of the course.

During the mid-1950s, Illinois offered "Rhetoric x101," a correspondence course for students like Margaret P. Perkins, who had postponed college education until her three children had grown and left home. In "Rhetoric and I" (1955) she describes the benefits the course provided for her. Like her young fellow-students on campus, she found that the assignments fostered her appreciation of the qualities of good writing: "Writing these essays has made me more aware of sentence structure . . . consciousness of word choice and meaning" (8). Also like the students at Urbana, she felt that she had begun to improve her spelling, "but punctuation . . . is still a big stumbling block" (8).

Perkins does not explain the effect Rhetoric x101 made on her other course work, as it had been her first and only college class to that point. She does, however, articulate the effect it had on her life. All the things that she felt she learned were nonacademic: the habit of rising early to be able to include study in her busy daily schedule; improved time management; more interesting conversation with her husband; appreciating the difficulty of her own children's school lives, especially with grades. She sums up the value of the course this way: "The satisfaction of completing the course, despite adverse conditions has been worth the struggle. It has been good discipline" (9). Perhaps Charles Roberts included "Rhetoric and I" in the *Green Caldron* because from her vantage point, removed from the distractions of campus life, Perkins could articulate the ideal value of freshman English as no adolescent undergraduate could.

Another benefit claimed for students in freshman English was intellectual and psychological growth. Textbooks frequently used language reminiscent of the biological sciences to describe the desired effects of the course—words such as "liveliness," "growth," "maturity," "ripening," "naturalness." This kind of vocabulary reflects a sustained metaphor in the discourse of freshman English—learning is an organic process that takes place naturally if impediments to growth and development are avoided. Growth was thought to produce an emotionally, intellectually, and socially mature individual. Hayford and Vincent, in discussing the ultimate effect of literacy—mastery of thought itself, describe the goal of a successful freshman English student: "The person who is sensitive to the emotional implications of an experience, who can share another's feelings and express his own, has more to give as he writes, and receives more through his reading. D. H. Lawrence . . . wrote of 'Man in his wholeness, wholly attending.' Man in his wholeness learns all he can of his own inner workings" (296). Growth as a reader and writer bestowed this "wholeness," a maturity that allows an individual to give, as well as to receive from others. Instructors at Wheaton, Northwestern, and Illinois expended much effort to help their students reach this level of maturity. One of the problems of the course, however, lay in the distance between the whole student hypothesized by Hayford and Vincent, and the actual opinions of students such as those Dudley Bailey interviewed in 1958, who recollected with disgust that in their freshman courses they only "read some stories" and "wrote some more stories" (234).

Without doubt, many students felt the latent hostility that Bailey tapped; most probably expended their negative energy in conversation or in satiric writing that never crossed the teacher's desk. Once in a while, however, a student turned to irony that proved compelling, as in "My

Troubles—Bitter Words" ("Individuality"), or "The Advantages of Being a Hermit," published in the *Green Caldron* in March 1949.

In his essay, Charles W. Eckert satirizes the triviality of the rhetoric classroom, in particular, impromptu writing.

> There comes a frustrating, half-mad moment in every rhetoric student's life when he or she faces a blackboard upon which are scrawled a group of cryptic phrases, known in the trade as "assigned theme topics." The titles usually run like this: "Should the Federal Government Subsidize Wool-Raising?" "My Favorite One Thousand Books and Why," or "The Two Franklin D. Roosevelts—Man and Aircraft-Carrier." But these are only examples. The topic I am forced to write upon for this theme is "The Advantages of Being a Hermit." (11)

Eckert proceeds to attack the topic by writing a ridiculously fanciful tale about an "Octopus named Homer." He comments parenthetically, "and remember, Mr. Instructor, you asked for this" (11). Homer lives in a cave under the Pacific, and gets in trouble when he claims to be clairvoyant. The essay cleverly pokes fun at anti-Communism through Homer's nemesis, Boris the Red-Herring, who threatens in a mock-Russian accent, "Come out before we comink in after you, already!" (12). Homer escapes by predicting the end of the world, which comes about for Boris and his goons due to the atomic test beneath the Bikini Atoll. The hermit survives, and Eckert concludes by displaying his mock-erudition: "The fish-folk all worship him as a prophet, and his fabulous reputation makes the Oracle at Delphi and the Cumaean Sibyl look like tea leaf readers by comparison" (13). He thumbs his nose at his instructor one last time in his conclusion: "Thus ends the story" (13). Although Eckert calls attention to the triviality and artificiality of impromptu essays, his composition received acclaim because it displays the very values that he tries to mock. In one class period, he was able to concoct a clever essay that demonstrates his mastery of the mechanics of writing, a sophisticated style, and an impressive fund of knowledge. Ironically, the cleverness with which he mounts an attack on the course itself demonstrates its effectiveness in developing his emotional, intellectual, and social maturity.

MY PREVIOUS CHAPTER "Instrumentality" describes the function of freshman English within the departments of English and within the academy as a whole. The stated purpose of the course was to raise students from all backgrounds and disciplines to a level of literacy that would enable them to succeed in higher education; however, in practice it served as a scapegoat for the sins of illiteracy.[6] When the inevitable differences appeared between academic or public expectations and the perceived performance of students in their reading, writing, speaking, or thinking, freshman English provided the place at which the problem could be localized. The course also provided a similar service for the departments of English. When complaints arrived at the English chair's desk he (no women served as chairs of English during the postwar era at Wheaton, Illinois, or Northwestern) had a convenient hedge, especially considering that freshman English was taught by department members with the least status. He could either deflect the complaints by citing his own staff's relative inexperience; or he could come down hard on the accused staff member without fear of provoking the argument or retaliation he might expect from a powerful colleague.

In addition to relieving the rest of the department of the responsibility for developing students' literacy, the course also provided a bottom rung on the English career ladder. At Illinois, the rhetoric courses provided a place where graduate assistants could gain classroom experience while readying themselves for positions as teachers of literature. Northwestern had few assistants, and Wheaton none; however at both, the freshman English program provided a place to which the weak could be consigned, and from which the ambitious could launch their careers. Although no formal position existed at Wheaton, and Peter Veltman resisted being given this responsibility, through the 1950s he served as the de facto head of the writing program. When he finished his doctorate at Northwestern in 1959 he was appointed head of the Department of Education, and later became dean of the college. Falk Johnson served as chair of the Division of Rhetoric at Navy Pier from 1949 until 1966, by which time the Chicago Undergraduate Division had moved to its Chicago Circle campus (now the University of Illinois at Chicago) and had become a degree-granting institution. Shortly after he had completed his doctorate in linguistics at the University of Chicago, Johnson moved from Rhetoric and English to the newly formed Department of Linguistics. Fred Faverty first headed the English A committee at Northwestern in the late 1930s, and later succeeded to the department chair. Other influential figures—Ernest Samuels, Harrison Hayford, and Wallace Douglas—began by teaching or administering English A. Intelligent and resourceful persons, such as Veltmann, Johnson, Faverty, Samuels, Hayford, and Douglas, may have achieved their academic prominence had there been no freshman English programs at all; however, in practice, during the postwar era the course served as a point of departure for many.

On a broader scale, freshman English was thought to develop and strengthen democratic society. Commentators including Kenneth Oliver, Robert Saalbach, and Hans Guth connected the development of the individual claimed for freshman English with the survival of democracy. In the aftermath of World War II, proposals such as the Harvard Committee's *General Education in a Free Society* articulated the public agenda for college education. This document called for an emphasis on "education for an informed responsible life in our society" (4) in both the high schools and the colleges. In its conclusion, the document echoes the perception that once World War II had ended (James Bryant Conant's introduction is dated 11 April 1945, just a month before V-E Day) every person had to assume a personal responsibility for the peace that the nation had been forced to seek at such a high price:

> Not very long ago the mass of mankind could and did leave peace-making . . . to statesmen. Today most people feel some of its weight on their shoulders. . . . Among and beyond all the local and personal motives which drive men to pursue education, this budding collective responsibility year by year grows in power. . . . The desire to get on in the world or to advance the status of its workers . . . [is] being transformed . . . into wider interests more favorable both to growth in democracy and to the final cause for which society itself is only a means. (267)

Although this conclusion is part of the committee's proposal for adult education, it reveals the function of all education in a capitalistic democracy. The nation needed academically literate people not only to provide the basis of a satisfying, orderly, economically productive society, but also to build a bulwark of rationality against a return of the madness that had run rampant in the world. David Russell maintains that *General Education for a Free Society* "might have been titled 'General Education for the Cold War'" (252). He notes that the report called for composition to be taught through general education. At Harvard, which instituted some of the reforms Bryant called for, "Ironically, the pedagogy best able to develop democratic generalists was to be reserved for an elite group of students confined to their narrow disciplines" (255). As noted in chapter I, attempts to modify the course without addressing its essentially instrumental nature did not succeed.[7]

Freshman English at Wheaton, Northwestern, and Illinois reflected this national agenda for education. In his history of Wheaton College, Paul Bechtel notes how, in response to the influx of returning war veterans, the Wheaton faculty had to reassess their curriculum and educational philosophy. In September 1946, the entire faculty met in a workshop at Winona Lake, Indiana. They discussed the influence of the postwar New Humanism espoused by educators, such as Robert Hutchins, Mortimer Adler, Norman Foerster, and Mark Van Doren, and its relationship to Wheaton's admittedly conservative Christian philosophy. Bechtel summarizes their conclusions: "A Christian philosophy of education . . . acknowledges that there is a large body of valid data about humankind and the world based on observation and experience and recorded in the humanities, social sciences, and natural sciences. That reservoir of experience constitutes the cultural heritage of western civilization, available to Christians and others alike, which Christians will want to appropriate, evaluate in the light of God's revelation and authority, and apply to the needs of their lives" (184). The Wheaton faculty agreed with the new humanists' goals of the "reconstruction of society through the recovery of intellectual and moral values" (184), but sought to locate them in their particular Christian context. Bechtel commented on changes he saw at the college as a result of the self-examination that began at Winona Lake. "There seemed to be in classroom, in discussion, in print, in the spirit of the times, a keen awakening to academic excellence, intellectual curiosity, scholarly confidence in the contributions evangelicals at Wheaton could make within the larger society" (217).

The students, too, felt the same impetus to use their learning to heal a wounded world. In 1971 the Social Studies department conducted the "Wheaton History Project." Students in various courses researched important events in the history of the college by examining back issues of student publications and by interviewing alumni. In a paper produced for this project, "Post War Student Attitudes Toward World Affairs," Michael Waggoner comments: "Many GI's wanted to go back to the war torn countries as Christian missionaries because they felt the Gospel would fill vacuums that the war had created." One of the alumni he cited described the general attitude on the postwar campus: "At that time people were talking about Wilkie's one world and we had a strong feeling about God and country. Christianity and Americanism were felt to go hand in hand. The students were idealistic . . . concerning America's place, Her responsibilities overseas" (3). Waggoner sums up the attitudes he found in this way: "It seems that students were at once idealistic . . . and realistic. They were conscious of their responsibility as Christians to a war torn world" (3).

One Wheaton student in particular embodied the Christian sense of New Humanism. Ed McCully attended Wheaton from 1945 to 1949. He made an impact on the school as a talented athlete, as a leader (he won the presidency of his senior class by acclamation), and as an orator. In 1949 he competed in the Hearst Oratorical Contest in San Francisco and took first place with a speech on Alexander Hamilton (Elliot 49–50). The speech traces Hamilton's rise from a hard childhood in the West Indies as the illegitimate son of a Huguenot expatriate to a brilliant six-hour speech at the Continental Congress. McCully praises Hamilton because "though condemned to a lowly position by the society in which he found himself, he was willing to suffer the remorse, the pain, the tiring work, the thankless struggle which would someday break the shackles of oppression which bound him" (2). McCully urges his audience to admire Hamilton for having achieved personal liberation, but calls for them to hear "the challenge" that the patriot accepted: "The excelsior of its cry rings out to every American—to you, no matter what your position may be, your color of skin, your lot of race, hear this challenge from a man who rose from obscurity, to a position of service to the world" (4). His use of Hamilton's story as "a challenge to every

American" to engage in public service illustrates what the Wheaton faculty intended by encouraging the "recovery of intellectual and moral values" in a Christian context.

After graduation, McCully devoted his life to the principles he espoused in the speech. He returned to his hometown of Milwaukee to attend Marquette University law school, but after one year felt the call to pursue a vocation as an evangelist. With his Wheaton classmates Jim Elliot and Nate Saint, he joined a group of missionaries in Ecuador. In 1956 he, Elliot, Saint, and two other young men were murdered by the suspicious Auca Indians they were attempting to contact.

The ongoing concern of the Wheaton faculty with the impact of higher education on the world political order is reflected again in an article by Samuel Schultz, "Education for Citizenship," reproduced in the November 1955 *Faculty Bulletin of Wheaton College*. In this article, Schultz describes general education as "the password . . . in today's educational program to train the student for living in a democratic society" (n.p.). The Department of English at Wheaton took their part in this educational program seriously, especially through Writing 111 and 112. In 1956 they proposed to the entire faculty higher standards in writing throughout the curriculum. After debating for several months the problem of substandard writing among upperclassmen at Wheaton, the English department proposed changes in the content of its own courses and in the college's guidelines concerning writing. They did not make these proposals to satisfy a need for self-reform, but out of concern for the public performance of their graduates, many of whom—like Elliot and McCully—became teachers or ministers.

At Northwestern, the reading material for English A and the topics upon which students wrote show that there, too, freshman English served to prepare students to assume leadership in America's postwar milieu. One book in particular was used to broaden the students' worldviews— Vincent Sheean's *Personal History*. From first-hand experience, Sheean described international tensions and problems before, during, and after World War II. His autobiography provoked considerable discussion. From 1942 to 1953, the Department of English published an intramural journal, "The English 'A' Analyst," to present discussions and interpretations of the various titles included on the English A reading lists. In 1947 "The English 'A' Analyst" included correspondence between Sheean and Rabbi Samuel Teitelbaum, of the local Hillel chapter. The exchange of letters was provoked by Sheean's anti-Zionist opinions regarding the political turmoil in what was then Palestine. "The English 'A' Analyst" published Teitelbaum's letter and Sheean's response, as well as the rabbi's lengthy letter to the English A faculty. Discussion of *Personal History* extended well beyond the classroom, and the department encouraged broadening the scope of English A by publishing these letters.

Theme assignments and examination questions also reveal how the course reflected the national political agenda. "Suggested Topics for A10 Themes" (1959) lists as one possible writing assignment a paper based on logic: "Arguments operating from general assumptions. Inductive papers based on personal investigation. National Security and Individual Rights. The Press. Business Enterprise on Public Opinion." The assignment links individual growth and development (the argument was to be "based on personal investigation") with an increased awareness of major social, political, and economic issues. The final examination for English A10-3 (10 June 1958) asks students: "Write an essay in which you show the relevance of any two of the following quotations [from Henry James, Thoreau, de Tocqueville, and twentieth-century social commentators such as Henry Bamford Parkes and George F. Kennan] for contemporary American attitudes toward the subjects of the quotations. Some of the subjects dealt with are: technology, recreation and leisure time, foreigners and Americans, law and morality, and intellectual maturity." In this particular section of A10, the students would be evaluated on how well they were able to present their own experience in correct, attractive prose; moreover, they were asked to present themselves as participants in public dialogue concerning important social, economic, moral, and intellectual issues. To succeed in English A10 would indicate readiness to assume one's place not only within the academy or the workplace, but within a democratic society.

Just as the Wheaton faculty reassessed their curriculum in light of postwar political realities, the University of Illinois also undertook a set of studies that led to the establishment of a Division of General Studies in 1944. The university accepted DGS courses in Verbal Expression in lieu of Rhetoric 101 and 102. One of the planning documents from the Chicago Undergraduate Division, "Objectives in General Education," expresses more pragmatic justifications for the liberal arts than did the Wheaton faculty, but arrives at similar conclusions. It states, "The justification for education largely at public expense is to be found in the increased contribution which this education enables the individual to make to society, local, national, and international." The Division of Rhetoric, as part of the College of Liberal Arts, contributed to a student's general education. In a 1957 article, "The Unprepared Student at the University of Illinois," the director, Charles Roberts, suggested the connection between academic literacy and the national social agenda, referring to "our American democratic ideal of a sound education for all" (98). In it, he outlines the reforms he had helped bring about in the freshman English program.

The reading list included in the *Freshman Rhetoric Manual and Calendar* for 1949 and 1950 also suggests what a general education at Illinois was thought to include. Each semester, students were required to submit reports on three books from the list, which was organized according to categories of prose nonfiction, prose fiction, and drama. The nonfiction list alone contains 800 titles, annotated as "biography," "travel," "science," "arts," "essay," or "social points of view." The titles representing "social points of view" include works on economics, anthropology, race relations, nonviolence, international relations and foreign cultures (especially Germany, the Soviet Union, China, India, Britain, and Japan), sociology, and history (especially concerning the westward expansion of America and World War II). In the mid-1950s, students were not receptive to radical opinions. Bob Perlongo, a columnist for the *Daily Illini,* called them "the Hollow Generation. Imaginations are being stepped on all over the place nowadays . . . and instead of vitality and vigor there is a deadly white national pasty-faced expression of indifference" (quoted in Ebert 17). Given this pervasive apathy, it may seem unusual that freshmen were being encouraged to read diverse titles: Saul Alinsky's *Reveille for Radicals,* Franz Boas's *Race and Democratic Society,* John Dos Passos's *State of the Nation,* W. E. B. Du Bois's *Color and Democracy,* *These Are Our Lives* by the Federal Writers' Project, Margaret Mead's *And Keep Your Powder Dry,* Benito Mussolini's *My Autobiography,* Jawaharlal Nehru's *Toward Freedom,* Mbongu Ojike's *My Africa,* James Reston's *Prelude to Victory,* Edgar Snow's *Red Star over China,* or Wendell Willkie's *One World.* Despite the conservative nature of composition instruction and the self-indulgent mood on campus and throughout society, students seem to have been encouraged to inform themselves on a huge range of topics that differed from or even contradicted commonly held public opinion. Given the large and diverse corps of instructors at the University of Illinois, some must have encouraged students to challenge the dominant beliefs and values of mainstream American democracy. Yet these books may have served a much more mundane purpose. Just as the topics for writing provided convenient occasions for students to demonstrate how they had accommodated themselves to the discourse of freshman English, these books represented a wide spectrum of opinion—from Alinsky to Mussolini—so that potentially subversive texts could be contained and neutralized by the prevailing political and social ideology.

A report on a moderately controversial book from this list illustrates how one student handled a text that challenged the prevailing sociopolitical milieu. In 1960 Donald Lee Fox responded to *Grapes of Wrath* with his essay, "Steinbeck and Brotherhood." Fox found that in Steinbeck's critique of American capitalism "anger provided the vitality for a moving literary work" (9). Fox recognizes Steinbeck's theme of universal brotherhood, but claims that "when Steinbeck attempts to offer a solution for mankind's lack of vision . . . he begins to falter" (10–11). Fox sees Casy's abandonment of Christianity and the book's implicit endorsement of socialism as "perfectly normal and even predictable . . . under the then prevailing socio-economic circumstances. The majority of the civilized world's intellectuals were holding regular wakes for capitalism at that time" (11). Fox vehemently objects, however, that "in his [Steinbeck's] bitterness he excludes from the great community of mankind a large and important segment of mankind—the 'haves'" (11). He finds Steinbeck's portrayal of the rich to be "infuriating" and "ludicrous"; on the other hand, he objects to the "deification of the destitute and an absolution from responsibility for at least some of their own acts" (11). Fox is entitled to his opinion of *Grapes of Wrath,* but he does not use his opposition to Steinbeck's views as a point of departure from which to address the validity of a socialist critique of capitalism, or the relationship between art and politics. Instead, he salutes the canonical status of *Grapes of Wrath,* cancelling the opportunity for debate by regretting that Steinbeck's attitudes toward the rich "kept the work from being an ageless classic and very nearly destroyed it" (9). His paper reveals how a potentially subversive text was "contained and neutralized by the prevailing political and social ideology." Fox is not upset that his own world of privilege might be shaken by the story of the Joads, but that Steinbeck's edgy opinions have kept this book from achieving the respect that he would like to accord a text that many others consider a "great book." The fact that the rhetoric staff chose to publish "Steinbeck and Brotherhood" in the *Green Caldron* suggests that they sanctioned Fox's method of sanitizing a text that challenged his core values—capitalism and individual initiative—by encapsulating it in its status as a "classic." Richard Ohmann summed up the use of countercultural texts such as *Grapes of Wrath* within the discourse of freshman English with this sardonic comment: "I now think that our [teachers of composition] function is extremely valuable: namely, to ensure the harmlessness of all culture, to make it serve and preserve the status quo" (63).

Another feature of the freshman English course at Wheaton, Northwestern, and Illinois was the paradox of its frequent modification, yet its resistance to change. Forces outside the academy, for example the "enormous shifts in the size and composition of the student body" during the postwar era noted by Robert Shattuck (69), required that the colleges and universities seek new approaches to freshman English. However, the entrenchment of the current-traditional paradigm channeled the forces for change into ways of making the existing system more efficient, rather than questioning its ideological basis. The many changes proposed and enacted for the freshman English programs at Wheaton, Northwestern, and Illinois served not to question the basic purpose or structure of the course, but to bring students into conformity with the paradigm with less effort and expense.

At various times, all three schools exempted some students from freshman English based upon their entrance examination scores. In 1956 Wheaton experimented with exempting forty-eight students with the highest entrance scores from taking Writing III. This move did allow talented students to develop their potential more rapidly by taking other courses in the department's writing program; but it also made money available for staff who could work intensively with remedial students. The program was continued the next year, but with only twenty-four students, and then was dropped because the department eliminated its writing major when it could not attract enough qualified students. At

Northwestern, the top 10 percent of incoming freshmen were exempt from English A, mainly for reasons of economy. Northwestern used few graduate assistants, part-time faculty, or lecturers to teach English A, and kept class sizes below twenty students; hence, it was an expensive class to maintain. Illinois also exempted some students from Rhetoric 101 and gave them three hours' credit based on their entrance examination scores, but this was not an innovation as it had been at Wheaton and Northwestern. In all cases, however, such exemptions were made in order to streamline freshman English as a delivery system of academic literacy.

All three schools also made changes to deal more efficiently with those students who had had difficulty meeting minimum standards in their freshman English classes and in the other disciplines. Changes proposed to the Wheaton faculty in 1956 by Clyde Kilby stipulated that the college establish a "writing clinic," that entering students who proved themselves deficient in their knowledge of grammar and spelling be required to take a noncredit remedial course, and that the college enact a referral system by which students whose writing was identified as deficient by any members of the faculty could be referred to the English department for remediation. The faculty implemented only one of these proposals—the last. At Wheaton as at Illinois and Northwestern, attempts to broaden the responsibility for academic literacy beyond freshman English programs never succeeded.

Northwestern attempted to deal with "poor students" through individual counseling. In the early 1950s, the English department provided a tutor and required additional work of those not meeting the expected standards. Later, in 1962, the number of class meetings was reduced from four to three per week in order to provide more conference time for individual problems. Eventually, the department was absolved of responsibility for every student's competence in writing when the university abolished English A10 in 1968 as part of its revision of the undergraduate curriculum. The persistence of freshman English revealed itself when, five years later (15 May 1973), the English composition committee reported that they "question the wisdom of giving up our service to the University that took the form of the once compulsory freshman English."

Illinois, with the most diverse clientele and therefore with the greatest number of remedial students, had the most complex system of all three schools. Students who revealed a lack of basic skills on the entrance examination were required to take a noncredit course, Rhetoric 100, before they could proceed on to 101 and 102, both of which were graduation requirements. Those who earned lower than a B in 102 were required to take the English Qualifying Examination; if they failed, they had to earn a passing grade in Rhetoric 200 before graduating. The Writing Clinic offered individual help for students preparing to take the Qualifying Examination. In its attempts to make the freshman English program more efficient, the University Senate Committee on Student English revised this system in the late 1950s. First, Rhetoric 100 was phased out between 1956 and 1960. In 1964 Rhetoric 200 was reduced to a noncredit course and made optional—students could repeat the Qualifying Examination if necessary. In 1968 the entire mechanism was abolished. Each of the changes was made in order to streamline the program by shifting responsibility for competence in academic literacy from the program of rhetoric courses to the students themselves. Yet, the more responsibility was shifted to the students, the less competence they displayed. If the students' writing depended upon "the natural powers of the mind" (Young 31), the changes implemented at Illinois should have brought improvement. However, the students' steadily worsening performances reveals that their natural propensities did not incline them toward the production of correct, stylish expository prose.

The changes made to exempt some students or to provide remediation for others were the work of committees, or even of entire departments. As such, they reflected institutional will and affected the organization of the course, but not its content. Changes aimed to modify the current-traditional paradigm came from the initiative of individual teachers. At all three schools, various instructors attempted to convert freshman English into a more interesting or useful course. In all cases, however, the impact of these attempts was limited to the sections taught by the individuals themselves. In 1954 at Wheaton, Curtis Dahl instituted a special section of freshman English in which the students focused their attention on classical literature. "Composition through World Literature" abandoned a concentration on correctness, the modes of discourse, and the qualities of effective style for the sake of reading Homer, Aristotle, Dante, Thomas More, Cervantes, and T. S. Eliot. As enthusiastic as Dahl seemed—he wrote, "I am thoroughly convinced of the real worth of basing freshman composition on the best authors of all ages" (2)—there is no evidence that the course entered the Wheaton catalog, or was ever taught again. Roger Shuy brought his background in linguistics to bear upon freshman English at Wheaton in the late 1950s. Departmental policy required that students buy a handbook and a dictionary, but the instructor was free to assign a third text. He used Altick's *Preface to Critical Reading* to introduce language issues into the class and sought to generate collaborative writing processes. "I wanted a community effort, not a dictatorial one. . . . What grammar I taught was more from what is now called a sociolinguistic perspective—usage determines practice, not dictionaries, grammar books, or god" (personal letter 15 August 1988). Shuy's colleagues shunned his approach; by 1964 he had left Wheaton. The grading standards cited earlier in this chapter suggest that the current-traditional model upon which Writing 111 and 112 were based continued unchanged.

At Navy Pier, another linguist, Falk Johnson, attempted to change the content of Rhetoric 101. Over the course of two years, 1957 and 1958, he and two other interested faculty members, Andrew Schiller and Willis Jackman, investigated the usefulness of basing the course upon structural linguistics. The experiment with these "structural" sections proved inconclusive. A few members of the department continued to use some of the methods, but most teachers of Rhetoric 101 and 102 adhered to a current-traditional paradigm. Another member of the faculty there, Arthur Greenwald, had studied general semantics with S. I. Hayakawa at the Illinois Institute of Technology and with Irving Lee at Northwestern. When he began teaching at Navy Pier in 1949, he taught what he thought he was expected to—the current-traditional curriculum; however, after one year he simply inserted his interest in general semantics into the course and continued to do so well into the 1980s. In the mid-1950s, Robert Pirsig taught sections of Rhetoric 101 based upon the philosophical search for a definition of quality, the same theme that led him to write *Zen and the Art of Motorcycle Maintenance* in 1974. As with those interested in structural linguistics, Greenwald's and Pirsig's innovations remained limited to their classrooms alone.

At Northwestern, "young turks" like Wallace Douglas, who had studied with Porter Perrin at Colgate, and Harrison Hayford wanted to make the course less artificial. In the early 1950s, they began to choose reading material tailored to students' interests and to teach writing as a process.

Berlin points out that process theory originated much earlier, in the "postwar [WWI], Freudian-inspired, expressionistic notions of childhood education that the progressives attempted to propagate" (*Rhetoric and Reality* 3). He notes that some expressionists in the 1950s, especially Barriss Mills of Purdue, argued "against the current-traditional version of the composing act" (119). Given the materials and directions used by teachers and students at Northwestern, however, it is doubtful that Douglas and Hayford were following Mills's suggestions. Porter Perrin's *Index to English,* Northwestern's required handbook, describes the writing process as having nine steps: "There is usually an outside stimulus that turns the writer's mind to a theme, a period of gathering material, either from memory, from observation, or . . . from a period of specific research; the material crystallizes into some form . . . and then there is writing and revision and preparation of copy" (8). This description limits itself to externals consistent with the current-traditional paradigm. It follows the typical "select-narrow-amplify" pattern and does not address the possibility that the act of writing itself might generate ideas. When Perrin does discuss the production of text, he confines his comments to mechanical techniques, for example, dividing a long paper into manageable portions, leaving wide margins on a rough draft to facilitate revision, and making the first draft longer than it needs to be because it is easier to edit material out than to add it in later.

Even though Douglas and Hayford may have recognized the shortcomings of the current-traditional paradigm, the materials used in their classrooms suggest that they did not escape the limited discourse that an instrumental course imposed. Even though they revised the catalog description of English A three times between 1949 and 1957 and introduced more contemporary readings, the course remained within the current-traditional paradigm; eventually it escaped that model, but only by being abolished entirely.

The experiences of Dahl, Shuy, Johnson, Greenwald, Pirsig, Hayford, and Douglas illustrate what Robert Shattuck has called "the primary fact about American higher education: its stability" (69). The stability of practices typical of freshman English depends upon an ideology that has proved resistant to change through a century of its existence. Just as Rhetoric 101 at Illinois absorbed readings that represented politically or socially subversive points of view by making them topics within which students could practice their rhetorical techniques, so the freshman English programs at all three schools absorbed diverse pedagogies by making them elective approaches to one unchanging institutional goal. An instructor might choose to teach the course via diverse approaches: classical literature, sociolinguistics, structural linguistics, general semantics, philosophical inquiry, or process theory. Sharon Crowley has pointed out, however: "Despite attempts to update or expand the definition of its service ethic . . . the required introductory composition course has always been justified, at bottom, in instrumental terms" (*Composition in the University* 250–51). As the instrument by which students were indoctrinated into the prevailing system of institutional beliefs and values, freshman English could absorb and therefore neutralize many different and competing forces, even subversive ones. At Northwestern, it could even survive the abolition of the course in which it was embodied.

More than naming a specific course, "Freshman English" names a system of beliefs and values—a discursive practice. So long as the presumptions upon which it is constituted remain unquestioned, a discursive practice has the power to continue unchanged, despite the diverse settings in which it may be located.

eight

The Student

$\mathcal{J}$AMES F. GRANT, A STUDENT AT THE UNIVERSITY OF ILLINOIS in Urbana, wrote "Doubt Gets You an Education" for his Rhetoric 102 proficiency exam in 1948. His essay demonstrates how a competent freshman English student thought and wrote. A careful examination of his paper, reproduced below, reveals how a student achieved success by accommodating himself to the presumptions of the course.

DOUBT GETS YOU AN EDUCATION

When a person is attempting to absorb an education, he should have faith in the things propounded to him by his instructor, but for his own good and the increase of his knowledge he should reserve a particle of doubt. It is all very well to take what is offered, but to really gain insight into a subject there have to be doubts in the mind and independent research to verify or discourage those doubts.

In the universities of today very few instructors have the time to delve as deeply into all the aspects of a certain idea as they would wish to. For a student to really acquire a comprehensive knowledge, he has to take some of the instructor's words with a grain of salt and endeavor to find out for himself just what it is that doesn't ring true.

If, during the entire history of mankind, people had continued to believe fully the teachings and precepts of those who had gone before them, the world would still be at the intellectual level of the Stone Age. All the world's great thinkers in every field have been led on in their search for new knowledge by doubting some fact of the teachings of earlier scholars.

A complete education of any sort cannot be acquired by un-equivocal acceptance of age-old tenets in perfect faith. The same principle applies not only to formal education but to many things in the life of an average individual. "Believe nothing you hear, and only half of what you see," sounds perhaps a little exaggerated, but it really is an excellent idea.

If a person develops the habit of regarding with a bit of skep-ticism things which are represented to him as verities, that person will acquire a more complete and well-rounded education than the one who blindly accepts everything told to him. To be skeptical and to attempt to verify those skepticisms is to be a better educated man. (The *Green Caldron* published this essay in October 1948.)

Superficially, Grant's essay suggests an independent mind at work—the value placed on skepticism, the mistrust of instructors, the ques-tioning of "acceptance of age-old tenets in perfect faith." The author seems to declare independence from authoritarian teaching and from unsupported ideas, and to assert his right to think for himself. A more careful examination, however, reveals a writer who has conformed to the tenets of freshman English.

"Doubt Gets You an Education" is the classic five-paragraph im-promptu essay. It bears all the marks of Grant's applying the current-traditional model of invention that he had learned in Rhetoric 101. As he sat in the examining room, he scanned the list of topics and selected the quotation, "Believe nothing you hear, and only half of what you see." Next, he narrowed the topic within his range of experience. In this case, he turned to education, particularly the familiar world of a uni-versity student. Finally, he had to figure out how to amplify the topic and so develop his essay. He begins with a contrasting statement: a student should "have faith in the things propounded to him by his instructor" but "should reserve a particle of doubt." He establishes a dispassionate, polite tone and uses diction that reflects a well-read person: "propounded," "reserve," "particle," "verify," "discourage." In the first body paragraph, he gently chides his professors (he cushions his criticism by referring to "instructors," teachers of lesser rank) who would like to teach with depth, but are limited by a shortage of time. He is careful not to reject authority completely; he suggests questioning "*some* [emphasis added] of the instructor's words." In the second body paragraph, he broadens the issue to include "the entire history of mankind" and "all the world's great thinkers in every field," claiming that they, too, have discovered "new knowledge" through doubt. Having established the universality and effectiveness of the need for skepticism, he extends his argument from academia to "many things in the life of an average individual" and finds a seamless way to restate the topic without referring to the prompt itself. Grant concludes with a tidy summation. He does not overstate the issue; he calls only for "a bit of skepticism" and uses the comparative degree to make modest claims for improvement: "a more complete and well-rounded man," and "a better educated man." His essay contains sparse evidence—no paragraph contains more than three sentences—and none is specific enough to cause controversy. It addresses no particular audience, challenges no particular opponent, calls for no real change. "Doubt Gets You an Education" exemplifies a successful freshman English performance. It displays just enough resistance to convince his examiner that he has independent, original thoughts but at the same time does not transgress the tacit boundaries within which a student had to think and act.

Others have commented on the implicit subjectivity in freshman English. Susan Miller characterizes the composition student as "divorced . . . from any reality but the . . . objectless activities of responding to and generating written language" (*Textual Carnivals* 99). From the inception of freshman English at Harvard, the first-year student was defined (tacitly by the design of the entrance exam) "as the lower and in some ways the 'animal' order, in need of scrubbing" (85). According to Miller, introductory composition courses presume that students are "relatively young, relatively certain to take a freshman writing course as a freshman and before other studies, relatively sure of the financial and cultural norms that result in finishing undergraduate work in a regularly sequenced four-year period, and certainly needing to revere the values that nineteenth-century English programs were established to entrench" (88–89). Sharon Crowley claims that students in freshman English "must produce discourse that will satisfy their teachers . . . and beyond. In other words, the subjectivity produced by the requirement can be characterized as something like 'docile student'" (*Composition in the University* 217). Richard Ohmann describes the skills ("fluency, organization, analysis") and attitudes ("caution, detachment, cooperation") that freshman English communicates in order to indoctrinate young people into "the technostructure and . . . the smooth functioning of liberal (not liberated) society" (302). In another chapter of *English in America,* he describes how the course serves to train students to conform to the attitudes, values, and work habits of "a society most of whose work is done on paper and through talk. . . . We . . . discipline the young to do assignments, on time, to follow instructions, to turn out uniform products, to observe the etiquette of verbal communication. . . . Most of these are unwilled consequences, and, since they also run counter to the egalitarian ideology of the larger culture, it is not surprising that the English department fails to point them out when justifying its pay" (230). Miller, Crowley, and Ohmann note how the boundaries within which students had to operate also applied to the course itself. Miller notes that "the intransitive student's subjectivity is . . . transferred to the field of composition studies itself. . . . New programs in composition and other 'new' institutional approaches to student writing do not automatically redefine it, or its writers, as something other than the 'problem' it was established (literally) to correct" (201).

During the postwar era, some students seemed to escape the subjectivity that the course imposed. The postwar influx of GIs did not fit the profile of young, docile, compliant freshmen. Through their experience as GIs they had forged a powerful sense of self and a fund of knowledge that allowed them to write with eloquence that seemed to transcend the marginality of freshman English. Personal essays in the *Green Caldron* and the *Pier Glass* from 1946 to 1955 drew upon experiences that seemed to demonstrate that topics provided to younger undergraduates could be powerful sites for invention.

Earnest F. Nelson very likely wrote "My Trip through Hate" (1947) in response to a prompt like this one from the 1952 English Qualifying Exam: "Racial segregation, like slavery itself, is a malignant growth in a democracy." Nelson uses the topic to describe his experience after he had volunteered for the Army Air Force in 1941. He claimed that his training as an aircraft engine mechanic "wasn't hard. . . . Until the sign— 'Niggers don't drink this water, Whites Only'—appeared over the water fountain" (1). His experience became more troubling when he was sent to Maxwell Field, Alabama. At the train station he was greeted by "one sign [that] said 'The Cradle of the Confederacy'; on the side of a restaurant a sign said, 'Keep Off These Grounds, Niggers'" (1). He describes humiliation and threats that culminated in a severe beating he received because, even though he was in uniform, he sat in the front of a bus. He concludes that he "was glad to leave for overseas duty. . . . The German uniform would be different from mine, and I could fight back" (2).

Michael J. Smith uses a typical comparison and contrast structure to develop "A Sailor and a Doctor." He describes "the two men who, more than any others, helped give my life shape and direction." Smith depicts the sailor with a few sure strokes: "A man who had seen the world with her lipstick smeared and her hair uncombed. He was a navy-raised, navy-trained man who had run away from a dust-filled coal mine in a squalid little West Virginia town when he was seventeen. The Navy had given him shoes and shelter, and had even taught him to read and write. He had a covenant with the Navy. . . . He had fought through two world conflicts in the company of amateurs. He was proud of his uniform, his work. He asked for nothing more" (7). This sailor, Charles Beauford Dischner, guided Smith through combat and taught him "to see things through, not to quit, ever" (7). Dischner was killed saving the life of a wounded man after "a twelve-inch gun on the cruiser *Boston* blew up" (7). The epitaph on his tombstone at Arlington National Cemetery reads: "He did what he came to do" (7). The "doctor" in Smith's essay was "the head of the Orthopaedic Surgery Department at a large Chicago hospital" (7). After being discharged from the Navy, Smith contemplated pursuing a career in medicine, but felt that he was too old to begin. When he told the surgeon, "after all, I would be thirty-one before I even started to practice. . . . He looked at me and said, 'How old will you be in six years if you don't study medicine?'" (8). Smith concludes, "A sailor and a doctor . . . set my feet down and turned my eyes upward. Let me only do what I came to do" (8).

In "Oh, Jesus, Help Me!" Dorothy Giller uses the "my most memorable moment" topic as the occasion to describe an experience as a nursing assistant with a team of obstetricians from the Chicago Maternity Center. She focuses on one particular event, the delivery of a baby in a tenement. She describes in graphic detail the squalor of the apartment, the poverty of the woman, and the horror and beauty of the birth. Like Nelson and Smith, she concludes eloquently:

> I went immediately to the washroom where I washed my hands. When I had finished, I washed them again. I went to the window and looked down at the people going in and out of the taverns.
>
> Yes, I could wash away the dirt and urine and blood, I thought to myself. I cannot so easily wash away the dirt of poverty and ignorance.
>
> I saw little boys and girls running in and out of the taverns and playing on the curbs. I thought of Toni Ann [the baby whose birth she had witnessed] . . . and then, I cried. (6)

The eloquence of Nelson, Smith, and Giller emerges from life experience that they brought to the campus and the classroom, not from the ideas they had drawn from their reading (e.g., "The Role of Mechanics in Writing," "The Color of Red," or "First Impressions") or from cleverness or irony (e.g., "Mr. Pseudoscorpionida Shares His Knowledge," or "The Advantages of Being a Hermit").[1] Unlike the students whom Miller, Crowley, or Ohmann describe, they seem self-assured and self-actualized. Perhaps their rhetoric classes helped them with organization and diction, but essays such as these were not written merely to please their teachers. Although they, too, use the "select—narrow—amplify" inventional strategy of "Doubt Gets You an Education," the power of the real experiences these writers present obscures their current-traditional pedigrees. Their essays appear forceful partly because they are juxtaposed with the usual and customary products of freshman English; nevertheless, they are the exceptions that test but do not overstep the boundaries. Just as freshman English could absorb and neutralize controversial texts, it also could contain the experience of nontraditional students within conventional genres and methods of invention and use them as vivid examples of the alleged power of the course. By being featured in journals such as the *Green Caldron* or the *Pier Glass,* they served not to disrupt the marginality of the course, but to confirm its role as, in Sharon Crowley's words, "the universal requirement . . . that creates in students a healthy respect for the authority of the academy" (*Composition in the University* 216–17).

A similar dynamic appears in the research papers that students produced for Rhetoric 102 at Navy Pier. They chose (or were assigned) topics of compelling interest that had the potential to generate significant arguments. Within the discursive practice of freshman English, however, these topics served to confine their writing within a safe mode of expository display.

Leon M. Goldberg researched the European and North American political intrigue that preceded the construction of the Panama Canal. "The American Acquisition of Isthmian Canal Rights" (1961) recounts the geopolitical maneuvering that produced the Clayton-Bulwer Treaty of 1850 between Great Britain and the United States; the machinations of deLesseps's French Panama Canal Company in the 1870s; Britain's ceding a sphere of interest in Central America to the United States via the Hay-Paunceforte Treaty in 1900; and Theodore Roosevelt's support of the Bunau-Varilla Revolution, resulting in Panama's separation from Colombia and the subsequent sale by the puppet government of the rights to a ten-mile-wide Canal Zone to the United States. Goldberg presents these historical developments in careful detail. His 1500-word essay contains forty-four footnotes and cites ten sources. Nevertheless, he never mentions the issue of imperialistic capitalism and its effect on third-world countries. He presents as if unremarkable the facts that the principal shareholder in the Panama Canal Company, Philippe Bunau-Varilla, obtained American protection through the influence of Senator Hanna; "organized and financed a revolution in Panama" with the aid of "American naval units . . . refusing to permit Colombian troops to land on the Isthmus"; and subsequently "negotiated a treaty which he had induced his nominal superiors in Panama to approve unseen" (28). Goldberg concludes, "The United States government could now construct, control, and fortify its own Isthmian canal" (28).

Goldberg's treatment of the Panama issue resembles the way other student-authors reported on evolution, surrealism, and biblical translations. In her conclusion to "Evolution: Its Growth and Acceptance through Controversy" (1962), Barbara Keys comments: "The scientific facts supporting evolution are becoming more concrete every day. It seems to me that science has eclipsed religion in this respect and dulled the glow of special creation. It now remains eminently *reasonable* [emphasis in original] to accept evolution. And yet reason and faith are opposite: there will always be a Dawson or a Wilberforce putting his faith against reason. Science and religion cannot really be resolved; evolution will never be an answer to all" (11). Keys stands at the verge of analyzing the deeper conflict between faith-based and scientific explanations for the origins of life. Clearly, she has chosen one side in the argument. Yet, in the end she retreats into a sterile, safe declaration: "There will never be an answer to all."

Lynne Miller researched a controversial movement in art. She begins to probe the connections between psychology and creativity, but at the end of "The Surrealists" (1962), she merely summarizes the tension between classical and modernist art: "Perhaps they were the introspective neurotics that they were called. Perhaps they were the talentless failures, unable to achieve in all the schools of art of the so-called masters, who rationalized to save their egos and formed their own school, where talent did not matter, where their imaginations, their dreams, their minds, were the acme of art. Perhaps they were but escapists in their denouncement of reality. In any case, they were the Surrealists" (8). Her "perhaps," coupled with the faint irony she implies with "talentless," "so-called," or "escapists," suggests her pro-Surrealist argumentative stance. However, her concluding sentence—"In any case, they were the Surrealists"— collapses the potential controversy into a catchy tautology that serves as a "clincher," a typical current-traditional stylistic device.

A final example of a research paper from the *Pier Glass* is "Biblical Versions and Translations" (1961). Shirley Osema lays out the territory she intends to cover in this fashion: "There is only one Bible, but in any given language it has many texts, which scholars call views. . . . Words differ because of literary choices, interpretations, translations from various texts, changes in meaning of words and expression, and also because scholars know more now than ever about Greek and Hebrew grammar, vocabulary, and script. Annotations also differ, often coinciding with the interpretations of a particular denomination, thus affecting the acceptance of a particular version by a particular church" (12). Osema's paper develops each of the three subtopics that she introduces in a factual manner: the different "views" of the Bible in English, examples of variation in key passages of the various translations, and finally, examples of annotations in various Biblical editions. Like Goldberg, Keys, and Miller, she writes to fulfill the terms of the research paper assignment. She uses the same process of invention as do the authors of impromptus and personal essays. She selects a topic (the Bible), narrows it to a manageable scale (how translations differ in terms of word choice and annotations), and amplifies it by collecting data from a sufficient number and variety of sources. She never touches on the explosive canonical and sectarian issues related to her topic. The rhetoric staff did not publish "Biblical Versions and Translations" because Osema makes a contribution to the ongoing conversation about power, doctrine, and scripture, but because her essay is clear, orderly, and well documented.

Sites of potential controversy were offered to students not to provoke their thinking, but to allow them to discover many published opinions without strenuous research. In the 1950s they would have had to conduct their searches using fairly cumbersome tools such as general reference books, card catalogs, and various periodical indexes. As beginners, they had to be given a hidden treasure that was not too hard to find. Students were expected to sift nuggets of information from the arguments of experts that they then could organize into attractive displays. Writing a research paper meant applying the current-traditional model of invention to a topic *outside* one's personal experience, as well as revealing mastery of technical skills such as composing footnotes or compiling a bibliography.

The archives at the University of Illinois at Chicago contain a small handmade book, *It Takes All Kinds,* edited by students in Marion Kerwick's Rhetoric 144 Advanced Writing Class at Navy Pier. Kerwick, with the help of Ethelreda Miller and Edwin Joew, assembled this collection of typed stories and essays for display at an open house in 1952. The fourteen original prose selections reflect the various experiences and interests of a group of urban undergraduates. The title story, for example, written by Miller, re-creates a scene that would be familiar to anyone who had grown up on the South Side of Chicago during that period. Two girls stand next to a playground fence, watching their younger brothers play "piggy move up" (a baseball game that can be played with as few as three or four players). As they watch, they talk about the routines of their lives—frustrated love and tedious work. They are diverted by the arrival of an old man of indeterminate ethnicity ("We never could determine what shade of the rainbow Casey was") whose pet chicken, Caldonia, will—for a dime—dance to the music of "the latest jive tunes" sung by the girls and their friends.

The selections reflect the students' diversity of interests and backgrounds. "The Life and Times of Hope Squirrel" is a melodrama of tenement life told through the voices of anthropomorphic squirrels. In "Sketch of a City," a young couple on a date venture to the one place in the city they'd never gone, Chicago's famous Bughouse Square. There, they witness the drama among the drunks and socialists and an elderly evangelist, Sister Edward, who endures their mocking as she attempts to bring Jesus to them. *It Takes All Kinds* also includes tales of Mexican immigrants as they try to cross the Rio Grande, a Chinese farmworker who returns to China after sweating in the cotton fields of Mississippi, and a young teacher who discovers her own racial prejudice on her first day in front of her own classroom.

Inside the front cover is taped a letter from Kerwick to the librarian, who wanted to know how to catalog the book. She describes her students' work in this way: "An opportunistic teaching philosophy that avoids the usual academic procedures of laying down principles, superimposing general assignments irrespective of student preference, and drawing up hard-and-fast plans for every week of the semester to which the student must adhere, accounts for the varieties of style and content to be found in *It Takes All Kinds*." Kerwick's description of Rhetoric 144 implies what it meant to be a student or a teacher in Rhetoric 101 and 102. Rhetoric 144 allowed its students to adopt unique fictional identities to convey their individual ideas. Freshman English required its students to adopt what they believed were unique and independent identities, but their uniqueness and independence, as Kerwick suggests, were superimposed on them.

MY EARLIER CHAPTERS, especially "Individuality," present the presumptions upon which freshman English was based. The notion that each person is a unique and independent individual permeated the discourse of freshman English. That notion itself reflects something constructed, not a metaphysical reality or an independent fact of nature. Berlin and Crowley point out the Romantic origins of this meaning of individuality, and both authors note that it is a construct, not a feature of human nature. In his discussion of the rhetoric of liberal culture, Berlin notes, "The writing cultivated in this rhetoric thus valued the individual voice, the unique expression that indicated a gifted and original personality at work. Of course, this personality could not be allowed to violate the strictures of a certain notion of cultivation and class" (*Rhetoric and Reality* 45). Crowley traces the origins of Romantic individuality in rhetoric to the theory of invention posited by eighteenth-century British new rhetoricians. She calls their work "impressive achievements," but points out the problematic nature of "introspective invention": "Even though it placed responsibility for the quality of invention squarely in an individual author's mind, introspective invention was never a paean to Romantic notions about individual creativity or originality. Rather, it insisted that the quality of any discourse could be measured by its adherence to a rigorous set of standards derived from psychology and logic" (*Methodical Memory* 53). Within freshman English, to be an individual meant to present oneself as rational, orderly, skeptical, and subtly complex. Moreover, to be a student meant to present oneself as fundamentally flawed, capable of improvement but not perfection.

In 1953 Harrison Hayford's teaching assistant wrote "Reliving and Remembering," an article Hayford hoped to use in a freshman English textbook he was planning. This unpublished article (now part of the Harrison Hayford papers at the Northwestern University Archives) explains how students could learn to write successful academic prose by "'re-living' as well as remembering" their past experiences, and committing them in all their natural organization and vitality to paper. It begins with the anecdote of a student who wrote a paper free of mechanical errors, but who nevertheless got a D. The student was angry and puzzled because his paper contained no corrections, but only marginal notes concerning "'organization,' 'sincerity,' 'vagueness,' 'appropriateness,' 'naturalness,' 'consistency,' 'dullness.'" The article explains the student's confusion over having produced what he thought was good work and receiving a low grade substantiated with these comments: "For just as

certainly as dullness, unnaturalness, disorganization are the most common and most serious faults of freshman theme writing, so too are these
the most difficult to overcome, the most difficult for the instructor to
point out in specific terms and to suggest specific remedies for" (1). This
student did not understand how to improve his writing because the
faults noted in his essay do not pertain to the text itself. Rather, they
represent a lack of correspondence between his understanding of how
to represent himself via a text and the expectations of the instructor,
who speaks for freshman English, the instrument of academic literacy.
For this particular student to solve his problem, he must first come to
accept the judgment that has been passed on his paper as the truth. Then,
he must reexamine his life in the light of this new awareness of truth
and finally must "relive" his past experiences so as to discover the unity,
honesty, clarity, timeliness, and vivacity that he had never realized they
contained.

This example, the analysis of it, and the solution suggested reveal
the nature students were considered to possess when they began freshman English and the nature they could assume if they learned their lessons well. Above all, students were considered faulty. Freshman English
made them acknowledge their shortcomings and accept whatever remedies the course offered. As flawed beings, however, students—and their
instructors—always had to be wary of backsliding. The course could show
them the way, but it could not guarantee that they would achieve or maintain perfection. Students learned to acknowledge their tendency toward
error and weakness and to remember the remedies when they began to
regress.

Mike Rose has explored the origin of medical terminology in the
teaching of English. The term "remedial" was first used in an early study
of dyslexia—then called "congenital word blindness"—by a Dr. Morgan, in
1896. Over the ensuing decades, as teachers began to notice other reading and writing difficulties, they continued to use Morgan's medical language. "People tried to *diagnose* various *disabilities, defects, deficits, deficiencies,*
and *handicaps,* and then tried to *remedy* them" [emphasis in original]
("Language of Exclusion" 350–51). Rose points out that this particular
language associated teaching with the status of objective science and reflected the nobly progressive desire to educate not only the children of
privilege but all students. "Nevertheless, the notion of remediation,

carrying with it as it does the etymological wisps and traces of disease, serves to exclude from the academic community those who are so la-belled. They sit in scholastic quarantine until their disease can be diag-nosed and remedied" (351–52).

Medical terminology of the type Rose describes figured prominently in the postwar classroom. Before being allowed to enroll in freshman English, and also in the first few meetings of the course itself, students were given "diagnostic" tests and essay topics. For example, consider this passage from the 1949 *Freshman Rhetoric Manual and Calendar,* cited previously in "Individuality": "If you submit papers which are not genuine evidence of your own ability, you are thwarting your instructor's efforts to diagnose your writing ailments and to cure them" (5).[2] To ensure consistently ac-curate and honest diagnosis, freshman English courses always included a number of impromptu essays as a guarantee that students were supplying unadulterated specimens for examination. The instructor in "Reliving and Remembering," in a term used frequently to describe the teacher's role, offers a "remedy" for the problems he sees in the paper. Students who did not respond to the regular classroom treatment were referred to various "clinics" where "specialists" could provide individual therapy for their speech, reading, and writing.

A lesser but significant flaw was weakness or underdevelopment. In September 1955, the University Senate Committee on Student English at Urbana distributed a "Memo to Undergraduate Teaching Faculty," urging more stress on written work in all academic areas. The Com-mittee requested that all instructors "assign whenever (by any devious pretext) the nature of the course permits, some composition work . . . as a means of aiding students to discover their ineptitudes and weaknesses in writing." The drills, exercises, and practices typical of the freshman English curriculum reinforce this image of the student as someone who is, if not ailing, at least out of shape. Moreover, students did not want to face their weaknesses, and so they had to be tricked into confronting them by "devious pretexts," much like Kitzhaber's example of children who must be cajoled or coerced into eating their spinach.

Another of the students' flaws was moral weakness. Their propen-sity to cheating threatened the very nature of freshman English, which did not depend upon the students' learning a particular body of facts or set of techniques (in which cheating is already problem enough) but upon their learning to "express themselves." Paradoxically, freshman English sought to make students aware of the inherent goodness and value of themselves and their singular experiences, thoughts, and beliefs; yet at the same time it warned them of their equally natural tendency to misrepresent themselves. Students at Illinois were required to sign a pledge of honesty for each paper they submitted. According to the 1949 *Manual and Calendar,* these written pledges served "to keep you out of trouble and to remind you of the importance of honesty and originality in your work" (4–5). This statement presupposes students' propensity to trouble and dishonesty, and that such proclivities can be contained only long enough to produce one true and honest text before they must be asked to rein them in again. This pledge of honesty suggests the expectation that students will write dishonestly unless constantly and forcefully enjoined not to.[3]

A less culpable but still noticeable flaw was lack of commitment or responsibility. One of the comments on the paper discussed in "Reliving and Remembering" noted a lack of "sincerity"—it did not appear dishonest, but neither did it convey the vigor and forthrightness that a truly complete person would exhibit. In their introduction to *Pro and Con,* Matlaw and Stronks justify their textbook's use of controversy as the organizing principle by supposing that this approach will preclude a "retreat into a bland non-committal position" (xi), the stance students would adopt unless somehow provoked. In his 1961 survey, *Attitudes Toward English Teaching,* Joseph Mersand cites Dr. Clark of American University regarding the status of composition students: "Instructors in freshman composition . . . agree that there is no sense of responsibility about language, no recognition of the power of words" (49). Part of students' faulty natures was their undeveloped or rudimentary respect for thoughts and words. Like Matthew Arnold's apostles of equality, freshman English instructors had to stimulate or revive the students' moral commitment to think and write as the academy bade them.

Perhaps the least culpable flaw, but a flaw nonetheless, was the students' lack of polite graces, a kind of amusing immaturity. Teachers of English have often directed their condescending laughter at the malapropisms, non sequiturs, misspellings, and other infelicities that inevitably crop up in their students' writing. The *Green Caldron* featured sidebar lists of "boners" from students' essays; the same feature found its way into the *Pier Glass* and also onto the inside cover of the early issues of *College Composition and Communication* under the heading "Rhet as Writ." Sharon Crowley identifies such manifestations as "a historical practice in current-traditional composition, where for many years students were imagined as stupid and irresponsible louts who couldn't learn to spell or punctuate properly no matter how hard institutions tried to teach these skills to them" (*Composition in the University* 223).

Colleen Aycock, in her discussion of New Critical rhetoric, comments that "what the student does learn to value in the writing process is discrimination, subtlety, precision, conciseness, and wit" (156). Instructors expected to see a progression from simple, dogged writing (much like the correct but styleless paper in "Reliving and Remembering") to the cleverness, complexity, and subtlety that allowed an essay to hold up to a close reading. Perhaps students progressed in this fashion, but Howard Mindell, with the characteristic irony of a weary rhetoric student, points out another entirely possible reason for "improvement." In "The Inefficiency of Rhetoric" (1956), he comments:

> After eight or nine years of writing his thoughts on paper in a particular style or manner, the student tends to be immune to further instruction. This, of course, presents a challenge to the rhetoric instructors, and, to infuse greater spirit into the student, low marks are given at the beginning of the course. Gradually, of course, the marks become higher due to the rapid "improvement" of the student. It is more likely that high marks are given unconsciously by the instructor towards the end of the course, as he searches frantically for some form of improvement in his students. (22)

During this moment of rebellion, Mindell displays the qualities Aycock points out. At the end of his essay, however, he retreats into the role of "docile student." He apologizes for his attack on rhetoric classes, claiming that he has "just hastily scribbled down [his ideas] . . . for a new record in wordage for an impromptu." Then he concurs with his instructor that there really is one way by which a student can show improvement: "the careful and thorough examination of all mistakes, and a conscious effort while writing anything to try to include some of the things which make up good writing" (23).

All three flaws—lack of health, physical and moral weakness, lack of polish—are suggested by a passage from the 1953 *Freshman Rhetoric Manual and Calendar.* "Your Freshman Rhetoric instructor has been employed, first, to help you analyze the weak points and the strong points of your present ability . . . and, second, to indicate to you what you need to do to improve. His probing into your shortcomings may be painful at times, especially if your earlier efforts have not been exposed to searching criticism, but patience and application on your part and on his should eventually result in accomplishment of which you both may be proud" (3). The freshman English student was like a patient under the firm but compassionate hand of a doctor who could diagnose hidden weaknesses and prescribe remedies. Students lack the integrity and composure to endure the diagnosis at first and may respond with childish sensitivity. They have not yet developed a sufficient sense of value to recognize real quality in themselves or in their work. But with time and the endurance of some pain, they not only would recognize and remedy their weaknesses, but also achieve enough maturity and sophistication to gain some recognition within the adult world.

To succeed in freshman English meant to have reconstructed one's personality so as to minimize the impact of one's flaws upon written or spoken texts. In *A Rhetoric Case Book* (1953), Francis Connolly clearly states the qualities students had to develop first in themselves before they could produce effective writing:

> The source of a composition is the author himself. He is its efficient cause. . . . The author (as cause) must somehow express his own personality in the composition (the effect). Hence when we say that a good style is clear, vigorous, and interesting, we are assuming that these qualities in a composition must also be found in the cause—the writer. If the writer does not possess clear ideas, vigorous feelings, and vivid images, these elements cannot appear in his composition. Ultimately it is the writer's personality that shapes the style of a composition. (725–26)

To write well, students had to mend defects in themselves; persons who did not eliminate the unhealthily unfocused, uncommitted, bland selves they brought to freshman English were deemed incapable of joining the exchange of spoken and written words in the academy.

The therapy and guidance that freshman English provided might lead to improvement, but not to perfection. Students could never free themselves completely of the flaws that were part of their identity. The syllabus for Rhetoric 101 at Navy Pier (1960), for example, noted that "students should learn . . . how they might employ . . . some of the methods and devices good writers use." The syllabus places a distance between "students" and "good writers." Students are capable of employing only some of the devices; good writers presumably can use all of them. Students taking English A at Northwestern were expected to "develop, to the extent possible, a mature and realistic attitude toward the ideas and experiences that they attempt to communicate" ("Freshman Composition" 16). The maturity and sense of reality students might be able to achieve was limited "to the extent possible." The tentative, almost conciliatory tone in these statements ("might employ," "to the extent possible") masks an assumption that students would retain to some degree the limitations they had brought to the course.

Students, as students, were presumed to have an inescapably flawed nature. Therefore, the faculty assumed an ongoing responsibility to contain the inevitable backsliding. In his capacity as chair of the Joint Commission on Research in Student English, Ernst Matthews published "Student English—An All-University Problem" in the April 1949 *University of Illinois Faculty Bulletin*. Mathews had compared the scores of 335 students on two examinations—the English Qualifying Examination, and the university general examinations. He found that the quality of writing (as measured by an analysis of mechanical correctness, syntax, organization, and style) was far poorer on the general examinations than on the qualifying examinations. He drew the following conclusion: "Two-thirds of the extremely bad writing in examinations is done on the theory that careless English does the writer no harm. This carelessness might be regarded as harmless if it were merely a college pastime. The complaints of the employers of college graduates indicate, however, that bad writing habits are often carried away with the diploma" (n.p.). He ended his article with a plea for "increased surveillance by every member of the teaching faculty." A memo dated 4 April 1963 to the entire faculty from the Senate Committee on Student English at Navy Pier echoes Mathews's request: "Faculty members who teach courses other than Rhetoric or English are asked to admonish all students whose English composition or oral expression is noticeably poor. A warning from you, no doubt reinforcing what Rhetoric or speech instructors have already said, may well be doubly impressive and effective criticism." According to Mathews, students have a natural propensity toward "bad writing habits" that can only be kept in check via constant "surveillance." Like children, students lack the maturity to realize the full consequences of their carelessness; like parents, the faculty must watch them carefully, to keep their youthful indiscretions from causing them permanent harm.

Like Mathews, members of the English departments at both Wheaton and Northwestern cast themselves in this parental role and begged for cooperation from the rest of the faculty in preventing students from causing themselves injury. Members of the Wheaton Department of English planned a presentation to the rest of the faculty on the need for campuswide attention to students' writing (the following statements were recorded in the minutes of the department meeting of 7 November 1955). They spoke of their need to exercise guidance and control. They agreed, for example, that they "do no favor to the student or to the college in letting a student graduate who writes badly." It may have seemed cruel to deny a degree to a student who had not met the expectations discussed earlier in this chapter, but this sternness would ultimately serve the students' own interest, presumably by stripping them of their self-delusions and making them face the reality of their own weakness. As part of their presentation, the English faculty planned to offer as evidence of the problem some "horrible examples" of papers written by upperclassmen who had previously passed freshman English. Lest their colleagues from other departments take these papers as proof that the students should not have passed freshman English, the English faculty proposed the following explanation: "He [the author of one of the 'horrible examples'] will write satisfactorily while in the course, and then lose those standards at once unless required to uphold them throughout college." Freshman English, then, cannot effect a permanent change in the students; it can only temporarily block their flawed literacy. Students will write well only if compelled by outside forces, exercised by persons who appreciate, as the students cannot, the full consequences of one's actions.

In May of 1950, the General Faculty Committee of Northwestern University sent a letter to the entire faculty recommending "that all members of the university staff hold students to the highest possible performance in their writing and speaking of English. . . . No student passes the course [English A] who is not fairly proficient in the use of English. For the maintenance of this proficiency among upper-classmen, the English department cannot bear the sole responsibility." As at Illinois and Wheaton, the Northwestern faculty adopted a parental role in response to what they perceived as their students' inherent flaws. On their own, students were considered incapable of keeping themselves from reverting to the immature thinking and writing behaviors that they brought to the university. Like benign parents, the faculty realized that they could bring about only temporary change in their students; sternness in the face of inevitable backsliding was the kindest thing they could offer.

nine

The Teacher

SSESSMENTS OF TEACHING
FRESHMAN ENGLISH PUBLISHED during the postwar era fall into two
categories: anecdotal reminiscences, often the complaints of embattled
academic underdogs; or criticisms of the nearly universal policy of staffing the course with graduate students, part-time instructors, or newly
hired assistant professors. Typical of the former category is "Teaching
Freshman Composition," published by Keith Rinehart in *College English*
(1951). Rinehart describes his growth as a composition teacher between
1946 and 1950 while he worked at three different colleges. At each, he
absorbed a different philosophy of teaching. One department emphasized grammar, another logic, another general education. In doing so,
Rinehart began to realize the contradiction between the importance that
the institutions claimed for freshman English and his own lack of knowledge and power: "The university has turned over to us, its youngest, most
inexperienced teachers, the course most important for the students' educational life both within and beyond the college walls. Our course is the
nucleus to which all other college courses are added. If we fail in our
jobs, if we fail to teach the freshman how to think, others are helpless;

for they can't get at him, unless, of course, he has learned to think for himself" (453). Rinehart would concur with Ken Macrorie's tradition-alist teacher, George, who cried out, "My God! The first line of the war for the mind may be the freshman writing course!" (Macrorie, "Writing's Dying" 208).[1] He recognizes the magnitude as well as the impossibility of the task he has been assigned, especially considering his own sense of inadequacy. Rinehart concludes his article with the sardonic suggestion that in light of what he has come to realize about teaching freshman English, he should perhaps go back to the safety of teaching grammar.

A similar picture of teaching freshman English emerges from sev-eral books and articles, published between 1961 and 1976. Some of these consider the first-year course by itself—Albert Kitzhaber's *Themes, Theories, and Therapy* (1963), Robert Gorrell's "Freshman Composition" (1965), and Martin Steinmann's "Freshman English in America" (1965). Others treat the course within the context of English studies as a whole—Joseph Mersand's *Attitudes Toward English Teaching* (1961), Robert Shugrue's *English in a Decade of Change* (1968), Thomas Wilcox's *Anatomy of College English* (1973), or Richard Ohmann's *English in America* (1976/1996). These studies discuss many aspects of freshman English, especially its ever-changing cur-riculum, its instrumental role within the institution, the generally un-favorable impressions of students' progress, and the disproportionately heavy demands it makes upon teachers. What they do say about the po-sition of the teacher within the practice of freshman English amounts to a restatement of Rinehart's complaint that the least powerful were entrusted (or burdened, depending upon how pessimistic the author chooses to be) with the most demanding of all the classes offered by the Department of English. They usually call for less reliance on graduate students and instructors as staff for freshman English programs; some studies even propose that senior faculty assume a greater proportion of the classes.

Neither the anecdotal accounts of teaching experiences nor the comprehensive surveys, however, recognized the complicated interaction among teachers, students, and the course. Discussing freshman English meant proposing changes in one or more of the factors (changing the curriculum, enrollment standards, or staffing policies) in order to bring about more favorable results (heightened student literacy). None of these writers—not even Ohmann, whose study critiques the discipline of English historically and politically—considers freshman English as a practice with its own values, beliefs, and history. To enter into freshman English required students, as well as their teachers, to assume a distinct, inescapable, but unacknowledged function.

An examination of the practices at Northwestern, Wheaton, and Illinois reveals that despite marked differences among the faculty at the three schools, those who taught freshman English made the same presumptions and occupied the same problematic position within their respective institutions and within the teaching profession.

Northwestern, Wheaton, and Illinois staffed their freshman English programs in different ways. In interviews, Jean Hagstrum and Harrison Hayford described the situation of those who taught English A at Northwestern. All English faculty generally were required to teach the course in rotation, a policy that assigned the freshman course to junior faculty as well as to senior professors such as Richard Ellmann and John Spargo. Northwestern did not employ part-time instructors, and according to Fred Faverty's report to Dean Simeon Leland (28 June 1953) the new instructors and the few graduate assistants were supervised by "older men especially assigned to the task." That year, eleven assistants worked in the department, and Faverty wrote that he intended to lower the number by five because he felt too much responsibility was being placed in inexperienced hands. Teaching rosters from the 1950s reveal that Northwestern employed few women in the English department; presumably English A was taught for the most part by men.

No one person embodies what it meant to teach English A at Northwestern better than Wallace W. Douglas. He grew up on Chicago's West Side, but went east to obtain the academic pedigree that made him attractive to a competitive institution like Northwestern. He studied at Colgate with Porter Perrin, one of the pioneers in Composition as a discipline. Perrin's doctoral research on the theory and practice of Rhetoric in early American schools was reflected in his *Index to English,* one of the first textbooks to recognize the legitimacy of spoken American English. At Northwestern, Douglas maintained his mentor's quest for democratic values in his students' writing, in departmental affairs, in the teaching profession, and in American life. "Rhetoric for the Meritocracy," his scathing account of the origins of the Composition course at Harvard, typifies the values he absorbed from Perrin. In that essay, he mocks those who attempt to legitimize "the many practices of current composition teachers" by searching for their origins in classical rhetoric. "The interesting questions," he claims, "are those that ask why and how rhetoric in its truncated and debased modern form has been able to survive, and indeed flourish, as the study of written composition, or as practice in the production of written compositions and communications" (98–99). He came home to the University of Chicago, where he earned an MA in 1937, and then taught at Indiana University in Bloomington.

In 1940 Douglas headed east again to Williams College. He taught there while he specialized in the poetry of William Wordsworth during his doctoral studies at Harvard. He developed a curious attachment to the dual attitude toward the world of academic privilege that Cambridge represented. On the one hand, he felt attached to it; yet on the other, he resented it. At Douglas's memorial service, Jane Connor Marcus described him as "a charming and quirky mentor to the Left and a lone advocate of the importance of teaching to empower one's students." Because she had earned her BA at Harvard, he would tease her about their "common experience in the enemy's camp. . . . I hated the place with a passion, and Wally always used to call me 'Harvard' to get my goat." Nevertheless, he retained a sense of superiority that must have come from his experience in Cambridge; why else would he, in a memo critical of what he perceived to be his colleagues' retrograde ideas, have mocked a proposal's contents as being "unexceptional and unexceptionable . . . in conservative and provincial (not to say parochial) places like Illinois or at junior colleges with faculties made up largely of former high school teachers" (memo to Jean Hagstrum, 17 September 1973).

According to Harrison Hayford, Douglas did not last as director of English A because he was too "outspoken and acerbic" (personal interview, 2 March 1989). Although he did not control Northwestern's Composition program for long, his passion for empowering students and teachers made him continue to promote more egalitarian pedagogies wherever he could. In his eulogy for Douglas, Hayford described him as "put[ting] up a lonely and often losing fight for some curricular reform, or against some hidebound petty regulation that hampered students— his face glowing red, his hands and voice shaking with outrage" ("Wally Douglas Memorial—25 April 1995"). That sense of outrage, as well as his puckish humor, motivated him to continue fighting for reform all through his career. In a memo to Dean Simeon Leland (1 February 1963), Jean Hagstrum described Douglas as "a man of great independence and originality of mind [who] has decided to serve the profession rather through pedagogy than through scholarship. There is no doubt that his intellectual qualifications for scholarship are very high; but driven by a strong social conscience, he prefers to engage in those activities that most immediately affect the students—both on and below the college level." Benjamin H. Slote, a Northwestern undergraduate who went on to earn his doctorate at Yale and to teach at Allegheny College, recalled going to Douglas's apartment on Sherman Avenue for independent study sessions. Slote articulated how this mentor differed from other professors. His "subject" was the actual work that students performed, and his ability to find value there set him apart. "The scene of our independent study is particularly memorable because [of] the subject, the student's writing and thinking, that which Wally so personally served. . . . The sort of attention Wally gave students made them feel as if they deserved it." According to a self-assessment, "Accomplishments," Douglas counted as most significant his development of the English Curriculum Study Center (1964), through which several thousand teachers learned how to "get as far beyond writing-as-exercise" as they could. He also considered his role in establishing the Northwestern graduate program in English Education as an "accomplishment of some value."

Douglas edited two textbooks and published over thirty articles, chapters, and reviews related to composition, its history, and its teaching. He published only one monograph in his thirty-five years of teaching—*Wordsworth: The Construction of a Personality*, a version of his 1945 dissertation at Harvard. His service to composition and to pedagogy kept him from finishing the revisions until 1968. This choleric, demanding, yet endearing teacher devoted his professional life to trying "to help students say what they want to say, to help them express their feelings, their hopes, their dreams, and their fears" ("An Interview" 62). Nevertheless, his death notice in the *New York Times* identified him as an "expert on Romantic poets" who "focused on Wordsworth, and wrote many articles about the poet's complex politics and business dealings" (Saxon 10). In his memorial speech, Harrison Hayford described Douglas's reaction when some "hapless one of us might blunder into saying [something he disagreed with] about person, place, or thing. His jaw would drop. He would gasp incredulously." No doubt he would have responded to the obituary Wolfgang Saxon wrote about him as he did to other blunders: "That is bizarre! Bordering on the fantastic!"

At Wheaton, regular faculty taught the freshman English course; however, one group within the department handled Writing 111 and 112 while another devoted itself to advanced writing courses or to literature. Staff rosters in "Resources for an Evaluation Study" reveal that between 1952 and 1968 approximately one-fourth of the faculty were women. Minutes of department meetings from the 1950s reveal that those who taught Writing 111 and 112 included faculty members who began teaching at Wheaton without their doctorates and had settled into the freshman program more or less permanently, as well as new faculty who taught freshman courses while working toward their doctorates. Many of the latter group moved out of English or away from Wheaton once they had completed their degrees.

One such figure was Peter Veltman. Veltman was educated in his home town—Holland, Michigan. Hope College, a local school, awarded him a BA in English in 1938. He proceeded to Western Reserve (now Case Western Reserve) in Cleveland for an MA in British literature a year later. His master's thesis, "Milton and Vondel," turned out to be the apex of his literary career. For the next eight years he taught English, first at Chicago Christian High School and then in the same schools from which he had graduated, Holland Junior High and Holland Senior High. He was ambitious and energetic. He published a dozen articles in local educational and religious journals, participated in five different professional organizations, sponsored an award-winning newspaper, the *Holland High Herald,* and in his last year served as department chair in English.

Newspaper clippings in his biographical file at the Wheaton College archives reveal the concepts that shaped Veltman's work in middle and high schools. On the one hand, he used democratic, almost Deweyan language to describe his teaching philosophy. In "Serving the Community" (1949), he wrote: "Journalism is a project in community living and that community includes school, home, city, state, nation, and world." At Michigan State's statewide competition in 1947, his newspaper at Holland High won a special trophy for service to school and community. "The Other Side of the Fence," a 1948 article for *School and Society,* however, describes a more elitist notion of what the community needed to face postwar challenges. He decries those who were "flinching these days from teaching the classics and English grammar," and he criticizes the promotion of manual training classes in the schools. "America is engaged in a struggle to keep the world at peace. How will that peace be kept? By a lathe turner, by a drug-store clerk, by a shoe salesman? It may well be. But, above all, by those who can think clearly, who do not flinch because problems are at hand" (208).

That same year, Veltman published "Implications for Present Day Education in the Popularity of Comic Books" in *Michigan Education Journal*. Given his endorsement of grammar and classical literature as subjects that would promote clear thinking, his take on popular literature is surprising. He found comic books a time-saving teaching tool. He commented, "Is this not the age when economy is sought in all things?" He described them as attractive and useful, something a teacher could use for valid pedagogical purposes. He found the problem not in the cartoons or in the students who read them, but in the teachers' attitudes: "These, then are the implications of the comic book 'problem.' Will it remain a problem with youth getting all the blame, or will you help solve it by the means at your command, as an expert in diagnosing the ills of students and suggesting a solution or a substitution?" (193). Veltman did not adhere to a consistent theoretical point of view; instead, he seemed to use popular wisdom and common sense to generate an eclectic, pragmatic solution for each problem that he encountered.

It must have been Veltman's pragmatism that led him to apply for a teaching position at Wheaton College. It offered him a step up in salary and prestige, and he fit their needs. On his appointment questionnaire, Veltman could attest that he had been saved "for about 13 years," attended church, had married a Christian woman who shared his beliefs and supported his career, and was more than willing to subscribe to Wheaton's doctrinal platform. He did not belong to any "secret society" (Jonathan Blanchard considered Masonry "a conspiracy against God and the human race" [Bechtel 35]); did not smoke, take drugs, drink, dance, play cards, attend plays, go to movies, or engage in "other worldly practices." To the question, "What is your opinion of the theory that man is biologically descended from and/or genetically related to other forms of animal life?" he answered, "It is un-Biblical, unscientific, unreasonable, and pure hooey." In a recommendation for Veltman (22 August 1955), President V. Raymond Edman suggests the reasons that Wheaton considered him as a job candidate: "[The] excellent response from his students . . . is indicative of the high regard in which he is held by the undergraduates. . . . His teaching in the field of writing has been . . . superior. . . . It is far more difficult for us to secure a qualified instructor in writing than one in literature." Wheaton welcomed the young Dutch Reformed high school teacher because he had enough education (at the time, the department had only two people with PhDs, Clyde Kilby and Paul Bechtel), was sympathetic to young people, had an admirable record of teaching and publishing, pursued no beliefs or behaviors contrary to its standards, and was willing to teach writing.

The same pragmatism that led Peter Veltman to a position as a teacher of writing led him away from it as well. After his first seven years at Wheaton, perhaps when he had first come up for tenure review, he began to contemplate earning a doctorate. At first, Veltman considered pursuing a journalism degree at Northwestern. He had already taken courses there in romantic and contemporary literature, but he would have had to take fifty or sixty additional hours in political science, economics, and sociology. His dean, John H. Fadenrecht, wrote to Oswald Tippo, dean of the Graduate College at Urbana, as well as to the deans of several other midwestern universities asking for suggestions. He noted that Veltman "is not planning to be a professional journalist, but rather is planning to continue as a college teacher of writing and of elementary journalism." Fadenrecht added that Veltman was not "ready to start over again on a professional degree since he is well along in his graduate work in English (with the tendency being to concentrate on literature)." Although Veltman claimed that he wanted to continue as a teacher of writing, in 1955 he entered a PhD program in education at Northwestern. He never took another course in literature. His dissertation, "A Study of Pre-service and In-service Training of Full-time Teachers in Coeducational Protestant Church-related Junior Colleges," explored issues of teacher training and administration. Upon completing his doctorate in 1959, Veltman was moved from English to the department chairmanship of Education. After seven years, he left that position to become dean of the college.

In an address to the new faculty in 1968, he described the educational milieu of Wheaton, where students "are taught by teachers, not by scholars." Veltman continued, "Wheaton expects competence in classroom performance as well as empathy for the young learner as he attempts to resolve his conflicts, master his lessons, and integrate the subject matter with newness of life in Christ" ("What Wheaton Expects of You," n.p.). He shared none of the passion for academic sparring that Wallace Douglas relished in his professional life, and none of the attachment to Composition as a discipline. Douglas would have found Veltman's theology and his abandonment of Composition for educational administration "bizarre . . . bordering on the fantastic." Nevertheless, both men shared an essential feature of freshman English: devotion to helping students satisfy their needs to express their deepest desires and ideas.

At Navy Pier, established in 1946 to provide for the wave of returning veterans, the faculty resembled Wheaton's. According to Falk Johnson, many had master's degrees and had been recruited from secondary schools or from other disciplines, such as education. Others were working toward doctorates at Northwestern or Chicago and left the freshman program once they had completed their studies. Unlike Wheaton, Navy Pier employed a fair number of part-time instructors solely to teach Rhetoric 100, 101, or 102. Lists of staff members from that period reveal that half to two-thirds of the Rhetoric faculty were women.

Falk Johnson, who headed the Division of Rhetoric at Navy Pier until the university moved into its own campus in 1966, reflects the institution where he taught and the students who went there. In an interview (18 October 1988), he described his rural origins and his economic motives for pursuing higher education. "I come from a little mountain village . . . I'm a hillbilly, to a considerable extent. . . . I had the feeling that nothing ever happens in Mars Hill, where I lived." After completing his education at Wake Forest (BA, 1935; MA in English, 1936), boredom with small-town life led him to inquire about jobs he saw advertised in big-city newspapers. "New York didn't want me. Philadelphia didn't want me. Northwestern University wanted someone in public relations, and I've been in Chicago ever since."

Falk Johnson began taking graduate courses while working at Northwestern, but lost his job after a year. His wife, a fellow student from Evanston, "insisted that I shouldn't get my doctorate at Northwestern— it wasn't good enough. . . . So I transferred to the University of Chicago, and I started my work in English there." When World War II erupted, he had just taken his qualifying exams. In his words, "The war messed up my life." He spent a year and a half in Europe with the army "doing code and cipher work." He developed an interest in languages; upon his return, the difficult prospect of rereading all the work he had left behind during the war as well as practical financial considerations led him to reconsider his academic plans. "I went into linguistics . . . for the wrong reason. I thought, now, there is in English no commercial competitor for my services; but in linguistics, there are dictionary companies . . . and I would probably make more money." He found that lexicography paid the same as teaching, however, and wound up at Navy Pier.

Even though he expressed regrets at not having sought a position in linguistics right away, he stayed with composition because he was "interested in what [he] was doing, pretty well satisfied." He and his colleagues may have lacked the academic cachet of their colleagues at Northwestern or the missionary spirit of those at Wheaton, but they were competent and experienced. Johnson claimed, "Even in '46 . . . there was no one who came in to face students for the first time in freshman English. . . . Over the years, we developed a remarkable faculty for the freshman composition course . . . Bernard Kogan, Eugene Vest, Harry Runyon." It is clear from memos and accounts of department meetings that they felt a great sense of ownership in their Rhetoric program. In contradiction to Douglas's snide reference to "conservative and provincial . . . places like Illinois . . . with faculties made up largely of former high school teachers," Johnson and the Navy Pier staff displayed cleverness and spirit as they defended themselves against interference from high-handed, nosy administrators, and from their well-established colleagues in Urbana. At a meeting on 15 November 1960, the staff considered a request from Associate Dean R. W. Bailey that students who were failing Rhetoric at midterm be allowed to withdraw. Their response: "[We] thank Dean Bailey for the letter, but . . . we do not think that Deans should make judgments about rhetoric papers" (H. W. Bailey, Memo to R. P. Hackett, et al.). At the same meeting, they also considered "new approaches to the handling of increased enrollments in rhetoric" that Urbana was testing, including a lecture and quiz format in which one professor, assisted by graduate students, would teach sections with hundreds of students. Navy Pier instructor James Friend made a motion that his colleagues passed: "That physical accommodations be enlarged and that a staff at a more appropriate salary be provided to meet the present and future enrollment emergency rather than the experimental plan suggested by the Administration" (H. W. Bailey, Memo to A. D. Pickett). They instituted the "yellow slip" program that both Urbana and Wheaton copied and founded the *Pier Glass* because, according to Johnson, they "had specialized so much in dealing with the remedial students, that we felt we should do something for our superior students."

Johnson resigned from his leadership role to protest a new direction being forced upon the Division of Rhetoric. "Shortly after the transition was made to The Circle [Navy Pier's new campus west of downtown Chicago] . . . the course was downgraded, in my mind. It was to be taught by graduate assistants." By that time the wave of GIs—for whom Johnson had an intuitive sympathy—had moved on, and the administration was retooling Navy Pier to serve a different clientele. Faculty members retained after the Chicago Circle campus opened were said to have been "eclipsed." Rather than watch the program he had developed and the people with whom he had worked for over a decade be eclipsed, in 1966 he moved into the fledgling Department of Linguistics.

In 1988, twenty-two years after he had moved on, Falk Johnson still regretted that he had never been able to get his university and the profession at large to define clear objectives for composition instruction. He contrasted the satisfaction of working in a disciplinary field with teaching composition: "In linguistics . . . I get a sense of accomplishment, because the students have learned the facts. But in the composition course? How often do your students' grades go up during the teaching of the course? Why do they go up? Do you measure accountability? What you're doing is not measured, and . . . it's rather disillusioning. . . . You spend a lifetime, and you haven't made a measurable difference." Like Veltman, he shared the core values and experiences of his students; like Douglas, he felt a frustration with the bureaucracy that he thought prevented the Composition course from succeeding. Although they had clear ideas about how to assist their students and their colleagues in accomplishing educational goals, they did not succeed in reforming freshman English. Veltman and Johnson moved inward from the margins to more comfortable fields. Douglas stayed in composition, but the adjectives James Sledd and Jean Hagstrum used at his memorial service to describe him—"outrageous . . . irreverent . . . never dully complacent, conventionally agreeable, or placidly acquiescent"—reveal his never-ending struggle to challenge its boundaries.

For decades, Urbana had used the system that Falk Johnson wanted to resist. In 1952 the University Senate Committee on Student English produced "Provisions for Rhetoric and the Rhetoric Staff," an updating of Charles Roberts's 1942 survey. According to this document, the department strove to limit staffing to 75 percent graduate students, but generally the percentages ranged upward from 90; in 1952–1953, "98.66 percent of the rhetoric teachers were graduate assistants" (3). These teachers tended to be older than one may have expected, the average age being thirty; most were married men with children; all of them used their teaching as a means of support while working on doctoral degrees in literature. Although they were emotionally and intellectually mature, they had little background in Rhetoric. The 1952–1953 study noted: "The undergraduate preparation of the entire 1941–42 Rhetoric Staff included an average of thirty-two hours of work in literature but an average of only ten hours in the field of English language and composition, *including required freshman rhetoric courses* [emphasis in original]. Hence, the average preparation of our staff in this field is small, being approximately equal to that of high school teachers of English" (3). The 1952 report noted that since Roberts's assessment in 1941 the English department had begun to offer Rhetoric 480, "The Theory and Practice of English." During the 1952–1953 academic year, however, only three graduate assistants in Rhetoric were taking it. Falk Johnson noted the challenge that the Director of Rhetoric faced: "The course was taught in Urbana almost exclusively by graduate students . . . [and] the graduate assistants down there needed to be guided." From 1939 to 1960, the man who provided that guidance was Charles Roberts.

Roberts grew up in Sterling, Illinois, a blue-collar town that used to call itself the "Hardware Capital of the World." On a biographical form filled out in 1958, he listed his father's vocation as "iron moulder" and his mother's as "housewife." He attended Cornell College in Iowa for one year, then transferred to Ohio Wesleyan where he completed his bachelor's degree in 1924. Roberts, like Veltman and Douglas, returned to the region he had come from to begin his teaching career. He taught English and history at Morrison High School in Morrison, Illinois, for three years, then moved to the State University of Iowa (now Iowa State University, in Ames) where he studied English literature and worked as an editorial assistant for the *Midland Magazine*. He earned his master's degree in June 1928, then came to Urbana as a teaching assistant while he worked on his doctorate. He was appointed to an instructorship in 1938, just after he completed his PhD. One year later, after Bernard Jefferson's unexpected death, he began directing freshman Rhetoric. He kept that position, even though he tried to resign from it in 1953, until 1960.

Roberts had strong opinions and was not afraid to express them. Lynn Altenbernd, who headed the English department from 1959 to 1964, noted that he had a "peppery personality . . . but the pepper was applied in the interest of a sound rhetoric program" (personal correspondence, 27 June 2002). In Altenbernd's estimation, "Roberts was not popular with his aides and colleagues, but he got good results." He worked both within and outside the department to make the freshman Rhetoric program effective. His annual *Manual and Calendar* provided a day-by-day syllabus for his inexperienced staff. He established the freshman reading room at the university library, where students could find works from the comprehensive list in the back of the *Manual and Calendar*. In 1931, while still a teaching assistant, he began the *Green Caldron*, which continued publishing exemplary work from Rhetoric classes until 1970. He worked closely with the University Senate Committee on Student English to help it address the problem that President Willard noted in 1940: "Too many students graduate from the University of Illinois who use poor English in expressing themselves both in speaking and in writing, notwithstanding our requirement of one year of rhetoric" (Senate Committee on Educational Policy 2). Roberts and Jessie Howard, the Executive Secretary of the University Senate Committee on Student English, produced detailed background surveys, gathered statistical data, published studies and handbooks for the faculty, helped to administer the English Qualifying Exam three times each semester, and even graded the exams.

In their "Memorial to Charles Walter Roberts," three colleagues from the Division of Rhetoric, John Hamilton, Frank Moake, and Harris Wilson, noted that Roberts "had that rare courage to support a cause wholeheartedly and openly if he thought that the cause was right." Roberts campaigned throughout his career against what he deemed "educational nonsense," "lunatic ideas on education," or "creeping kindergartenism." In the guise of "The Last of the English Teachers," he used to deliver a set speech about how the English language and its teachers would become extinct. He adopted the Orwellian role of the lone remaining English teacher in 1999. This character blamed the decline and fall of the subject and the profession on a mistaken sense of democracy, abetted by permissive notions of child psychology, that led schools to abandon educational standards. "The young people who could read and write began to take on airs and consider themselves a bit better than the hand-minded ones who could not. . . . So in the interests of restoring the democratic spirit in the schools, the three R's were eventually abandoned for all the children of all people" ("English Teachers" 12). "English" slipped to "language arts," then to "communications." Books were replaced with film strips and sound recordings; Rudolph Flesch's "yardstick of readability" reduced literature first to the foot, then to the inch. "The Readable Inch version of *Hamlet* was very popular in the schools and was later put into an excellent two-frame strip in technicolor" (12). Once English had been eliminated as an American school subject, political attention shifted from defeating communism to defeating British "Creeping Socialism." "The Last English Teacher" told how Americans, after they had defeated the Russians and the Chinese, began "the final Crusade against the Creeps. It was during this . . . police action with the Creeps that the English language and English literature were finally seen in their true subversive light and were forever banned from our schools" (12).

During a panel discussion at Urbana in 1958, Roberts drew a distinction between education and training: "We train animals. We educate human beings. We cannot educate animals. We can, of course, train human beings, and in their infant stage, we must" ("'Creeping Kindergartenism'" 26). Roberts defined "the truly educated man" as someone not bound by his own circumstances, who can "roam through vast reaches of time and space to become acquainted with all manner of men . . . [who] knows that the world does not revolve around him as it seemed to when he was a child; yet they also know something of the power of the human mind to bring the world to heel and to further ennoble the human race" (26). In contrast, he criticized child psychology, "the ugly duckling of the sciences," because it had produced teachers, administrators, and theorists who were trained, but not educated. "Perhaps if we had ignored them [the psychologists] and had spanked a few more playsuits then we would not have to shoot down so many leather jackets today" (26). After criticizing permissive elementary and high schools, Roberts expanded his critique to the international level: "While a totalitarian state like the Soviet Union may be able to exist by simply training its young people, a republic of democracy like ours can survive and flourish only if the great majority of our young people are truly educated" (26).

The event that Roberts considered the apex of his career, the elimination of Rhetoric 100, emerged from the kind of thinking he articulated in those two speeches. He did not pretend to wave a magic wand to solve the problem of what he called "illiteracy" at Illinois. He based his proposal to the board of trustees upon demonstrable educational and fiscal reasons. He used his position as director of freshman Rhetoric as a platform for speeches about the decline of students' performance and backed his assertions with statistics. He established biannual conferences that brought secondary English teachers to Urbana to share ideas with their college English counterparts. He began a program by which the graded placement exams of incoming freshmen were returned to their high schools, so the teachers could see how their own graduates were performing. He and his staff prepared a handbook, the University of Illinois *Stylebook of English,* and sent it to every high school in the state. The *Stylebook* included the expectations for incoming freshmen and illustrated the department's grading standards with sample essays from the placement exams. He did not see dropping Rhetoric 100 as a punitive action, but as a recognition of the responsibility that each level of education should accept and as a reassertion of the university's proper role. Roberts thought that elementary, secondary, and university teachers and their students should benefit. "If we [English teachers] respond to the challenge, we may ultimately find greater appreciation for our efforts and a more respected and rewarded position in our American society" ("Reading, Writing Come First" 8).

Roberts also worked both regionally and nationally to improve conditions for students and teachers. From 1941 to 1949, he edited the *Illinois English Bulletin,* a journal for secondary teachers. Beginning in 1944, he devoted one issue of the *Bulletin* per year to publishing "Best High School Poetry" and "Best High School Prose," a feature that continues today.

In addition to publishing student work in the *Green Caldron*, Roberts and his colleague Leah Trelease edited *Student Prose Models* (1940), using samples of student work from Illinois Rhetoric classes. In 1949 he helped John Gerber found the Conference on College Composition and Communication and served as the editor of its journal from the first issue in 1950 until 1953. Hamilton, Moake, and Wilson claimed that Roberts "gave increased dignity and importance to the freshman writing program and to the administration of it both through his activities in this organization and his personal stature."

Roberts began teaching at the University of Illinois when he was twenty-six. His retirement letter to acting department chair Burton Milligan (25 January 1965) betrays his weariness after having run the Rhetoric program for twenty-one years. "I will be sixty-three next July 15. . . . I am taking the early retirement while we [he and his wife, Evelyn] still have enough vigor and enthusiasm to do some of the things the stern voice of duty has been denying us. . . . I would prefer to withdraw from the scene of active duty as quietly as possible. . . . Let's have no Banquo banquet now." Two and a half years later, he died. In their memorial, his colleagues stated that "with him passed an era in academic life. For that era, no better symbol of dignity, of high principle and purpose, of dedication could be found than Charles Roberts."

Douglas, Veltman, Johnson, and Roberts are quite different from one another, as are the programs they served. On a deep level, however, all four share a common subjectivity that freshman English creates for its practitioners. Susan Miller has noted the diversity of those who teach the course, yet the sameness that the ideology of "composition teaching" imposes: "When we look at the particularity of people . . . who teach composition, we may find enormous variations in their interests, education, experience, and self-images as teachers. But when we examine the ideological 'call' to create these individuals as a special form of subjectivity for composition teaching, we see them in a definitive set of imaginary relationships to their students and colleagues. Particularities are masked by an ideologically constructed identity for the teacher of composition" (123). The differences among the teaching staffs at the three schools—differences in age, experience, temperament, gender, and professional rank and ambition—did not affect the shape of the discursive practice within which they worked. They shared common presumptions.

The most pervasive was the belief discussed in my earlier chapters, "Priority" and "The Course," that freshman English existed to supply the necessary basis for all other disciplines. This belief enmeshed the faculty in a paradoxical web. They attempted to identify the linguistic, semantic, or psychological precursors to academic literacy and to invent effective pedagogies for them. The more they did so, however, the more they reinforced the tyranny of the "current-traditional" curriculum that they hoped to escape.

In the final two chapters of *The Methodical Memory* ("What's Wrong with Current-Traditional Rhetoric?" and "The Limits of Modern Epistemology"), Sharon Crowley discusses how freshman English served to muzzle both the real inventive selves of students, and the real teacherly selves of instructors. Academics supposed that because writing is "natural," anyone could do it; because of its potential power, however, it was circumscribed. "In its institutionalized form . . . writing instruction served the academy as a useful mud-fence, guarding it from the unsupervised and uncontained sprawl of self-initiated analytical or critical student discourse" (153). She presents the problem of freshman English in hero/villain dualities, i.e., classical invention vs. the controlled activity that passes for invention in a current-traditional classroom; or classical rhetoric's notion of knowledge as located in particular social, political, or economic circumstances vs. the notion of knowledge-as-commodity that limits the boundaries of allowable texts. She sums up her objections to current-traditional rhetoric in this way: "Because it standardizes and forecasts how the writing process should develop, the current-traditional theory of invention elides differences among rhetorical situations, denies the location of any rhetorical act in a given community, and transfers discursive authority away from individual rhetors and onto the academy" (167). Crowley implies that freshman composition might work were it to show students how rhetoric is not a mere "system of rules for arranging words," but a means by which "language, effectively used, can change the way people think and can move them to act." Echoing Foucauldian claims for the power of language, she envisions Rhetoric classes through which students would learn what skilled rhetoricians know—"how to invent culturally effective arguments . . . [how] to exert noncoercive control over those who don't suspect the power that is resident in language" (*Methodical Memory* 168).[2] I would maintain, however, that the peculiar shape of freshman English as a discursive practice (in "Composition's Ethic of Service," Crowley describes this discursive practice as "a nexus of power relations" [258]) renders any change in philosophy moot. No matter which content or pedagogy was inserted into the discursive practice, the results were the same. The experiences of faculty members at Wheaton, Northwestern, and Illinois bear this out.[3] Some attempted to subvert the current-traditional paradigm by introducing innovative techniques into their classrooms; however, these innovations never succeeded in enlarging freshman English beyond the marginal role it always had served.

Faculty members managed to escape freshman English in two ways. Most abandoned the subject, moving into literature, linguistics, education, or other fields; some engineered the transformation of the course into something other than a universal program of academic literacy, as at Northwestern where the university eliminated the English A requirement and introduced a new curriculum that included a variety of elective freshman seminars. Abolishing freshman English entirely—or narrowing its scope as did Illinois—did not eliminate the perception that students needed to acquire certain skills before being able to participate in true academic discourses. These kinds of reforms merely displaced the responsibility onto others—high school teachers, the staff at writing clinics, private tutors, or the students themselves. For example, after Rhetoric 100 was discontinued at Navy Pier, the Division of Rhetoric tried several approaches to forestall an increase in the failure rate in Rhetoric 101. The bookstore was asked to stock various self-help books, and a variety of tenth-grade high school textbooks and handbooks were placed on reserve in the library. Not surprisingly, these resources were not well used and did not stem the rise in failures among students taking 101.

Literary values also pervaded freshman English. Virtually all instructors of freshman English—both graduate students and regular faculty—had devoted themselves to studying literature and had received what little pedagogical training they had in a literary context. Wallace Douglas had studied Wordsworth at Harvard; for his dissertation, Charles Roberts wrote about the authorship of "Gammer Gurton's Needle"; Falk Johnson prepared his master's thesis on Poe as a critic of poetry and his dissertation on pronunciation of American English before 1850 as revealed in phonetic texts and alphabets; even Peter Veltman had written on

Milton for his MA and first intended to pursue a doctorate in English, not education. Martin Steinmann aptly describes these four men, as well as many of their fellow-teachers of freshman English: "Their studies, if they have prepared them to do anything, have prepared them to teach literature, not composition, and to do research in literary history and criticism, not in grammar and semantics and in rhetoric" ("Freshman English: A Hypothesis" 27). Besides encouraging a distaste for teaching composition or infrequently causing the course to be converted into an introduction to literature, the common literary training of most freshman English teachers brought about more pervasive effects. Teachers of freshman English conducted their classes with an Arnoldian sense of high moral purpose. At the very least, their belief in the innate value and positive moral influence of literature determined the kinds of materials they assigned and the responses they expected. Yet, far more pervasive was the emphasis on what John Heyda has called the "character building" aspects of the course. Despite the arbitrariness of its content and their lack of preparation and motivation to teach it, the instructors at Wheaton, Northwestern, and Illinois took freshman English very seriously.

Another aspect of the literary values that permeated freshman English originated in the pervasive influence of New Critical theory during the postwar era. As established in my earlier chapter, "Correspondence," nearly everyone who began teaching English after World War II accepted close reading as the technique by which they and their students could deal with texts. At Wheaton, Northwestern, and Illinois, teachers devoted extensive class time to the close reading of literary samples in the belief that by doing so their students would manage to absorb into their own writing the subtly interrelated organic unity they would discover in literature. As Colleen Aycock states, teachers had learned "to value . . . clear, coherent, graceful, and interesting prose" (156). At all three schools, a successful writer in freshman English was expected not only to produce error-free texts, but also to exhibit a style that lent itself to close reading.

Instructors at these three schools based their teaching on assigning personal essays that they scrutinized for errors. The few graded examinations and papers to be found in the archives bear comments that deal primarily with surface errors like spelling, punctuation, and standard English usage. A memo that the Senate Committee on Student English at Navy Pier sent to all members of its faculty (13 May 1957) begins:

"The first goal of student writing—in all departments—is the clear, accurate statement of facts and ideas. But we feel that it should also be
reasonably *correct* [emphasis in original], as English."[4] The memo offers
several suggestions on how to deal with poorly written work: to refuse
to grade "ungrammatical" work at all, to lower the grade, or to "criticize serious errors wherever they occur." It includes a sample of a paper
in the student's own handwriting, on which a Rhetoric teacher has cor-
rected five spelling errors, one needless repetition, one verb tense shift,
and one faulty parallel structure marked "grammar." In the right margin,
the committee has typed the comment, "Do you criticize *your* students
for the errors listed on the next page?" The next page, which contains the
reminder "to save this page and use it in marking future papers," lists
seven "frequent mechanical errors" that teachers were urged to mark:
poor penmanship, misspelling (with a suggested limit of one error per
page), comma splices, incomplete sentences, subject-verb agreement
errors, pronoun-antecedent agreement errors, and faulty verb tenses.
Wheaton and Urbana also used rigid scales of these sorts of errors, especially misspelling, to lower the marks given to a paper. Those marks,
however, were first determined by the overall "feel" of a paper, based
on the degree of organic complexity the writer revealed in dealing with
a topic.

For example, in 1959 a student in Harrison Hayford's English A10
class submitted a paper that attempts to describe her ambivalent feelings
about having taken, on the recommendation of her advisor, a course
entitled "Human Geography." Her paper reveals tension between her
accustomed behavior in front of faculty members and what she really
wants to admit: "I could tell you that I hate it, but I won't, I can't, I
musn't [*sic*]." Hayford noticed traces of the kind of personal revelation
he had been looking for in freshman papers, but could not accept its
mechanical and stylistic flaws. He commented: "This is a peculiar paper.
It comes closest of any you've written so far to being what I'm after in
honesty, tone, and personal language. At the same time it is pretty sloppy
in mechanical details of spelling and punctuation. And more important it doesn't put in the specific details. So it's both a B and an F." He
went on to request a rewrite. Reassuring the author that she need not
fear to tell the truth, Hayford commented that "the truth you tell will
be held in your favor, because writing can't be any good if it doesn't get

honest." For Hayford, as for most freshman English instructors of the era, "honesty" consisted of a writer's arranging carefully selected details so as to convey a subtle, ironic, variegated yet orderly self. The expectation of this "honesty," as well as the texts that would be able to reveal it, originates in the common background of New Criticism Hayford and many of his colleagues shared.

In addition to having come from a common literary background, teachers of freshman English assumed a painfully problematic position within the academy, what Robert Gorrell described as "the constant self-examination and the frequent despair characteristic of any gathering of teachers of freshman English" (98). Incessant concern for and attention paid to the freshman English courses at Wheaton, Northwestern, and Illinois emerge from their archival records. Departments and committees spent countless hours discussing the importance of the course, its manifold problems, and possible solutions. It would seem from this kind of evidence that a course accorded this much energy and attention would attract the most dynamic, ambitious faculty. Freshman English, however, effected a great deal of attention not because it was central to the effort of the departments of English and to the university, but precisely because it was marginal. As Sharon Crowley has put it, freshman English "literally underwrites the authenticity . . . of mainstream academic work" ("Derrida" 179). By defining the boundaries, by exorcising the unwanted, it affirmed what was of value—what it was not. The course underwent constant examination because of its irreconcilable goals. It needed to provide anything that students required to succeed in whatever kinds of literacy they would encounter, both within the academy and in rest of their lives. Yet at the same time it could not usurp the content and function of the disciplines it was meant to serve.

The men who devoted their professional lives to freshman English have commented on the conflict they felt because they had to work in the margins of their departments. In an undated statement entitled "Accomplishments," Wallace Douglas reflected, "As I think about accomplishments, I am a little dismayed by the amount of my time that has gone into writing proposals and final reports, committee and consultant meetings, and talks to teacher groups—activities which, on the whole, are not easily noticed by the scholarly, academic community. . . . Whether any of the publishing I have done would constitute accomplishments in the community's view, I am not sure." On 19 May 1953, Charles Roberts wrote to his department chair, Gordon Ray, asking to resign from the directorship of freshman Rhetoric. Although Roberts does not specify his reasons, he implies the difficulty he felt when he mentions that he had "decided against volunteering a report and a set of recommendations to the Dean and to the Senate Committee on Student English. Such a report, I fear, would become a bill of complaint, a relief to my own feelings, but would contribute little to harmony in the department." In the interview cited earlier in this chapter, Falk Johnson described his work as head of the Rhetoric department at Navy Pier as "without prestige, and without rewards, partly because it is without prestige. . . . It [teaching rhetoric] shouldn't be treated [without respect]. But it's still true. It's non-prestigious." As leaders of the largest contingent of teachers in their departments, these men exercised considerable authority and responsibility, especially Charles Roberts, who in 1953 was responsible for seventy-five Rhetoric staff members, the majority of them inexperienced graduate students. Nevertheless, they felt unappreciated and powerless. In "The Sad Women in the Basement," one chapter of *Textual Carnivals,* Susan Miller provides an explanation that matches their conflicted experience: "It [composition teaching] is an employment that in the majority of its individual cases is both demeaned by its continuing ad hoc relation to status, security, and financial rewards, yet given overwhelming authority by students, institutions, and the public, who expect even the most inexperienced composition teacher to criticize and 'correct' them in settings entirely removed from the academy. The perduring image of the composition teacher is of a figure at once powerless and sharply authoritarian" (139). Developing the image in the title of her chapter, Miller discusses how "composition teaching codes the individual of either sex as a woman." She maintains that part of the inferiority presumed of those who support freshman English is a translation of "an older social identity" of English, which was "first coded . . . as 'female' among 'hard' disciplines" (139). Miller suggests that the heavy burdens and lack of appreciation that Douglas, Johnson, and Roberts had to endure manifest traces of unacknowledged sexism.[5]

In practice, the teachers of freshman English were drawn by the tantalizing sense that just around the corner they would find something that would satisfy the impossible demands of the course. All fields experiment with pedagogy, but during the postwar era teachers attempted to use an incredible array of techniques and approaches. They were driven to experimentation partly by a belief, substantiated by apparent progress in secondary schools in the late 1950s, that the problems of freshman English could be solved. But they were also driven by desperation. As Ernest Samuels said, "It can be a desolating experience to try to teach freshmen to write." Samuels, John Gerber, Charles Roberts, and other directors of freshman English programs banded together in the early 1950s to form the Conference on College Composition and Communication, first of all because they felt a need for mutual support that came from neither their departments nor their institutions. In a letter to David Russell (6 October 1986), Douglas described why the organization began. Even though he cautions that his memory may be "faulty and prejudicial," he claims that "the outfit was founded as a meeting place for the burgeoning first-year courses in the state universities and municipal colleges. . . . Discussions in the early meetings tended to be managerial and seldom fell into pedagogy or philosophy." In his address to its 1988 convention, David Bartholomae explained that the CCCC was formed in response to two pressures: "the senior professor of literature . . . [and] the pressure of numbers" (40). The forces that gave rise to CCCC seem to have endured. As recently as 1998 one commentator, Sharon Crowley, has described CCCC as existing "in order to help its teachers manage the universally required course and to protect them from exploitation" (*Composition in the University* 253).

The course itself grew, first with the influx of returning veterans, then with the tide of students that began to inundate campuses in the mid-1950s. The corresponding increase in faculty hired to deal with these numbers increased the size of the problem. Programs for the yearly CCCC conventions during the postwar era reveal a constant search for a solution to the problem of freshman English—the communications approach, structural linguistics, clinical and empirical psychology, the rediscovery of classical rhetoric. In an interview published in 1980, Douglas confirmed that the restless search had continued. He commented on what he called the "new set of masks" that composition had assumed. "We've got rhetoric. We've got some interest in the notion of the two hemispheres of the brain. . . . I think we are going to be going off on semiology or semasiology or some variant of that collection of words. . . . Where we used to find ourselves behind grammar, sentence diagramming and things of that sort, we are now going to hide ourselves behind the mechanisms of rhetoric, the topics, questions of audience and one thing and another" ("Interview" 54). Unlike other fields, in which experts tend to consolidate knowledge before moving on to challenge the status quo, freshman English begat an eclectic organization that encouraged its members to seek out and follow new kinds of knowledge almost yearly. Except for rare calls for the abolition of freshman English itself, as Warner Rice proposed at the 1959 NCTE convention, the CCCC (which included among its early animators and contributors Ernest Samuels, Harrison Hayford, and Wallace Douglas of Northwestern, and Falk Johnson, Harris Wilson, and Charles Roberts of Illinois) did not question whether it ought to be promoting a course like freshman English.

Contemporary scholarship has tried to address that question. Some commentators, like Robert J. Connors, see the *raison d'être* of freshman English in benign terms. In his introduction to *Composition-Rhetoric,* he comments that we [those involved in the teaching of composition] need to band together by listening to our common story, because we have the opportunity to do good. He calls it "the unequaled moral power of composition studies as a college discipline. We have always thought that our mission was nothing less than to save the world" (19). Marjorie Roemer, Lucille M. Schultz, and Russell K. Durst claim: "The flexibility of this site [freshman English] has allowed us to explore so many different, context-specific options within it. . . . Not only is there not just one freshman course, but we could never wish that to be the case. To imagine uniformity is to imagine mechanized, teacher-proof programs that substitute the integrity of a set of topics for the integrity of a teacher's vision of rhetorical consciousness" ("Reframing" 386–87). Connors, Roemer, Schultz, and Durst see optimism in a course that has been trying new things for over a century. Others, like Sharon Crowley, see required freshman English in negative terms: "The universal requirement has obscured the potential of composition instruction at the college level, and it has delayed the development of composition studies as well" (*Composition in the University* 262). Richard Ohmann commented fatalistically, "I would not look to change freshman English without changing American society, too" (160).

I would not state the issue in terms of whether freshman English should be praised, modified, or abolished, but in terms of what we might come to know and do because we have examined its internal dynamics as a discursive practice. Understanding the problematic context within which freshman English, its students, and its teachers were operating during the postwar era may help us recognize—as Richard Miller suggests —our "storehouse of lived experience that necessarily includes successful strategies for navigating a bureaucratic system and ideas about ways to make the system function more efficiently, if not more humanely" (*Learning* 213).

Conclusion

ARLY IN THIS STUDY, I AN-
NOUNCED MY INTENTION TO TAKE "the representations of the practices of freshman English as a text to be 'solicited' . . . to reveal its
structure, the source of its power, and the mechanism of its durability."
The archival evidence from Northwestern, Wheaton, and Illinois has revealed a discursive practice that operates through a (mainly) tacit system
of interrelated presumptions. I have inferred these presumptions—
instrumentality, priority, efficiency, individuality, transmission, and
correspondence—from the documented words and actions of administrators, teachers, and students involved in freshman English from 1947
to 1963. This solicitation reveals with some clarity a discursive practice
whose primary traits were transparent to those involved in it at the time.
Revealing this formerly transparent structure offers many possibilities.

For those who hold with, as Nan Johnson has called it, "the expository nature of history" (Octalog 9), this study provides a scrapbook of
family memories. I have gone through the trunks in the attic and the
boxes in the basement (in some cases, literally) and, from the castoffs
and heirlooms I found there, have pieced together a collage of an era.

Especially for those who have invested themselves in the teaching of composition, it is interesting to see the pictures and read the anecdotes of our forebears in the profession. The majority of the people cited in these pages appear nowhere else in our disciplinary histories; yet, truly, the words and deeds of persons such as these constitute the basis of composition studies. Anyone conversant in the discipline ought to know about the figures profiled in the standard histories, but we should also have the opportunity to hear the voices of Wallace Douglas, Peter Veltman, Falk Johnson, and Charles Roberts, as well as their collaborators and students.

For those interested in the relationship between freshman English and the profession of English, *Practicing Writing* offers one view of the inner dynamics of composition during its predisciplinary period. In *Rhetoric and Reality,* James Berlin has discussed the same period. He chose to analyze the broad movements of the postwar era of freshman English: general education, communications studies, the founding of the Conference on College Composition and Communication, New Criticism, linguistics, and the fledgling revival of rhetoric (92–119). As my study shows, all of those forces touched the freshman English programs at Northwestern, Wheaton, and Illinois. However, something much more powerful than any of these reforms informed the practices of freshman English during this period. Berlin calls this force "current-traditional rhetoric." He comments, "For the majority of English teachers, it has been a compelling paradigm, making it impossible for them to conceive of the discipline in any other way" (*Rhetoric and Reality* 9). *Practicing Writing* reveals the interrelated beliefs and values of the discursive practice that made it so compelling. Composition and its practitioners were composed by the discursive practice itself, whose tenets were so obvious and commonsensical that they were unremarkable. Since then, composition has changed. Beginning in the early 1960s, those in the discipline (Stephen North's historians, philosophers, critics, experimentalists, clinicians, formalists, and ethnographers) have interrogated it in ways that would have been inconceivable before 1958, when "English-the-school-subject" came to be considered as "English-the-discipline" (North, *Making of Knowledge* 9). However, "English-the-school-subject" (in this study, "freshman English") was not a void upon which the spirit of the Basic Issues conferences of 1958 breathed. The discipline of composition in which many work today emerged from the predisciplinary, preinterrogation practices that *Practicing Writing* documents and analyzes.

Practicing Writing depicts freshman English as a practice-based phenomenon with a durable ideological apparatus, not a theory-based phenomenon with practical implications. In his introductory overview to *Rhetoric and Reality*, Berlin states: "In examining the variety of rhetorics that have appeared in the English departments of American colleges in the twentieth century . . . I will be concerned with the rhetorical theories that have appeared. . . . But I want also to examine the concrete classroom practices to which those theories have led" (5). In contrast, I begin with the assumption, as does Robert Connors, that freshman English did not emerge from theory, but from practice. It was "created to solve a social problem and not by the evolution of a body of knowledge" (Octalog 7–8). Given the genealogy of this site of academic activity, I think that the primary reality of freshman English lies not in rhetorical theory, but in concrete practices. I propose that a valid history of such a phenomenon would look *first* (not "also") at the classroom practices invented to address the concrete social problems, then infer the theories that inform these practices. As Jean Ferguson Carr suggests, we need to reexamine texts that we thought were "empty" or insignificant because they are so simple. "We need to rethink the notion that influence and tradition are produced in straight lines, that theories are uttered and then get 'implemented' somehow and the influence spreads down and out until it is diffused in the hinterlands" ("Rereading the Academy" 97).

Fifty years after "the birth of modern Composition, capital C" (North 15), compositionists have achieved a self-awareness of their relationship with their fellow scholars, and with the academy at large. Unlike their forebears in the 1950s, they have begun to articulate to one another the "what they do does" that Foucault claimed people often do not know (Dreyfus and Rabinow 187). Clearly, however, few outside the academy appreciate the progress that composition scholars feel that they have made. Neither do many in the larger academic community perceive what composition teachers believe they are doing. For example, in 1992 Lester Faigley commented on outsiders' perceptions of his discipline: "If current philosophical and literary theory appear in nonacademic forums only in extremely simplified and distorted form,

composition theory is almost totally unknown" (*Fragments of Rationality* 77).
We can see an example of the limited understanding of Composition in
Joan S. Stark and Lisa R. Lattuca's 1997 study, *Shaping the College Curriculum:
Academic Plans in Action*. One of their chapters, "Influence of Academic
Fields," uses English composition as an illustrative case of what they call
"symbolic communication fields." They comment, "English composition
instructors . . . believe they are engaged in teaching students a body of
skills to be learned and applied. . . . Although they may belong to a
community of scholars with respect to other courses they teach, such as
in literature, they do not see the field of composition as either an organized body of knowledge or as a group of scholars" (155). It seems that
commentators in the popular media and educational specialists outside
Composition do not understand its history as an academic subject, nor
do they appreciate the struggle of scholars to understand the intricacy
of teaching and learning academic literacy. Perhaps *Practicing Writing* can
help these observers understand the complicated bind in which composition programs and teachers must operate. Like Harrison Hayford's
student, a composition teacher could tell her critics and her colleagues
from other disciplines that "I hate it, but I won't, I can't, I mustn't."
Teachers such as Jeff Smith want to do work that they believe is valuable,
but swallow their own critical awareness and their pride to do what they
are bidden. He writes, "In general, teachers don't like seeing their work
as instrumental—as aspects or stages of a large enterprise whose aims
they can't dictate" ("Students' Goals" 315). Nevertheless, he realizes, "We
cannot secede from the rest of the curriculum. . . . I am willing . . . to
try to make what I teach *useful* [emphasis in original]" (318–19). Notwithstanding the good will of teachers such as Jeff Smith, composition is
constrained at best or denigrated at worst by those who Lester Faigley
describes as worrying whether "teachers of writing . . . [do] anything
other than teaching students the proper use of semicolons" (*Fragments of
Rationality* 77). Reflecting on the opposition to Linda Brodkey's proposed
E306 Rhetoric curriculum at the University of Texas, Sharon Crowley
commented, "It is as though the curriculum of freshman English is
owned by the community at large" (*Composition in the University* 230). In a
historical sense, freshman English *has* been "owned" by the academic
community at large (e.g., the University Senate Committee on Student
English at Illinois, or the General Faculty Committee at Northwestern),

although it has usually been abandoned at the doorstep of the English Department. I hope that *Practicing Writing* might help everyone with a stake in freshman English to understand and take appropriate action concerning what they own, but have not owned up to.

The teachers of composition in the 1950s did not have the opportunity for critical self-reflection that their successors can have, if they choose to look for it. Virtually any teacher of composition today has easy access to the insights that scholars have developed concerning the history, ideology, and best practices within the discipline. Nevertheless, in terms of what happens within classrooms every day, many still adhere to the same paradigm that their predecessors did.

In 1986 George Hillocks published his metacognitive study, *Research in Written Composition*. The studies he analyzed included thirty that dealt with writing by college freshmen (189). Hillocks concluded that research demonstrates the effectiveness—and ineffectiveness—of certain modes and foci of instruction for grades 6–13. Those modes of instruction that research showed to be more effective were the Rousseauian "natural process" and the Deweyan "environmental" methods. The least effective was the "presentational" mode, what Sharon Crowley has castigated as "full-frontal teaching." As she says, "In current-traditional pedagogy, students don't perform: teachers do" (*Methodical Memory* 147). Hillocks is gentler: "The findings indicate that the dimensions of effective instruction are quite different . . . from what is practiced in schools and colleges (the presentational mode)" (246). He also found certain foci of instruction to be ineffective: "traditional school grammar . . . teaching from models . . . [and] free writing" (248–49). The effective foci— sentence combining, the use of evaluative scales that students apply to their own and to others' writing, and inquiry methods—reflect the approach that Crowley also endorses, that of classical rhetoric. Hillocks would agree with her that effective writers learn, as do skilled rhetoricians, "how to invent culturally effective arguments. Thus they are able to exert noncoercive control over those who don't suspect the power that is resident in language" (*Methodical Memory* 168).

In 1999, with *Ways of Thinking, Ways of Teaching*, Hillocks revisited the composition classroom. He and his assistants observed and interviewed nineteen instructors of introductory composition in "a large urban community college system." He chose these teachers because he intended "to determine the extent of change in teaching practices as a result of an intensive seminar on research into the teaching of writing" (30). He found a diversity of content that he considered necessary. "Given the breadth of possibilities for inclusion in a writing course, selection is a necessity: no teacher could include everything possible" (116). Nevertheless, the case studies he presents reveal little change from the presentational methods he discredited thirteen years earlier. He gives examples such as Professor Danziger, who teaches students to improve their writing by including absolute phrases and by eliminating their use of passive voice; Professor Dobbs, who emulates successful athletic coaches by dictating lengthy passages that students must copy verbatim, and by drilling them in mechanics; or Professor Rose, who teaches the five-paragraph essay. Over two years of observation, Hillocks found that more than 70 percent of instructional time was given over to delivering declarative knowledge. In transcripts of classes, 89 percent of the lines reflected teacher talk. Less than 5 percent of classroom time was devoted to generating ideas, or even to generating rhetorical forms (41). He comments, "For most teachers in the sample, teaching is an act of telling, as though they are able to transfuse their ideas directly into the minds of students. And when the ideas do not hold, it is simply that students have not applied themselves to the task of learning what was put forward for them to learn" (93). In his concluding section he comments, "The cluster of knowledge that the teacher garners over a career appears to remain stable. . . . It may be that understanding teacher knowledge will permit greater change. After teaching in various institutions for over 40 years, [however,] I can remember witnessing few dramatic changes." Hillocks notes that "this is not a very optimistic view of teacher knowledge," but he remains hopeful that if teachers could change their attitudes or epistemological stance, they could bring about improvement in the teaching of writing (125).

In "The Teacher," I offered examples of two ways in which the experience of teaching freshman English was evaluated in the postwar era: global assessments of teaching practices, and personal anecdotes about the vicissitudes of teaching the course. If Hillocks's two studies together represent a relatively current general assessment of the state of teaching practices, then Lad Tobin's *Writing Relationships: What Really Happens in the Composition Class* offers the extended personal anecdote of an enlightened teacher attempting to make sense of his classroom experience. At one point, Tobin relates the experience of reading a bowdlerized version of *Snow White* that one of his daughter's friends had brought to a sleep-over. The little girl's mother had scratched out all the phrases in the fable that conveyed brutality or harshness and had replaced them with euphemisms. Tobin surmises: "We in the process movement have written our own basalized story of our classroom. . . . The enemy is traditional teaching and teachers [i.e., current-traditional teaching], the heroes are—well, *we* are the heroes. The only problem is that . . . this happy talk does not match the pictures and does not reflect much of what happens in our classrooms or the way we actually feel about our day-to-day teaching" (143–44).

Tobin analyzes his own classroom experiences, his office conferences, and even conversations with his fellow-teachers in order to explore the connection among the relationships between teachers and students, students and students, and teachers and other teachers. He attempts to tease out the complex dynamics of "product, process, and control" he observes there. As he puts it, "the real question is, how can writing teachers shape these [classroom] relationships to make the writing and reading processes productive for students and for themselves?" (16). He presumes that these processes are malleable, and that teachers can make them become more productive. Just as Hillocks hopes that deeper knowledge about effective teaching will bring about change in "the culture of teaching writing" (50), so Tobin hopes that understanding the "writing relationships" he alludes to in his title will allow the process movement to transform the teaching of composition. He admits, though, that actual practices rarely match the theoretical promises. "As soon as we stop talking about idealized classrooms and start talking about our students and ourselves, we are forced to confront the tension, competition, misunderstanding, frustration, resistance, and disappointment that are inevitable aspects not only of the writing process but also of the relationships that are established within the writing class" (145). Both George Hillocks and Lad Tobin are enlightened observers of the actual practices in contemporary composition classrooms. Both desire, deeply, that teachers and students of composition succeed in achieving the goals James Berlin holds out for writing instruction: "In short, the writing course empowers students as it advises in ways to experience themselves, others, and the material conditions of their existence—in methods of ordering and making sense of these relationships" (*Rhetoric and Reality* 189). The conclusions I draw from both, however, suggest that in the years since the birth of Composition, capital C, the practical experience of teachers and students in "the first-year course" (no longer "freshman English") is not all that different, for all the fine talk, from that of the 1950s.

What can we conclude, then, from this "solicitation" of the practices of freshman English? First, I am tremendously impressed by the course's elasticity and by its tenacity. It has survived through the tumultuous second half of the twentieth century and shows no signs of losing its contentiousness or its vitality. Second, I am convinced that the "problem" of freshman English cannot be "solved" by manipulating one or another of its variables, as was attempted during the postwar era at Northwestern, Wheaton, and Illinois. It is a weblike phenomenon. Participants in the discursive practice adhere—usually tacitly—to presumptions that take on the quality of articles of faith:

1. Academic literacy is based on a fundamental and general set of skills.
2. This set of skills must be acquired prior to participating in the specific discourses of the academy.
3. The best methodology for inculcating these skills has not yet been discovered, but will be.
4. As a person acquires these skills, his or her true self becomes more clearly defined.
5. The texts that represent this body of skills convey essential values.
6. A person must learn a proper way of reading so as to perceive the true value of such representative texts as well as the value of the texts a person produces.

As in a creed, each of these tenets requires the acceptance of all the others. Reforming any one requires reforming all of them and would generate a different discourse that would be a not-freshman-English. Rejecting any one means rejecting all. It would seem to me that this structure accounted for the resiliency of freshman English during the postwar era and may account for it now.

A "solicitation" such as the one I have attempted to perform in *Practicing Writing* should reveal not only the structure of this discursive practice, but the source of its power, and the mechanism of its durability as well. Those who dealt with freshman English in the 1950s tried to shake its structure in a variety of ways, but could not rearrange or modify its essential nature. No one was able to find a way to dissolve it, except for Northwestern. Even then, the discursive practice did not disappear, but moved into another location. At various times in its history, leaders in Composition have called for the abolition of freshman English, from Warner Rice's "A Proposal for the Abolition of Freshman English, as It Is Now Commonly Taught, from the College Curriculum" in 1960 to Sharon Crowley's "A Personal Essay on Freshman English" in 1990.[1] Nevertheless, as Crowley herself points out at the beginning of her recent (1998) study, *Composition in the University,* "The student body of freshman composition comprises all but the very few members of each year's entering class who manage to get out of the requirement as well as the students at the dozen or so elite private universities that do not impose one" (1). I do not see fissures in the structure of freshman English that can be widened so as to make it crumble. Freshman English derives its power from popular and academic notions of literacy, and I do not see those changing soon. Lynn Z. Bloom connects the course with middle-class American values: "The middle-class pedagogical model, replete with Franklinesque virtues, has remained normative and dominant from the emergence of composition as a college course in the late nineteenth century to the present" ("Freshman Composition" 658). In the same vein, Richard Ohmann reiterates in his 1996 edition of *English in America* what he first observed in 1976: "I no longer think that we could collectively make our writing about writing and our teaching of it, larger in spirit by internal reform. . . . I no longer see freshman composition as *perversely* confining. Its thinness is socially useful. I would not look to change freshman English as a whole without changing American society too" (*English in America* 159–60).

Ohmann's connection between freshman English and American society and its capitalistic culture suggests topics for further exploration beyond the scope of *Practicing Writing,* but related to issues that it raises. In "Individuality," I cited Lester Faigley's question, "Why [are] . . . college writing courses . . . prevalent in the United States and rare in the rest of the world?" ("Competing Theories of Process" 539). *Practicing Writing* documents overt connections between freshman English and the promotion of democratic ideals in the postwar era, but the course seems to reflect in a deeper way the individuality and egalitarianism that typify life in the United States. Ohmann's "Freshman English and Administered Thought," one chapter of *English in America,* and Wallace Douglas's "Rhetoric for the Meritocracy" in the same volume connect freshman English with the North American economic and political agenda; but neither compares freshman English with written composition as an academic subject in other cultures. Freshman English reflects the culture of the United States in obvious ways: it includes a large, diverse population; it claims to provide access to power and status for anyone willing to work hard; it sees its goal as a practical problem to be solved expediently. Examining these as well as the more subtle connections between the course and national culture might reveal provocative insights about both. One way to begin this kind of examination would be to compare the development of academic literacy in the United States with the process in another English-speaking country that has a similar culture, such as Australia. Another would be to compare freshman English in the United States with its counterpart in another country that has a similarly large, diverse, economically mobile population, such as Brazil.

Practicing Writing raises another set of issues related to the structure of the discursive practice that constitutes freshman English. First, this study might be used as a model for interrogating the history of courses in other disciplines, especially those that serve instrumental purposes. Although freshman English is the most ubiquitous of general education requirements, large numbers of students also are required to take introductory courses in mathematics, the social sciences, the natural sciences, the humanities, and languages other than English. What structures might a solicitation of the practical experiences of these courses reveal, and what might that tell us about the "what they do does" of disciplines other than English, and of the academy as a whole? Second, I do claim that freshman English has a distinct structure as discursive practice in the predisciplinary period I have explored here. I suspect that this structure accounts for the durability of the course over the last fifty years, but I do not claim to have demonstrated that. Composition scholarship and practice alike have changed since the 1950s. At the end of *Rhetoric and Reality,* Berlin discusses the principal influences on Composition after 1975: poststructuralist literary and cultural criticism, expressionistic and epistemic rhetorics, classical rhetorics, and cognitive studies of the composing process (183–86). In his introduction to the 1996 edition of *English in America,* Ohmann sees multiculturalism —African-American studies, Chicano studies, queer studies, women's studies—as the dominant new issue in Composition (1). I would add the impact of electronic media to Berlin's and Ohmann's lists. Without doubt, these influences combined with four decades of disciplinary status have affected freshman English. Studies such as George Hillocks's and Lad Tobin's suggest, however, that the discursive practice that constitutes postmodern Composition may share the same presumptions as did freshman English in the 1950s. Despite all of our reflection and analysis, what remains transparent to us today? It would be provocative to study archives from the 1980s, for example, to see what they might reveal.

Some composition scholars invest the freshman English class with tremendous significance. Susan Jarratt, for example, sees the importance of the course and its history in these terms: "When a history changes the way writers behave in the classroom (both instructor and student) in ways that allow for the recognition of inequity and oppression; that give voice to silence; that create the means for just action, as well as open negotiation over what constitutes 'justice'—then that history is a good one" (Octalog 45). The outcomes Jarratt sees as coming from a good history, which in turn activates the potential of the classroom, are monumental. They include nothing less than the defeat of the forces of oppression and the creation of an open, equitable, free, just society. James Berlin outlines the value of the course in more personal, but no less significant, terms. "Although . . . [composition] courses have . . . undergone periodic assaults from teachers, administrators, and students, they remain one of the few permanent features of the college curriculum. The freshman writing course has somehow managed to prove itself indispensable to a student's education. While there are, doubtless, numerous and complicated reasons for this fact, one obvious explanation is that the student's ability to use language effectively is perhaps the single most important result of a college education" (*Writing Instruction* 85).

For Berlin, the freshman course is nothing less than the cornerstone of the university itself, and of the knowledge that students acquire there.

I would contrast Berlin's and Jarratt's opinions with Lynn Z. Bloom's. She ascribes the course's resiliency to its intimate connection with the middle-class values upon which the United States is based. She recognizes the course's ubiquity, but sees its value quite differently: "One of the major though not necessarily acknowledged reasons that freshman composition is in many schools the only course required of all students is that it promulgates the middle-class values that are thought to be essential to the proper functioning of students in the academy. . . . Like swimmers passing through the chlorine footbath en route to plunging into the pool, students must first be disinfected in Freshman English" ("Freshman Composition" 656). *Practicing Writing*, in a way, validates both points of view. It shows how the course was invested with tremendous significance for the individual student, for the university, and for society as a whole. It shows how freshman English withstood many "periodic assaults." The course has demonstrated the ability to absorb and neutralize nearly any attack or modification and still retain its shape as a discursive practice. It also shows the course as a scapegoat for faculty and students alike. Having a particular vision, or desire, or sense of possibility, or sense of scorn for the phenomenon of freshman English does not mean that we can transform it into what we would have it be. "What really happens in the composition class" is both far less than what the scholars and—especially—the practitioners may realize, and far more. Our individual words and actions are generated by and absorbed by the discursive practice; but those same words and actions permit the discursive practice to endure.

For my fellow-practitioners of composition, this study suggests the true value of our day-to-day experience. Some, I think, romanticize the events that occur within the classroom. Patricia Harkin, for example, notes that some teachers "think of teaching as a site or moment when we are free, behind closed doors, to be eclectic, to ignore recognized procedures, to do what needs to be done, . . . to escape the panoptic gaze of the disciplines for a silent, secret moment of postdisciplinary knowledge" ("Postdisciplinary Politics of Lore" 138). To my way of thinking, however, no one who operates within a discursive practice (such as composition teachers) can "escape the panoptic gaze of the disciplines." Rather than being under the surveillance of a disciplinary gaze that can be evaded by shutting the door, I would say that we are "written" by the discursive practice in which we are participating. We do not "use" the discipline so much as the practices of the discipline use us. This does not mean, however, that our words and actions in the classroom have no value. On the contrary, I maintain that the discursive practice of freshman English *consists in* what we say and do.

Without doubt, freshman English would cease if no one agreed to teach it. For the past 130 years, however, many men and women have agreed, some enthusiastically, to do so. What other single course has generated its own professional organization? The Conference on College Composition and Communication has grown from John Gerber's session, "Three Views of Required English," at the 1948 NCTE convention in Chicago to an international organization with more than 10,000 members and its own annual convention.[2] Something about freshman English compels interest and commitment. It has compelled me, as I mentioned in the introduction, to try to perceive what gave shape to my classroom experience. What I have come to understand is this: the "problem" of freshman English does not respond to theoretical or practical solutions. Freshman English is not a problem to be solved, but a problematic event. We cannot find a solution, but we can choose an approach. In "A Comprehensive Unity: Response to Chiara Lubich, Dr. Ed. honoris causa," David L. Schindler alludes to Michel Foucault in his assertion: "The order of things—of all things, analogically understood—lies most profoundly, not in relations of power among entities but the 'powerless' beauty of giving and receiving" (23–24). Those of us who practice freshman English touch on one aspect of the order of things that Schindler refers to. Despite—or better, because of—the frustrating powerlessness that defines the experience of students and teachers in freshman English, we experience something fulfilling and attractive. In "A Doctorate in Education," the address that Schindler was responding to, Chiara Lubich describes the force that compels the best practices in this course, and in many others: "Every authentic educational approach includes a utopian thrust, that is, a guiding principle which stimulates people to build together a world which is not yet a reality, but ought to be" (14). To participate in freshman English is to enter a utopia in both senses of the word: etymologically, it is an academic "no-place"; yet symbolically, it contains the hoped-for perfection that authentic teachers may never reach, but are compelled to seek.

Notes

Introduction

Personal communication from Michel Foucault, cited by Hubert L. Dreyfus and Paul Rabinow in *Michel Foucault: Beyond Structuralism and Hermeneutics,* 187.

1. John Brereton mentions Nan Johnson and Sharon Crowley in his preface as examples of historians writing since 1970 whose approaches privilege theory over practice. I would include other familiar names as well: Albert Kitzhaber, James Berlin. Brereton's most recent book, *The Origins of Composition Studies in the American College, 1875–1925,* calls for attention to the actual practices and products associated with writing instruction. David Russell's *Writing in the Academic Disciplines, 1870–1990* approaches the history of composition from a different angle than the rest (writing instruction outside the English department). Russell does incorporate much practical material from colleges and universities throughout the nation.

2. Program descriptions and syllabi can be a deceptive source. Albert Kitzhaber notes in *Themes, Theories, and Therapies:* "What actually goes on in the classroom usually has some relation to the syllabus but in varying degrees, depending on the closeness of supervision and on the predilections of the individual teacher" (9). Susan Miller comments dryly, "There are, of course, many slips between the cup of program descriptions and the lips of the majority of teachers and students" (*Textual Carnivals* 105).

3. Brereton has noted this limitation in Berlin's methodology. In his review of *Rhetoric and Reality,* in the November 1991 issue of *College English,* Brereton comments: "And a limitation of Berlin's decision to stick so close to the 'official' journals is that we miss a sense of what student writing looked like, how exam questions read, what textbooks covered, and how composition fared in its ongoing struggle for a place within English studies" (828).

4. In his introduction to *Composition-Rhetoric: Backgrounds, Theory, and Pedagogy,* Robert Connors also takes exception to the "current-traditional" label, first coined by Richard Young in 1978. He comments: "What we have reified as a unified 'current-traditional rhetoric' is, in reality, not a unified or an unchanging phenomenon. . . . Since, therefore, the methods and theories associated with teaching writing in America after 1800 are neither changeless, nor unified, not seriously 'current' in today's scholarly field, not strongly related to traditional rhetoric, I propose to eschew the term 'current-traditional

rhetoric' and to refer instead to older and newer forms of composition-rhetoric" (5-6).

5. Connors names the era from 1910 to 1960 the "modern period," a time marked by lack of scholarly research and a domination of textbooks as "absolute arbiters of classroom content and practice" (*Composition-Rhetoric* 15). He sees roots of the revitalization of composition-rhetoric in three developments from the 1940s: the communications movement in general education, the rise of New Criticism as a dominant scholarly apparatus, and the expansion of graduate schools due to the influx of students under the GI Bill (204).

6. Other schools evidently followed the same practice that Stiker did at Lewis College. "Syllabus for English 102 (1965 Version)" from Loyola University in Chicago contains the following heading: "Ultimate Disposition of all Written Work. All of the written assignments, both exercises and themes, must ultimately be *returned to the teacher* [emphasis in original] at a time designated by him—to be destroyed at the end of the course." Students were required to relinquish their papers so as to discourage plagiarism; but from a perspective outside the context of the course, this requirement calls attention to one of the many paradoxes of freshman English. The course was cited as the most important in the department, if not in the university, and students were urged to approach the work they did in their freshman English classes with utmost seriousness. Nevertheless, the integral historical traces of what happened in the course—the very texts through which students demonstrated that they had achieved the goals of the course—were systematically destroyed.

"One may well ask," notes Richard Miller, "why on earth should that material have been preserved? It is a reasonable question." Besides exemplifying the paradoxical marginality of the course, Miller sees in the lack of samples of student work "another trace of the belief that 'the student' functions as a transhistorical subject whose work remains everywhere and in every way the same. . . . Such a question may just be another way of saying that student work warrants as little attention as one can get away giving it" (*Learning* 45). I discuss the identity (or, better, *non*identity) of freshman English students in "The Student."

Federal law in the United States has unwittingly contributed to the difficulty that historians might face in uncovering archival evidence. The 1974 Federal Education Rights and Privacy Act (FERPA) states: "The parent or eligible student [i.e., one over eighteen] shall provide a signed and dated written consent before an educational agency or institution discloses personally identifiable information from the student's educational records." According to some archivists, such as David B. Malone at Wheaton and Patrick Quinn at Northwestern, this regulation may make it illegal for them to make student papers available, even if they had them, unless the student has provided written permission to do so.

7. Illinois has already replaced its seal with a stylish logo "as elegant and memorable as the Nike swoosh" ("Tradition at the University of Illinois" 2). Northwestern has tried to change its seal as well, but the traditionalist senti-

ment that created the classical seal to begin with forestalled this change. In February 2001, Alan Cubbage, Vice President for University Relations at Northwestern, announced that his office had accepted the advice of a marketing firm to cut back on the seal's use and substitute a more modern-looking logo. He was quoted as saying in the *Daily Northwestern:* "It's somewhat old-fashioned. It's this wonderful old Methodist heritage that really doesn't have anything to do with the university right now" (Talcott 2). Four months later, a chastened Cubbage announced that "there really is a lot of affection and affinity toward (the seal). Some of the elements in it are very old-fashioned, but at the same time people had an affection for those elements" (Talcott and Murtaugh 1). One student, however, made a comment that suggests a less affectionate reason for retaining the seal. Sejal Shah said, "The seal looks Ivy League-ish. It shows that we're an institute of higher education and learning" (2). Evidently John Evans's comment about saving money by sending his children to Northwestern instead of Yale or Harvard still holds true.

8. I harbor no pretensions that this small study adds appreciably to the Foucauldian enterprise. Despite its importance as a subject in American schools from elementary to college levels, I think that composition does not wield the level of power in society as do the practices Michel Foucault chooses to analyze in *The Order of Things*—economics, biology, and linguistics; or those of his subsequent investigations—medicine, insanity, the penal system, or sexuality. Nevertheless, reading Foucault has to some degree inspired the structure of this study. I use the term "discursive practice," as does Sharon Crowley, to name the system of rules (usually tacit) that determines what counts as meaningful in a given discipline during a particular milieu. For example, during the postwar era, some kinds of controversial reading material, including articles from pulp magazines, drugstore novels, or comic books, were excluded from freshman English. Other kinds of controversial reading material, books by Saul Alinsky, Franz Boas, W. E. B. DuBois, and Benito Mussolini, were included. Within the discursive practice of freshman English at that time, the former group of texts was irrelevant to the political and social ideology students were expected to absorb from their reading and so display in their writing. The latter group, although they contradicted prevailing political views, provided material with which students could represent themselves as politically and socially astute, a relevant self-construct in postwar America.

9. For example, in the foreword to *Rhetoric and Reality* Donald Stewart criticizes those who cling to their own nonhistorical notions of the role of the English department, calling them "anachronisms, impeding the work of an English department with a broad and deep perspective on its past and a comprehensive view of its structure and mission in the years to come" (xi). Susan Miller concludes *Textual Carnivals* with these words: "Those who teach and conduct research about limited, initiative writing are inevitably implicated in limited, initiative roles. But they also have alternatives in rethinking their images of the students they teach" (201). Sharon Crowley describes the value of *The Methodical Memory* for practitioners in these terms: "When teachers are not

allowed access to alternative theoretical and pedagogical models, it is difficult even to know that alternatives exist" (xii). Certainly, enlightened teachers are better teachers. I believe, however, that within the discursive practice of freshman English, individual perspectives, thoughts, and choices of pedagogical models have less overall effect than we might imagine. In the last three chapters and in the conclusion, I discuss this resistance to change.

Chapter 1

1. Henry Giroux uses the term "instrumental ideology" to name the positivistic influence in social studies based on "the assumption that there is a unitary scientific method which recognizes no distinction between the physical world and the human world" (*Theory and Resistance* 210). I use the term in a less political fashion, although I readily admit that the reduction of academic literacy to a single course has strong political implications.

2. Other commentators from the 1950s saw the salvation of democracy not in the power of personal expression, as did Oliver, but in the wisdom to be gained from studying the humanities, especially literature. For example, in *Composition in the University,* Sharon Crowley notes that in 1957 Natalie Calderwood suggested that horrors like nuclear disaster would occur because "the mediators are either ignorant or defiant of the universal certainties—the truths in all human experience" (107). Calderwood's humanistic orientation reflects an issue that Berlin and Crowley claim was the hallmark of composition in the 1950s—the debate between the value of communications versus the value of literature. In "Transmission" I deal with that issue at length.

3. For example, in the early 1950s, DePaul University offered a special communications course within its College of Commerce (cf. Ward). Clyde Kilby, chair of the Department of English at Wheaton, frequently mentioned the program at Juniata College, the alma mater of his colleague Paul Bechtel. At Juniata, students did not take freshman English as such, but were taught rhetorical principles in the context of their major course work. Preceptorial systems, such as those at Knox College, the University of Chicago, and Alexander Meiklejohn's program at Minnesota (which the Department of General Studies at Illinois imitated) sought to present the liberal arts in a unified fashion, at least during the first year or two of a student's higher education. But these programs are the exceptions; sometimes—as in the case of DGS at Illinois and many other interdisciplinary "communications" courses—they proved to be short lived, or they have been maintained as an emblem of a determination to provide an alternative to the usual offerings in higher education.

David Russell discusses progressive programs, including Meiklejohn's (*Writing in the Academic Disciplines* 224–28). In *Rhetoric and Reality,* James Berlin discusses communications programs at the State University of Iowa and the University of Denver (97–104). Berlin sounds a sanguine note about such programs: "The communications course encouraged a fresh and worthy set of ideas in composition and finally made a substantial contribution to the development of writing instruction in colleges." Yet, he notes that "their decline was inevitable [due to] the threat they posed to departmental autonomy and academic specialization" (104). I would interpret the decline of communication programs as a result, at least in part, of their difference from "normal" freshman English. Because they did not fit within what Henry Giroux calls the "instrumental ideology" of English, the institutions let them die out.

4. In *Theory and Resistance in Education,* Giroux analyzes "three basic ideologies that characterize the various approaches to literacy." One of them, instrumental ideology, ties literacy to the culture of scientific positivism (209–10).

5. Charles Roberts took notes on this article and filed them with miscellaneous reports and notices he kept for the University Senate Committee on Student English. David Russell points out that Campbell had studied under Barrett Wendell, who subscribed to the notion that the great books would save democracy from devolving into "a caricature of government." Campbell, echoing his teacher, claimed that "the success of the democratic state . . . [lay] in cultivating the sensitivity of the individual" (quoted in *Writing* 170). In 1939 Campbell anticipates the function of freshman English as an instrument of post–World War II democracy.

6. In 1964 the campus moved to a permanent site, then called "Chicago Circle" after its location near the juncture of three interstate highways. Today, it is known as the University of Illinois at Chicago. During the 1950s the Chicago Undergraduate Division was commonly referred to as "Navy Pier." That is the name I will use in general references to events and practices at the Chicago Undergraduate Division.

7. Although the committee existed on paper, it seems to have functioned for the most part as an administrative gesture that the College of Liberal Arts cared about students' literacy beyond freshman year. In a letter to Dean Simeon Leland (18 December 1953), Fred Faverty relayed Frank Fetter's concern about weak writing. Faverty comments, "I recommended that he [Fetter] submit these papers because I thought that in a period of three years our committee should have at least some piece of evidence on English as used by upperclassmen." In another letter to the dean (16 September 1959) Wallace Douglas, with typical sarcasm, accepted Leland's offer to serve on the committee: "The Committee on the Students' Use of English. That's one of the really choice committees, unless you decide that we should have a meeting. I'll be glad to serve." The Northwestern University Archives contain no records of the work of this committee.

8. Connors does see, however, some light during what he construes as the dreary post–World War II era: "Some of the later developments in the culture of composition-rhetoric . . . are not so dark" (*Composition-Rhetoric* 203). In the postwar era he finds the beginnings of ferment that led to the reforms of 1963 and after. Commentators during the postwar era, however, described the status of composition professionals much as Campbell did a decade earlier.

9. In *Composition-Rhetoric,* Connors provides historical perspective on this phenomenon. He connects the increase in numbers of graduate students in American universities beginning in the 1890s with the rise of the freshman composition course (195–202).

10. A number of commentators have made this observation, including Martin Steinmann, Richard Lloyd-Jones in his brief biography of Richard Braddock (cf. Brereton, *Traditions*), Adolphus J. Bryan, and Robert Connors. Connors traces the history of composition instructors as indentured servants back to the turn of the century. "Thus, very early in the creation of the modern university system, was born the tradition—still, sadly with us today—of graduate students and young faculty members 'voting with their feet' against composition and in favor of teaching literature" (*Composition-Rhetoric* 197).

Chapter 2

1. In "Transmission" I discuss the relationship between composition and literature. Berlin sees the preference for literature as content in the composition course arising shortly after the turn of the century, as articulated by proponents of the rhetoric of liberal culture (*Rhetoric and Reality* 43–46). Robert Connors sees the first use of literary topics during the same era, between 1885 and 1910, a period that he designates "Consolidation Composition-Rhetoric." Students used the content of literature as material for practicing the "modes." He comments, "Literary assignments provided a way out of the world of personal writing that many found uncomfortable and were uncertain about the purpose of" (*Composition-Rhetoric* 325).

2. In *Composition in the University*, Sharon Crowley lists, in historical order, the multiple purposes that the first-year course has been expected to accomplish. "It has been argued that students should be required to study composition in order to develop taste, to improve their grasp of formal and mechanical correctness, to become liberally educated, to prepare for jobs or professions, to develop their personalities, to become able citizens of a democracy, to become skilled communicators, to develop skill in textual analysis, to become critical thinkers, to establish their personal voices, to master the composing process, to master the composition of discourses used within academic disciplines, and to become oppositional critics of their culture" (6). Her list sums up many of the functions this study analyzes in more depth, particularly, Instrumentality (liberal education, career preparation, democratic citizenship), Individuality (personality and voice), Transmission (taste), and Correspondence (textual analysis). The more recent additions, for example, academic discourse analysis and cultural criticism, to the agenda of the first-year course continue a pattern that has been part of freshman English since its inception.

Chapter 3

1. In *Rhetoric and Reality* (111–15), Berlin discusses the effect of structural linguistics, in particular the work of Harry R. Warfel, during the 1950s. Connors (*Composition-Rhetoric* 162–70) presents more detail, in particular the work of Charles Fries.

2. Charles Roberts and the rhetoric staff at Illinois followed in the footsteps of their colleagues at the turn of the nineteenth century. John Brereton notes in his discussion of the first composition program at Harvard: "In the early 1870s . . . Harvard . . . began to prod its preparatory schools about improving their writing instruction" (*Origins* 27). Connors notes the same phenomenon twenty years later. In the wake of the Harvard Reports of the 1890s, "The most notable college teachers of rhetoric . . . cried out for deliverance by some sort of secondary school *deus ex pedagogia*" (*Composition-Rhetoric* 131).

Chapter 4

1. See chap. 7 of Connors's *Composition-Rhetoric,* "Invention and Assignments in Composition-Rhetoric," for a thorough discussion of the practical considerations that led writing teachers away from classical rhetoric, and toward romantic rhetoric.

2. One of the participants at this workshop was Willie Nell Love, a member of the Department of Humanities and an instructor of freshman English at Navy Pier.

3. In her article, "The Question Concerning Invention: Hermeneutics and the Genesis of Writing" (1988), Lynn Worsham provides a similar answer to Faigley's question by considering writing as part of what Heidegger considered to be the identifying mark of modern existence—the dominance of technology. "Writing and writing instruction have become just another realm in which scientific and technological thinking manage Being by providing models and metalanguages that contain the event of writing and render it available as a means to achieve various ends, chief among them are self-actualization and knowledge, democracy and economic prosperity" (216). Sharon Crowley offers another explanation. In *The Methodical Memory,* she notes the irony inherent in current-traditional invention. On the one hand, a principal goal of current-traditional rhetoric was "putting the bones and sinews of writing on public display for everyone's potential appropriation"; classical rhetoric, on the other hand, presumed "that a writer's authority depended to some extent upon her reputation in the community" (150). Current-traditional rhetoric stripped all power of invention away from student writers; therefore, freshman English offers the illusion of participation in democratic public discourse, but sanitizes and encapsulates the statements students might make. I discuss this point further in "The Course," where I analyze the function of reading lists used in freshman English classes at the University of Illinois.

4. This syllabus is dated 1960, but Falk Johnson, the director of Composition at that time, said that these syllabi were produced every year. They varied only slightly to reflect choices of the new textbooks or other modifications in the surface features of the course. Their substance remained the same.

5. This stylebook was distributed free to all first-year students in all colleges. The story of this publication itself reveals a great deal about the function of the rhetoric course on the campus. The Committee published the

Stylebook after polling the faculty and finding substantial interest in providing a guide to correct English for all students at the university, no matter what curriculum they might be pursuing. But as Jessie Howard, executive secretary of the committee, noted in "Background Material to the Study of Faculty Cooperation in the Improvement of Student English": "Ever since its publication interest in the *Stylebook* has been almost nonexistent, in spite of every effort by the Committee to stimulate it" (7).

6. Indeed, a historian and critic as astute as Sharon Crowley claims "that the point of composition is to express oneself" (*Composition in the University* 14). But in the context of a "course [that] is universally required" (15), this phrase assumes a paradoxical tone.

7. In *Composition-Rhetoric,* Connors discusses how Buffon's aphorism reflects a monist influence in midcentury writing instruction. Because style was perceived as one aspect of texts that had organic unity, no separate canon of style could exist. Style emerged from all aspects of writing, as idiosyncratic to a particular text as a personality is to an individual (282).

8. As Connors points out, the medieval origin of the word, the Latin *plagiarius,* suggests kidnapping (*Composition-Rhetoric* 321, n. 8). It is interesting that the etymology used in this Wheaton document, which goes back one step further to the original Greek, makes the act of plagiarism seem less "vicious." Certainly man-stealing would be considered more depraved than merely being underhanded or oblique.

9. The language of the *Manual and Calendar* echoes the rules for moral perfection that Franklin enumerates in his *Autobiography.* In "Freshman Composition as a Middle-Class Enterprise," Lynn Z. Bloom discusses the Franklinesque middle-class values that suffuse the pedagogy and content of freshman English. One of the qualities she perceives in the course is "self-reliance, responsibility." A corollary of self-reliance is the injunction against plagiarism. "From sea to shining sea, as promulgated by American colleges and universities, the cardinal sin of plagiarism is a heinous affront to the middle-class value of honesty, manifested in respect for others' property" (659).

10. Here, too, Bloom perceives concealed middle-class values—"Respectability ('middle-class morality')"—in the self to be represented in the texts produced in freshman English classrooms. She cites two authors who discuss freshman English as a "contact zone"—Mary Louise Pratt ("Arts of the Contact Zone," *Profession 91* [New York: MLA, 1991]: 33–40), and Richard Miller ("Fault Lines in the Contact Zone," *College English* 56 [April 1994]: 389–408). "No matter what kinds of writing assignments we give, as middle-class teachers we expect freshman papers—on whatever subject—to fall within the realm of normative discourse in subject, point of view, values implied. By and large, we get what we expect. But when we receive a paper that incorporates what Mary Louise Pratt calls 'unsolicited oppositional discourse, parody, resistance, critique' and—intentionally or unwittingly—transgresses these normative boundaries, we go to pieces. In the social space of the classroom, which Pratt defines as a 'contact zone, where cultures meet, clash, and grapple with

each other, often in contexts of highly asymmetrical relations of power,' as Richard Miller points out in 'Fault Lines in the Contact Zone,' we are ill prepared to deal with alien topics or points of view that are, say, racist, misogynistic, sadistic, or otherwise debased or debasing. Our initial, middle-class impulse is to suppress the topic, to punish or try to rehabilitate the author, or to deliberately overlook the paper's attempt to wreak havoc in the contact zone" (659–60). Professor Bone of Wheaton or Charles Roberts of Illinois did not use the language of literary criticism ("oppositional discourse," "contact zone") as do Bloom, Pratt, and Miller. In the 1950s as well as in the 1990s, however, it appears that teachers of freshman English felt the squeeze between the stated expectation of "individuality" in students' work and the requirement that individuality be constructed according to a tacit system of rules.

11. In the fall 1988 *Rhetoric Review*, Donald Stewart discusses the connotations of the word "collaborator," especially for anyone who was aware of events during World War II. Stewart writes, "*collaborator* is a word which was relatively innocuous before the war, obscene during and after it" (66).

12. The director of freshman English at Minnesota, Martin Steinmann, and his staff published this handbook, *Themes and Exercises,* yearly from 1956 to 1962. It contained theme assignments, sample themes, and various appendices on composition issues including outlining, paragraphing, note taking, and types of essays. It also included study questions for literary selections required in the freshman courses and a schedule of reading assignments and lectures. *Themes and Exercises* was required in the fourteen different freshman English courses offered at Minnesota.

Chapter 5

1. In "Ministering to a Mind Diseased," a chapter in *As If Learning Mattered,* Richard Miller discusses the difference between the image of Arnold as the prophet leading a band of "apostles of equality" and his actual experience as an inspector of schools during much of his professional life. Miller uses Arnold as an archetype of "a disciplinary disinclination to consider how rarely the business of critique has a demonstrable impact on the work that students, teachers, and inspectors actually do in and for the schools" (53). Miller's close reading of what Arnold actually said and did during much of his career resembles what I am trying to do in this study with the experience of practitioners of freshman English.

2. Crowley claims that interest in the function of literature in composition classes during the 1950s increased in response to the threat that communications might replace literature in required first-year courses (*Composition in the University* 22).

3. Saalbach's sentiments reflect the "brahminical romanticism" Berlin cites as having arisen in the 1920s. "Most proponents . . . favored class distinctions and aspired to the status of an educated aristocracy of leadership and privilege" (*Rhetoric and Reality* 45).

4. For a thorough discussion of the history of the textbook as it applies to freshman English, consult Robert Connors's *Composition-Rhetoric*, chap. 2 ("Shaping Tools: Textbooks and the Development of Composition-Rhetoric"). Especially interesting to those concerned with the post–World War II era is his thorough analysis of James McCrimmon's *Writing with a Purpose*.

5. See Connors, again, for a discussion of *Harbrace*. Debra Hawhee also analyzes this textbook in a Foucauldian manner, pointing out how "handbooks write the discipline; and . . . they discipline the writer" ("Composition History" 504).

Chapter 6

1. One decade later, Wellek found that New Criticism "has, no doubt, reached a point of exhaustion." Brooks as well, in 1962, decried New Criticism's decline into an ossified routine. Graff comments, "With remarkable speed, the fortunes of the New Criticism in the university had gone from rags to riches to routine." He uses this example to opine that such pedagogical problems are not "technical matters to be worked out at the level of the individual course" but issues that reflect the very structure of academic institutions themselves (226–27). What Graff sees in the life cycle of New Criticism reflects what I am trying to demonstrate about the position of freshman English within the postwar academy. The solutions to most pedagogical problems were thought to be local issues, to be solved by adopting new textbooks or enacting new policies. The problem of freshman English, however, is *structural*, not pedagogical. Graff, of course, suggests that the solution to the problem he sees in literary studies is to foreground the "cultural text." I see a problem with this strategy in the teaching of composition. As Jeff Smith has pointed out, composition has certain ethical obligations to its clients. "I don't think it's fair to students to whipsaw them between the curriculum's values and my own. . . . I want what I teach to be good not just for people, not even just for citizens, but for future doctors and lawyers and organic chemistry majors. I am willing . . . to try to make what I teach *useful*" ("Students' Goals" 318–19).

2. Several other historians have noted the connection between New Criticism and composition during the postwar era. James Berlin comments that New Criticism, a politically safe way of addressing literature in the McCarthy era, served to "unify the diverse factions within the English department" (*Rhetoric and Reality* 107). Unified around a common critical apparatus, the English department moved to base the composition course as well "around what it knew best—the literary text" (108).

As noted earlier, Robert Connors sees three phenomena in the late 1940s that together changed the face of English as a discipline. Connors calls New Criticism "a species of rhetorical criticism" and notes that during the postwar era, "communications pedagogy and New Critical theory were everywhere discussed" among the young, new professoriat that developed following the war (*Composition Rhetoric* 204–5).

Citing William Cain, Sharon Crowley notes how New Criticism has become so much a part of the way of looking at texts (both student as well as literary) that it has achieved what David Russell calls "transparency." Crowley comments, "Since many teachers of writing were trained to be teachers of literature, and have no training in composition at all, it is only natural to transfer the set of assumptions made about texts in new criticism into their teaching of composition" (*A Teacher's Introduction to Deconstruction* 26–27).

3. Winterowd was her advisor on this dissertation.

4. In the same vein, Susan Miller comments in *Textual Carnivals:* "Over the period from 1920 to 1960, we see both an enormous variety of writing courses and their leveling into the generic forms that replaced them as New Critical literary principles became entrenched after World War II" (67).

5. In discussing freshman English during the postwar era, Berlin also connects the study of literature from a New Critical point of view with the development of individuality. He writes, "Literature was offered as the subject matter of the composition course because it was seen as preserving the integrity of the individual against the tyranny of the mob. . . . [It] was seen as serving the individual and acting as a safeguard against collectivist notions that might threaten the ideal of 'rugged individualism on the plane of the spirit' and, finally, on the plane of politics" (*Rhetoric and Reality* 109–11).

6. In *Composition-Rhetoric,* Connors discusses how Rorabacher's text—which he claims was popular at the time—illustrates the abandonment of the modes of narration, description, and argumentation in favor of exposition (238).

Chapter 7

1. For a thorough discussion of how classical rhetoric, especially invention, came to be reduced to exposition and argument, see Sharon Crowley's *Methodical Memory,* especially chap. 6, "EDNA Takes Over: The Modes of Discourse" (96–119). Also useful is Robert Connors's *Composition-Rhetoric,* especially chap. 7, "Invention and Assignments in Composition-Rhetoric" (296–327).

2. The *Manual and Calendar* from 1949 devotes a paragraph to the "Spelling Test." Students had to earn a score of 90 or face possible failure in the course. *Standards in Freshman Rhetoric at the University of Illinois* (1956) states under "Course Rules and Requirements" that a spelling test would be administered during the last week of the semester. Students had to earn at least a score of 80; "Failure to make this grade will lower your semester grade one letter, even to the point of failure in the course" (1). The penalties for spelling had softened slightly over the course of seven years, but had not been eliminated.

3. These "Guidelines" specify what qualities (or deficits) cause a paper to receive a particular grade, as well as the penalty to be imposed for "weaknesses" such as sentence errors, misspellings, errors in agreement, incorrect verb forms, poor penmanship, and the like. A copy from Robert Warburton's files at Wheaton and another from the files of Falk Johnson at Navy Pier are virtually identical (except for minor changes in nomenclature—Urbana used

E instead of F to indicate failure) to "Standards for Judging Freshman Rhetoric Written Work" in *Standards in Freshman Rhetoric at the University of Illinois* (1956). The influence of Charles Roberts's program at Urbana evidently reached across the state.

4. Debra Hawhee notes the military-style syntax of the instructions to students in the *Harbrace College Handbook*. "Once students learn the Harbrace codes and the required action, they have been effectively trained, and they respond automatically, obeying the sharp orders found in the beginning of the handbook" (517).

5. Little was done to ascertain the opinions of students in freshman English programs. Of all the studies and proposals made at Wheaton, Northwestern, and Illinois, none mentions having attempted to ascertain what students thought of the course. Even broader national studies such as Gorrell's and Kitzhaber's look at the course solely from the point of view of the teacher or administrator.

6. In a related but not identical idea, Jeff Smith openly acknowledges the course's "gatekeeping" function. The thought that a teacher's livelihood might serve merely instrumental ends is distasteful. "In general, teachers don't like seeing their work as instrumental—as aspects of stages of a larger enterprise whose aims they can't dictate. They don't like to see themselves as means to others' ends. . . . Yet that shouldn't really be so painful. Even the noblest human efforts are usually means to others' ends" (315). Smith frankly accepts the terms imposed by an instrumental course. At the conclusion of *Composition in the University,* Sharon Crowley recognizes the same limits, but draws different conclusions. She states, "I wonder why we think that our professional interests are served by continuing to speak discourses that are imposed upon us, hierarchical and exclusive as they are" (262).

7. Concerning Linda Brodkey's infamous E306 syllabus at the University of Texas, Sharon Crowley also enunciates reasons for the failure of attempts at reform of freshman composition: "Because of the universally required course and its unique function within the academic imaginary, composition studies is still associated with composition's earliest and most familiar pedagogy: the pedagogy of grammar, spelling, punctuation, and formal fluency. Because of this association, composition is regarded as instrumental or remedial work" (*Composition in the University* 256).

Chapter 8

1. See "The Role of Mechanics in Writing" in "Individuality"; "The Color of Red" in "Transmission"; "First Impressions" in "Transmission"; "Mr. Pseudoscorpionida Shares His Knowledge" in "The Course"; "The Advantages of Being a Hermit" in "The Course."

2. In *Textual Carnivals,* Susan Miller analyzes the ubiquitous "you" found in textbooks. On the surface, it appears to be "a pedagogue's direct personal friendliness" (89). But that breezy appellation masks a subjectivity imposed

upon students. Modifying Terry Eagleton's description of a literary subject to apply to a composition student, Miller points out that the "you" masks a "required subjectivity" that is used "to regulate and map individuals" (90). Although the student assumes that he or she is independent and free, in fact the student has become an object of an evaluative system. Referring to Foucault's "The Examination," in his *Discipline and Punish,* Susan Miller claims that "these instruments [records and grades] make a person an object of scrutiny who may be more or less 'normal'. . . with the result that a person is particularized in relation to a standard or 'norm' of health or achievement" (90).

3. See "Individuality," for a discussion of plagiarism, especially Connors's explanation of the connection between personal writing, research papers, and plagiarism.

Chapter 9

1. In 1952 Ken Macrorie published "World's Best Directions Writer," and eight years later he followed that article with "Writing's Dying." Both feature a dialogue between "Ed Zybrowski," who represents the new wave of emphasis on functional communications, and "George," who reiterates a more traditional notion of literacy. Like Rinehart, Macrorie's character invests freshman English with profound significance.

2. In "Composition's Ethic of Service," one chapter of *Composition in the University,* Crowley calls for a careful examination of the "discourse of student need" as a legitimizing term for freshman English. She sums up her suggestions for moving composition out of its instrumental position in the academy: "There is a place for composition in the university, and that place does not depend upon Freshman English" (265).

3. Compare the experience of teachers such as Curtis Dahl and Roger Shuy at Wheaton; Falk Johnson, Andrew Schiller, Willis Jackman, and Arthur Greenwald at Navy Pier; and Wallace Douglas and Harrison Hayford at Northwestern. These teachers and their attempts at change are recounted in "The Course."

4. In "Rhetoric for the Meritocracy," Wallace Douglas cites Leon Renfrew Meadows's 1928 dissertation on the teaching of composition in teachers' colleges. Meadows notes in his conclusions: "Independent thinking and clear, forceful, correct expression were strongly emphasized by our early teachers and writers in the field of composition" (97). Douglas comments wryly, "Accuracy in mechanical matters, a more or less specialized means of expression, and some evidence of originality, imagination, or independence in thinking . . . I suppose most English teachers today would agree that these about exhaust the aims they set for students" (98).

5. Of the individuals discussed in this chapter, Peter Veltman appears to have been least bound by the strictures of freshman English. It provided him an entree to academia, and then a point of departure into administration. He escaped the "perduring image of the composition teacher" (*Textual Carni-*

vals 139) that marked the personal and professional lives of Douglas, Johnson, and Roberts. Interestingly enough, of the three schools in this study, Wheaton, with its strongly traditional Christian identity, would seem to be the most patriarchal; yet it has the longest institutional tradition of affirming women. From the very beginning, Jonathan Blanchard considered the education of women a focus of his college. Perhaps Blanchard's open advocacy for the rights of women a century before Veltman's time created an ongoing atmosphere of tolerance that allowed him to avoid the sexist opprobrium implicit in freshman English, whereas the others mentioned in this chapter could not.

Conclusion

1. In his "Conclusion and Postscript on the Present," the last chapter of *Rhetoric and Reality*, James Berlin mentions six different calls for the abolition of freshman English between 1960, when Rice published his article, and 1973, when Ron Smith published "The Composition Requirement Today: A Report on the Nationwide Survey of Four-Year Colleges and Universities." Berlin concludes this section: "Smith's prognosis, like all other predictions of the demise of the freshman writing course, proved to be inaccurate" (180–82).

2. David Bartholomae offers a thumbnail version of the origins of the Conference on College Composition and Communication (CCCC) in "Freshman English, Composition, and CCCC," the text of his chair's address to the 1988 CCCC in St. Louis. Nancy Bird's dissertation, "The Conference on College Composition and Communication: A Historical Study of Its Continuing Education and Professionalization Activities" (Virginia Polytechnic University, 1977), offers a more thorough history.

Works Cited

Applebee, Arthur N. *Tradition and Reform in the Teaching of English: A History*. Urbana: NCTE, 1974.

"Appointment Questionnaire," 3 February 1943. Peter Veltman Records, Wheaton College (Ill.) Archives.

Arnold, Matthew. *Culture and Anarchy*. Ann Arbor: University of Michigan Press, 1965. Vol. 5 of *Complete Prose Works of Matthew Arnold*. Ed. R. H. Super. 11 Vols. 1960–77.

Aycock, Colleen Kay. "New Critical Rhetoric and Composition." Diss. University of Southern California, 1985.

Bailey, Dudley. "The Obvious Content of Freshman English." *College Composition and Communication* 9 (1958): 231–35.

Bailey, H. W. Memo to A. D. Pickett, 22 November 1960. University Archives, University of Illinois at Chicago.

———. Memo to Deans R. P Hackett, J. O. Jones, A. D. Pickett, and F. W. Trezise, 22 November 1960. University Archives, University of Illinois at Chicago.

Barker, Nicholas P., et al. *Themes and Exercises*. 6th ed. Minneapolis: University of Minnesota Department of English, 1962.

Bartholomae, David. "Freshman English, Composition, and CCCC." *College Composition and Communication* 40 (1989): 38–50.

Bechtel, Paul M. *Wheaton College: A Heritage Remembered 1860–1984*. Wheaton: Harold Shaw, 1984.

Berkhout, Helen. "The Role of Mechanics in Writing." *Pier Glass* 8 (1962): 14–15. University Archives, University of Illinois at Chicago.

Berlin, James A. *Rhetoric and Reality: Writing Instruction in American Colleges, 1900–1985*. Carbondale: Southern Illinois University Press, 1987.

———. *Writing Instruction in Nineteenth-Century American Colleges*. Carbondale: Southern Illinois University Press, 1984.

———. "Writing Instruction in School and College English, 1890–1985." In James V. Murphy, ed. *A Short History of Writing Instruction, from Ancient Greece to Twentieth-Century America*. Davis, Ca.: Hermagoras Press, 1990. 183–220.

Bloom, Lynn Z. "Freshman Composition as a Middle-Class Enterprise." *College English* 58 (1996): 654–75.

Bowen, Robert O. "The Purpose and Content of Freshman English Composition." *College Composition and Communication* 8 (1957): 109–11.

Bowersox, Herman C. "The Idea of the Freshman Composition Course—A Polemical Discussion." *College Composition and Communication* 6 (1955): 38–44.

Brereton, John C., ed. *The Origins of Composition Studies in the American College, 1875–1925: A Documentary History.* Pittsburgh: University of Pittsburgh Press, 1995.

———. "Review: Learning Who We Are." *College English* 53 (1991): 826–30.

———. *Traditions of Inquiry.* New York: Oxford University Press, 1985.

Bryan, Adolphus J. "The Problem of Freshman English in the University." *College Composition and Communication* 2 (1951): 6–8.

Bushman, John C., and Ernst G. Mathews, eds. *Readings for College English.* New York: American Book, 1951.

Callahan, Raymond. *Education and the Cult of Efficiency.* Chicago: University of Chicago Press, 1962.

Campbell, Oscar James. "The Failure of Freshman English." *English Journal, College Edition* 28 (1939): 177–85.

Carr, Jean Ferguson. "Rereading the Academy as Worldly Text." *College Composition and Communication* 45 (1994): 93–97.

Carver, Ron. "The Need for the Study of the Great Books." *Green Caldron* (October 1950): 1–3. University of Illinois at Urbana-Champaign Archives.

———. "The Menace of Television." *Green Caldron* (May 1950): 31. University of Illinois at Urbana-Champaign Archives.

A Community of Scholars: New Approaches to Undergraduate Education at Northwestern. Evanston: Northwestern University, 1968.

Connolly, Francis. *A Rhetoric Case Book.* New York: Harcourt, Brace, 1953.

Connors, Robert J. *Composition-Rhetoric: Backgrounds, Theory, and Pedagogy.* Pittsburgh: University of Pittsburgh Press, 1997.

———. "Personal Writing Assignments." *College Composition and Communication* 38 (1987): 166–83.

———. "Rhetorical History as a Component of Composition Studies." *Rhetoric Review* 7 (1989): 230–40.

"'Creeping Kindergartenism' Infects Schools, U.I. Professor Charges." *Champaign-Urbana Courier* 6 April 1958: 26.

Crowley, Sharon. *Composition in the University: Historical and Polemical Essays.* Pittsburgh: University of Pittsburgh Press, 1998.

———. "Derrida, Deconstruction, and Our Scene of Teaching." *Pre/Text* 8 (1987): 169–83.

———. *The Methodical Memory: Invention in Current-Traditional Rhetoric.* Carbondale: Southern Illinois University Press, 1990.

———. *A Teacher's Introduction to Deconstruction.* Urbana, Ill.: National Council of Teachers of English, 1989.

Dahl, Curtis. "Composition Through World Literature." *CEA Critic* 16 (May 1954): 2.

Douglas, Wallace. "Accidental Institution: On the Origin of Modern Language Study." *Criticism in the University.* Eds. Gerald Graff and Reginald Gibbons. Evanston: Northwestern University Press, 1985. 35–61.

———. "Accomplishments" n.d. Wallace Douglas Files, Northwestern University Archives.

———. Letter to David Russel, 6 October 1986. Wallace Douglas Files, Northwestern University Archives.

———. Letter to Dean Simeon Leland, 16 September 1959. Wallace Douglas Files, Northwestern University Archives.

———. Memo to Jean Hagstrum, 15 May 1973. Wallace Douglas Files, Northwestern University Archives.

———. Memo to Jean Hagstrum, 17 September 1973. Wallace Douglas Files, Northwestern University Archives.

———. Letter to author, 30 July 1988.

———. "Rhetoric for the Meritocracy," in Richard M. Ohmann, *English in America: A Radical View of the Profession*. New York: Oxford University Press, 1976. 97–132.

———. *Wordsworth: The Construction of a Personality*. Kent, Ohio: Kent State University Press, 1968.

Dreyfus, Hubert L. and Paul Rabinow. *Michel Foucault: Beyond Structuralism and Hermeneutics*, 2nd ed. Chicago: University of Chicago Press, 1982.

Dunstan, J. Leslie, ed. *Protestantism*. New York: George Braziller, 1962.

Dykema, Karl W. "The Problem of Freshman English in the Liberal Arts College." *College Composition and Communication* 3 (1951): 3–5.

Ebert, Roger, ed. *An Illini Century: One Hundred Years of Campus Life*. Urbana, Ill.: Board of Trustees of the University of Illinois, 1967.

Eckert, Charles W. "The Advantages of Being a Hermit." *Green Caldron* (March 1949): 11–13. University of Illinois at Urbana-Champaign Archives.

Edman, V. R. "Statement Concerning Peter Veltman," 22 August 1955. Peter Veltman Records, Wheaton College (Ill.) Archives.

Elder, Franklin. "An Example Paragraph." *Pier Glass* 8 (Spring 1962): 16. University Archives, University of Illinois at Chicago.

Elliot, Elisabeth. *Through Gates of Splendor*. Wheaton, Ill.: Tyndale House, 1956.

English A Analyst (1947). Northwestern University Archives.

"English A10-3 Final Examination," 10 June 1958. Wallace Douglas Files. Northwestern University Archives.

"English Composition Committee Report," 15 May 1973. Wallace Douglas Files. Northwestern University Archives.

"The English in this Paper is Unacceptable" [Checklist], 1956. English Department Records, Wheaton College (Ill.) Archives.

"English Qualifying Exam" (1951, 1953, 1958, 1960). University of Illinois at Urbana-Champaign Archives. 4/2/23, Box 5.

"English Teachers May be Extinct by 1955: Roberts." *Champaign-Urbana Courier* 12 November 1953: 12.

"The Evaluation of My Paragraphs." Student essay, 1959. Harrison Hayford Files. Northwestern University Archives.

Fadenrecht, John H. Letter to Dean Oswald Tippo, 16 March 1955. Peter Veltman Records, Wheaton College (Ill.) Archives.

Faigley, Lester W. "Competing Theories of Process: A Critique and a Proposal." *College English* 48 (1986): 527–39.

———. *Fragments of Rationality: Postmodernism and the Subject of Composition*. Pittsburgh: University of Pittsburgh Press, 1992.

———. "The Study of Writing and the Study of Language." *Rhetoric Review* 7 (1989): 240–56.

Faverty, Fred. Letter to Dean Simeon Leland, 18 December 1953. Northwestern University Archives.

———. Report to Dean Simeon Leland, 28 June 1953. Northwestern University Archives.

Fetter, Frank W. Memo to Fred Faverty, 18 December 1953. Northwestern University Archives.

"Final Examination, English A10," 1958. Wallace Douglas Files, Northwestern University Archives.

Foucault, Michel. *Discipline and Punish*. Trans. Alan Sheridan. New York: Random-Vintage, 1977.

Fox, Donald Lee. "Steinbeck and Brotherhood." *Green Caldron* (October 1960): 9–11. University of Illinois at Urbana-Champaign Archives.

Freedman, Nathan. "A Door Was Opened." *Pier Glass* 6 (1959): 8–10. University Archives, University of Illinois at Chicago.

"Freshman Composition Courses in Twelve Illinois Colleges." *Illinois English Bulletin* 39 (1951): 1–23.

General Faculty Committee of Northwestern University. "Memo to All Faculty," May 1950. Northwestern University Archives.

George, Diana, and John Trimbur. "The Communications Battle, or Whatever Happened to the 4th C?" *College Composition and Communication* 50 (1999): 682–98.

Gerber, John C. "The Conference on College Composition and Communication." *College Composition and Communication* 1 (1950): 12.

Giller, Dorothy. "Oh, Jesus, Help Me!" *Pier Glass* (Fall 1956): 2–5. University Archives, University of Illinois at Chicago.

Giroux, Henry. *Theory and Resistance in Education: A Pedagogy for the Opposition*. Exeter, N.H.: Heinemann, 1983.

Goldberg, Leon M. "The American Acquistion of Isthmian Canal Rights." *Pier Glass* 7 (Spring 1961): 25–27. University Archives, University of Illinois at Chicago.

Gorrell, Robert M. "Freshman Composition." *The College Teaching of English*. Eds. John C. Gerber, et al. New York: Appleton-Century Crofts, 1965. 91–114.

Graff, Gerald. *Professing Literature: An Institutional History*. Chicago: University of Chicago Press, 1987.

———. "The University and the Prevention of Culture." *Criticism in the University*. Eds. Gerald Graff and Reginald Gibbons. Evanston: Northwestern University Press, 1985. 62–82.

Grant, James F. "Doubt Gets You an Education." *Green Caldron* (October 1948): 17. University of Illinois at Urbana-Champaign Archives.

"Guidelines for Grading Compositions," 4 October 1968. English Department Records, Wheaton College (Ill.) Archives.

Guth, Hans. "Rhetoric and the Quest for Certainty." *College English* 24 (1962): 131–36.

——. *The Wadsworth Manual: A Guide for Teachers of Composition.* Belmont Ca.: Wadsworth, 1965.

Hagstrum, Jean. Annual report to Dean Simeon E. Leland, 12 June 1961. Northwestern University Archives.

——. Memo to Dean Simeon E. Leland, 1 February 1963. Northwestern University Archives.

——. Remarks at Memorial Service for Wallace Douglas, 25 April 1995.

——. Telephone conversation with author, 9 February 1989.

——. Teaching notes for English A 10-2, Fall 1956. Northwestern University Archives.

Hansen, Chadwick. Letter to author, 28 April 1988.

Harkin, Patricia. "The Postdisciplinary Politics of Lore." In *Contending with Words: Composition and Rhetoric in a Postmodern Age.* Patricia Harkin and John Schilb, eds. New York: Modern Language Association, 1991. 124–38.

Hart, John A., Robert C. Slack, and Neal Woodruff, Jr. "Literature in the Composition Course." *College Composition and Communication* 10 (1958): 236–41.

Harvard Committee. *General Education in a Free Society.* Cambridge: Harvard University Press, 1945.

Hawhee, Debra. "Composition History and *The Harbrace College Handbook.*" *College Composition and Communication* 50 (1999): 504–23.

Hayford, Harrison. "Literature in English A at Northwestern." *College Composition and Communication* 7 (1956): 42–45.

——, and Howard P. Vincent, eds. *Reader and Writer.* Boston: Houghton Mifflin, 1954.

——. Conversation with author, 2 March 1989.

——. "Wally Douglas Memorial—25 April 1995." Wallace Douglas Files, Northwestern University Archives.

Heyda, John Francis. "Captive Audiences: Composition Pedagogy, The Liberal Arts Curriculum, and the Rise of Mass Higher Education." Diss. University of Pittsburgh, 1979. Ann Arbor: UMI, 1981. 7924660.

Hillocks, George. *Research on Written Composition.* Urbana: National Conference on Research in English, 1986.

——. *Ways of Thinking, Ways of Teaching.* New York: Teachers College Press, 1999.

Hodges, John C. *Harbrace College Handbook.* 3rd. ed. New York: Harcourt, Brace, 1951.

——, with Mary E. Whitten. *Harbrace College Handbook.* 5th ed. New York: Harcourt, Brace, and World, 1962.

"Human Geography." Student essay, 1959. Harrison Hayford Files, Northwestern University Archives.

"An Interview with Wallace Douglas." *The Gypsy Scholar: A Graduate Forum for Literary Criticism* 7 (Summer 1980): 53–62.

Johnson, Falk. Conversation with author, 18 October 1988.

Johnson, Henry C., Jr. and Irwin V. Johanningmeier. *Teachers for the Prairie: The University of Illinois and the Schools, 1868–1945*. Urbana: University of Illinois Press, 1972.

Johnson, Mark. "The Color of Red." *Green Caldron* (March 1961): 11–12. University of Illinois at Urbana-Champaign Archives.

Keeton, Morris, and Conrad Hilberry. *Struggle and Promise: A Future for Colleges*. New York: McGraw-Hill, 1969.

Keys, Barbara. "Evolution: Its Growth and Acceptance through Controversy." *Pier Glass* 8 (Spring 1962): 6–12. University Archives, University of Illinois at Chicago.

Kitzhaber, Albert R. Letter to Wallace Douglas, 13 March 1961. Wallace Douglas Files, Northwestern University Archives.

———. *Rhetoric in American Colleges, 1850–1900*. Dallas: Southern Methodist University Press, 1990.

———. *Themes, Theories, and Therapy: The Teaching of Writing in College*. New York: McGraw-Hill, 1963.

Lamar, Wilmer A., and Ruth E. McGugan. "The Rhetoric Program at the University of Illinois: A Research Study," 1965. University of Illinois at Urbana-Champaign Archives. 4/2/23, Box 3.

Lubich, Chiara. "A Doctorate in Education." *New Humanity Review* 5 (2001): 5–16.

Macrorie, Ken. "World's Best Directions Writer." *College English* 13 (1952): 275–79.

———. "Writing's Dying." *College Composition and Communication* 11 (1960): 206–10.

Marcus, Jane Connor. Remarks at Memorial Service for Wallace Douglas, 25 April 1995. Wallace Douglas Files, Northwestern University Archives.

Martin, Harold C., and Richard M. Ohmann. *Inquiry and Expression: A College Reader*. New York: Holt, Rinehart, and Winston, 1961.

"Materials, Devices, Attitudes in the Composition Course: The Report of Workshop No. 3." *College Composition and Communication* 2 (1951): 3–5.

Mathews, Ernst G. Letter to H. W. Bailey, 13 November 1946. University of Illinois at Urbana-Champaign Archives. 4/2/23, Box 4.

———. "Student English—An All-University Problem." *University of Illinois Faculty Bulletin* (April 1949): n.p. University of Illinois at Urbana-Champaign Archives.

Mathieson, Margaret. *The Preachers of Culture: A Study of English and its Teachers*. Towata N.J.: Rowan and Littlefield, 1975.

Matlaw, Myron, and James Stronks, eds. *Pro and Con*. Boston: Houghton Mifflin, 1960.

McCully, Ed. "Alexander Hamilton" Student manuscript for a speech, n.d. Wheaton College (Ill.) Archives.

"Memorial to Charles Walter Roberts," n.d. Morgue File for Charles W. Roberts. University of Illinois at Urbana-Champaign Archives.

Mersand, Joseph. *Attitudes Toward English Teaching*. Philadelphia: Chilton, 1961.

Miles, Libby. "Review: Disturbing Practices: Toward Institutional Change in Composition Scholarship and Pedagogy." *College English* 62 (2000): 756–65.

Miller, Ethelreda, and Edwin Joew, eds. *It Takes All Kinds.* Handmade book of student essays and stories, 1952. University Archives, University of Illinois at Chicago.

Miller, Lynne. "The Surrealists." *Pier Glass* 9 (Fall 1962): 7–12. University Archives, University of Illinois at Chicago.

Miller, Richard E. *As If Learning Mattered.* Ithaca, N.Y.: Cornell University Press, 1998.

——. "Composing English Studies: Toward a Social History of the Discipline." *College Composition and Communication* 45 (1994): 164–79.

——. "Fault Lines in the Contact Zone." *College English* 56 (April 1994): 389–408.

Miller, Susan. *Textual Carnivals: The Politics of Composition.* Carbondale, Ill.; Southern Illinois University Press, 1991.

Mindell, Howard. "The Inefficiency of Rhetoric." *Green Caldron* (April 1956): 21–23. University of Illinois at Urbana-Champaign Archives.

Minutes, 7 November 1955. English Department Records, Wheaton College (Ill.) Archives.

Minutes, 20 May 1955. English Department Records, Wheaton College (Ill.) Archives.

Minutes, 8 September 1955. English Department Records, Wheaton College (Ill.) Archives.

Minutes, 26 April 1960. English Department Records, Wheaton College (Ill.) Archives.

Minutes, 29 November 1960. English Department Records, Wheaton College (Ill.) Archives.

"Minutes of the Faculty of the College of Liberal Arts," 10 December 1935. Northwestern University Archives.

"My Special Day." English Qualifying Exam, 13 April 1961. University of Illinois at Urbana-Champaign Archives. 4/2/23, Box 8.

"My Troubles—Bitter Words." English Qualifying Exam, 29 November 1951. University of Illinois at Urbana-Champaign Archives. 4/2/23, Box 8.

Myers, Greg. "Reality, Consensus, and Reform in the Rhetoric of Composition Teaching." *College English* 48 (1986): 154–74.

Nelson, Earnest F. "My Trip Through Hate." *Green Caldron* (March 1947): 1–2. University of Illinois at Urbana-Champaign Archives.

North, Stephen M. *The Making of Knowledge in Composition: Portrait of an Emerging Field.* Upper Montclair N.J.: Boynton/Cook, 1987.

Northwestern University Bulletin. 28 April 1947. Evanston: Northwestern University, 1947.

——. 20 December 1948. Evanston: Northwestern University, 1948.

——. 14 March 1955. Evanston: Northwestern University, 1955.

"Northwestern University Identity System." http://www.northwestern.edu/logo/logo.html. 5 August 2002.

"Objectives in General Education." n.d. English Department Records, University of Illinois at Chicago.

Octalog. "The Politics of Historiography." *Rhetoric Review* 7 (1988): 5–49.

Ohmann, Richard M. *English in America: A Radical View of the Profession.* New York: Oxford University Press, 1976/1996.

Oliver, Kenneth. "The One-Legged, Wingless Bird of Freshman English." *College Composition and Communication* 1 (1950): 3–6.

Osema, Shirley. "Biblical Versions and Translations." *Pier Glass* 8 (Fall 1961): 12–16. University Archives, University of Illinois at Chicago.

Parker, William Riley. "Where Do English Departments Come From?" *The Writing Teacher's Sourcebook.* Eds. Gary Tate and Edward P. J. Corbett. New York: Oxford University Press, 1988. 3–15.

Perkins, Margaret P. "Rhetoric and I." *Green Caldron* (March 1955): 7–9. University of Illinois at Urbana-Champaign Archives.

Perrin, Porter G. *An Index to English: A Handbook of Current Usage and Style.* Chicago: Scott, Foresman, 1939.

———. "The Remedial Racket." *English Journal* 22 (1933): 382–88.

Perrine, Laurence. *Sound and Sense: An Introduction to Poetry.* 2nd ed. New York: Harcourt, Brace, and World, 1963.

Peters, Marie H. "Mr. Pseudoscorpionida Shares His Knowledge." *Pier Glass* 3 (1956): 2–4. University Archives, University of Illinois at Chicago.

"Plagiarism and Other Dishonest Practices," 1960. Mimeographed. English Department Records, Wheaton College (Ill.) Archives.

Potthof, Edward F. "The Program for Improving Students' Use of English at the University of Illinois." *College English* 7 (1945): 158–63.

Pratt, Mary Louise. "Arts of the Contact Zone." *Profession 91* (New York: MLA, 1991): 33–40.

Pridmore, Jay. *Northwestern University: Celebrating 150 Years.* Evanston, Ill.: Northwestern University Press, 2000.

"Professional Biographical Data," Handwritten questionnaire, 4 October 1959. Peter Veltman Records, Wheaton College (Ill.) Archives.

"Proposals for Writing 111 and 112," 1957. Mimeographed. English Department Records, Wheaton College (Ill.) Archives.

"Reading, Writing Come First." *Champaign-Urbana Courier* 28 April 1958: 8.

"Reliving and Remembering." Student essay, 1953. Harrison Hayford Files, Northwestern University Archives.

"Report of the English Composition Committee," 1973. Northwestern University Archives.

"Resources for an Evaluation Study," 1968. Mimeographed. English Department Records, Wheaton College (Ill.) Archives.

Rice, Warner. "A Proposal for the Abolition of Freshman English as It Is Now Commonly Taught, from the College Curriculum." *College English* 21 (1960): 361–67.

Riddle, Donald W. Memo to Senate Committee on Student English, 9 March 1960. University Archives, University of Illinois at Chicago.

Rinehart, Keith. "Teaching Freshman Composition." *College English* 13 (1951): 450–54.

Roberts, Charles W. "A Course for Training Rhetoric Teachers at the University of Illinois." *College Composition and Communication* 6 (1955): 190–94.

———. *Freshman Rhetoric Manual and Calendar for 1948–49*. Urbana: University of Illinois, 1948.

———. *Freshman Rhetoric Manual and Calendar*. Urbana: University of Illinois, 1949.

———. *Freshman Rhetoric Manual and Calendar*. Urbana: University of Illinois, 1950.

———. *Freshman Rhetoric Manual and Calendar: 1953–54*. Urbana: University of Illinois, 1953.

———. *Freshman Rhetoric Manual and Calendar: 1956*. Urbana: University of Illinois, 1956.

———. Letter to Burton Milligan, 25 January 1965. Charles W. Roberts File, English Department, University of Illinois at Urbana-Champaign.

———. Letter to Gordon Ray, 19 May 1953. Charles W. Roberts File, English Department, University of Illinois at Urbana-Champaign.

———. "The Unprepared Student at the University of Illinois." *College Composition and Communication* 7 (1957): 95–100.

"Roberts 'Just Marking Time.'" *Champaign-Urbana Courier* 9 June 1954: 8.

Roemer, Marjorie, Lucille M. Schultz, and Russell K. Durst. "Reframing the Great Debate on First-Year Writing." *College Composition and Communication* 50 (1999) 377–92.

Rorabacher, Louise E. *Assignments in Exposition*. New York: Harper and Brothers, 1946.

Rose, Mike. "The Language of Exclusion: Writing Instruction at the University." *College English* 47 (1985) 341–59.

Rudolph, Frederick. *Curriculum: A History of the American Undergraduate Course of Study Since 1636*. San Francisco: Jossey-Bass, 1978.

Russell, David R. Letter to author, 12 October 1988.

———. *Writing in the Academic Disciplines, 1870–1990: A Curricular History*. Carbondale, Ill.: Southern Illinois University Press, 1991.

Ryan, Michael. *Marxism and Deconstruction: A Critical Articulation*. Baltimore: Johns Hopkins University Press, 1982.

Said, Edward W. "Traveling Theory." In *The World, the Text, and the Critic*. Cambridge, Mass.: Harvard University Press, 1983. 226–47.

Samuels, Ernest. Telephone conversation with author, 2 February 1988.

Saxon, Wolfgang. "Wallace Douglas, 80, Expert on Romantic Poets." *New York Times* 7 February 1995, late ed.: B10.

Schindler, David. "A Comprehensive Unity: Response to Chiara Lubich, D. Ed., Honoris Causa." *New Humanity Review* 5 (2001): 20–25.

Schultz, Samuel. "Education for Citizenship." *Faculty Bulletin of Wheaton College* (November 1955): n.p. Wheaton College (Ill.) Archives.

Senate Committee on Educational Policy. "Report to the Senate, April 17, 1941." University of Illinois at Urbana-Champaign Archives. 4/2/23, Box 1.

Senate Committee on Student English. Annual Report, 1953–1954. University Archives, University of Illinois at Chicago.

——. Memo to All Faculty, 4 April 1963. University Archives, University of Illinois at Chicago.

——. Memo to All Members of the Faculty, 13 May 1957. University Archives, University of Illinois at Chicago.

Shattuck, Roger. "Contract and Credentials: The Humanities in Higher Education." In *Content and Context: Essays on College Education*. Ed. Carl Kaysen. New York: McGraw-Hill, 1973. 65–120.

Shugrue, Michael. *English in a Decade of Change*. New York: Pegasus, 1968.

Shuy, Roger. Letter to author, 15 August 1988.

Siegel, Howard. "First Impressions." *Green Caldron* (April 1960): 8–9. University of Illinois at Urbana-Champaign Archives.

Simpson, C. J. "Annual Report of English Department, 1959–60." English Department Records, Wheaton College (Ill.) Archives.

Sledd, James. Remarks at Memorial Service for Wallace Douglas, 25 April 1995. Wallace Douglas Files, Northwestern University Archives.

Slote, Benjamin H. Remarks at Memorial Service for Wallace Douglas, 25 April 1995. Wallace Douglas Files, Northwestern University Archives.

Smith, Jeff. "Students' Goals, Gatekeeping, and Some Questions of Ethics." *College English* 59 (1997): 299–320.

Smith, Michael J. "A Sailor and A Doctor." *Pier Glass* 4 (Fall 1957): 7–8. University Archives, University of Illinois at Chicago.

Solberg, Winton U. *University of Illinois, 1894–1904: The Shaping of the University*. Urbana: University of Illinois Press, 2000.

"Staff Room Interchange." *College Composition and Communication* 9 (1958): 29–38.

Standards in Freshman Rhetoric at the University of Illinois. Urbana: University of Illinois, 1956.

Stark, Joan S. and Lisa R. Latucca. *Shaping the College Curriculum: Academic Plans in Action*. Boston: Allyn and Bacon, 1997.

Steinberg, Erwin R. "Some Basic Assumptions for Courses in English Composition." *College Composition and Communication* 2 (1951): 11–16.

Steinmann, Martin. "Freshman English: A Hypothesis and a Proposal." *Journal of Higher Education* 37 (1966): 24–32.

——. "Freshman English in America." *Universities Quarterly* 19 (1965): 391–95.

——. Conversation with author, 27 July 1988.

Stewart, Donald. "Collaborative Learning and Composition: Boon or Bane?" *Rhetoric Review* 7 (1988): 58–83.

Stout, George D. "A Why and How for Freshman Composition." *College Composition and Communication* 4 (1953): 25–27.

"A Suggested Outline for Judging Composition Papers," 1950. Mimeographed. Harrison Hayford Papers. Northwestern University Archives.

"Suggested Topics for A-10 Themes," 1950. Mimeographed. Harrison Hayford Papers. Northwestern University Archives.

"Syllabus for English 102 (1965 Version)." Mimeographed. Department of English, Loyola University Chicago.

Talcott, Sasha. "In Search of Applicants, NU Looking to New Logo." *Daily Northwestern.* (20 February 2001) www.dailynorthwestern.com/daily/issues/2001/02/20/campus/logo.shtml.

———, and Dan Murtaugh. "Officials Say NU Will Keep Current Seal." *Daily Northwestern.* (4 May 2001) www.dailynorthwestern.com/daily/issues/2001/05/04/campus/logo.shtml.

Thomas, Joseph M., et al., *Composition for College Students.* 4th ed. New York: Macmillan, 1937.

Tobin, Lad. *Writing Relationships: What Really Happens in the Composition Class.* Portsmouth, N.H.: Boynton/Cook Heinemann, 1993.

"Tradition at the University of Illinois." Online. http://www.english.uiuc.edu/dahlquist/TraditionWeb.htm. 5 August 2002.

University Senate Committee on Educational Policy. "Report to the Senate, April 17, 1941." University of Illinois at Urbana-Champaign Archives. 4/2/23, Box 1.

University Senate Committee on Student English. "Background Material for the Study of Faculty Cooperation in the Improvement of Student English," 1955. University of Illinois at Urbana-Champaign Archives. 4/2/23, Box 4.

———. "Guidelines for Grading Compositions," 1968. University of Illinois at Urbana-Champaign Archives. 4/2/23, Box 8.

———. "The Maintenance of Good Writing after the Freshman Year," 1964. University of Illinois at Urbana-Champaign Archives. 4/2/23, Box 4.

———. Memo to All Faculty, 4 April 1963. University of Illinois at Urbana-Champaign Archives. 4/2/23, Box 2.

———. Memo to Undergraduate Teaching Faculty, September 1955. University of Illinois at Urbana-Champaign Archives. 4/2/23, Box 2.

———. "Provisions for Rhetoric and the Rhetoric Staff," 1950. University of Illinois at Urbana-Champaign Archives. 4/2/23, Box 5.

———. "The Qualifying Examination in English: Background," 1962. University of Illinois at Urbana-Champaign Archives. 4/2/23, Box 4.

———. "Results of the Qualifying Examination in English, 1944–1967," June 1967. University of Illinois at Urbana-Champaign Archives. 4/2/23, Box 3.

———. *Stylebook of English.* Urbana: University Senate Committee on Student English, 1951. University of Illinois at Urbana-Champaign Archives. 15/7/807.

———. "The University of Illinois Faculty Looks at Student English," 1954. University of Illinois at Urbana-Champaign Archives. 4/2/23, Box 3.

Veltman, Peter. "Implications for Present Day Education in the Popularity of Comic Books." *Michigan Education Journal* 26 (October 1948): 192–93.

———. "The Other Side of the Fence." *School and Society* 68 (25 September 1948): 207–9.

———. "Serving the Community." *Scholastic Editor* 28 (February 1949): 7.

——. "What Wheaton Expects of You." Manuscript of speech to the new faculty, 4 September 1968. Peter Veltman Records, Wheaton College (Ill.) Archives.

Veysey, Laurence R. *The Emergence of the American University*. Chicago: University of Chicago Press, 1965.

——. "Stability and Experiment in the American Undergraduate Curriculum." *Content and Context: Essays on College Education*. Ed. Carl Kaysen. New York: McGraw-Hill, 1973. 1–63.

Waggoner, Michael. "Post-War Student Attitudes Toward World Affairs." n.d. Student essay. History Department Records, Wheaton College (Ill.) Archives.

Ward, Ferdinand J. C. M. "The Sub-Freshman English Student in the Day Commerce Department of DePaul University, Chicago." *College Composition and Communication* 7 (1956): 73–75.

"Wheaton College Style Book: A Guide for the Writing of Term Papers, Research Studies, and Reports." Wheaton: Wheaton College, 1949.

Wilcox, Thomas W. *Anatomy of Freshman English*. San Francisco: Jossey-Bass, 1973.

Williamson, Harold F. and Payson S. Wild. *Northwestern University, A History: 1850–1975*. Evanston, Ill.: Northwestern University, 1976.

Wilson, Harris W. "Illinois vs. Illiteracy." *College Composition and Communication* 7 (1956): 71–73.

Winterowd, W. Ross. "Post-Structuralism and Composition." *Pre/Text* 4 (1983): 79–92.

Worsham, Lynn. "The Question Concerning Invention: Hermeneutics and the Genesis of Writing." *Pre/Text* 8 (1987): 197–244.

Young, Richard E. "Paradigms and Problems: Needed Research in Rhetorical Invention." *Research on Composing: Points of Departure*. Eds. Charles L. Cooper and Lee Odell. Urbana: NCTE, 1978. 29–47.

Index

247